Francis Frith's

West Yorkshire

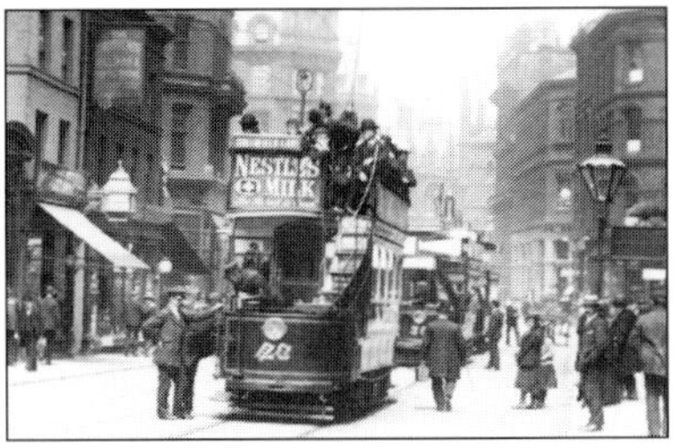

Photographic Memories

Francis Frith's
West Yorkshire

Robert E Preedy

FRITH BOOK Co

First published in the United Kingdom in 2000 by
Frith Book Company Ltd

Paperback Edition 2000
ISBN 1-85937-201-5

Hardback Edition 2002
ISBN 1-85937-602-9

British Library Cataloguing in Publication Data

Francis Frith's West Yorkshire
Robert E Preedy

Frith Book Company Ltd
Frith's Barn, Teffont,
Salisbury, Wiltshire SP3 5QP
Tel: +44 (0) 1722 716 376
Email: info@francisfrith.co.uk
www.francisfrith.co.uk

Printed and bound in Great Britain

Front Cover: Bradford, Market Street 1897 39509

AS WITH ANY HISTORICAL DATABASE THE FRITH ARCHIVE IS CONSTANTLY BEING CORRECTED AND IMPROVED AND THE PUBLISHERS WOULD WELCOME INFORMATION ON OMISSIONS OR INACCURACIES

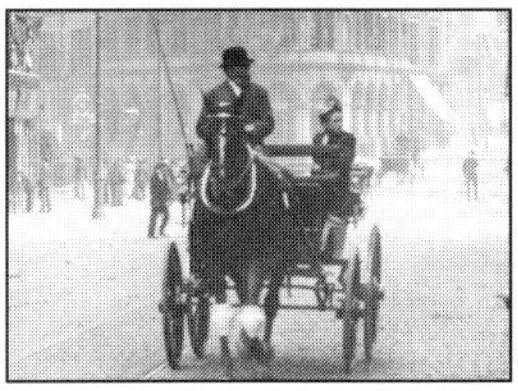

Contents

Francis Frith: Victorian Pioneer 7

Frith's Archive - A Unique Legacy 10

West Yorkshire 12

An a-z of West Yorkshire 15

Index 119

Free Mounted Print Voucher 123

Francis Frith: *Victorian Pioneer*

Francis Frith, Victorian founder of the world-famous photographic archive, was a complex and multi-talented man. A devout Quaker and a highly successful Victorian businessman, he was both philosophic by nature and pioneering in outlook.

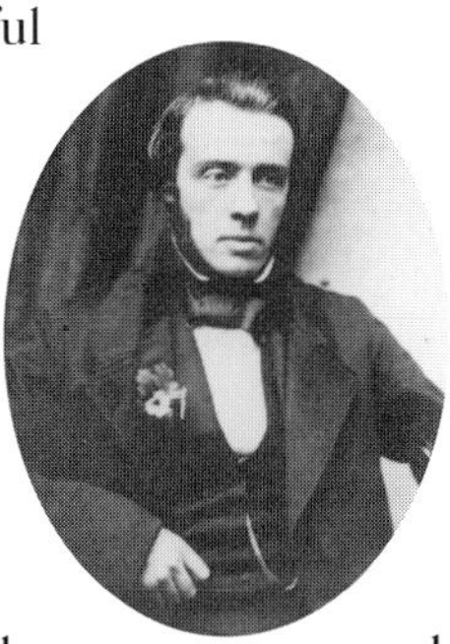

By 1855 Francis Frith had already established a wholesale grocery business in Liverpool, and sold it for the astonishing sum of £200,000, which is the equivalent today of over £15,000,000. Now a multi-millionaire, he was able to indulge his passion for travel. As a child he had pored over travel books written by early explorers, and his fancy and imagination had been stirred by family holidays to the sublime mountain regions of Wales and Scotland. 'What a land of spirit-stirring and enriching scenes and places!' he had written. He was to return to these scenes of grandeur in later years to 'recapture the thousands of vivid and tender memories', but with a different purpose. Now in his thirties, and captivated by the new science of photography, Frith set out on a series of pioneering journeys to the Nile regions that occupied him from 1856 until 1860.

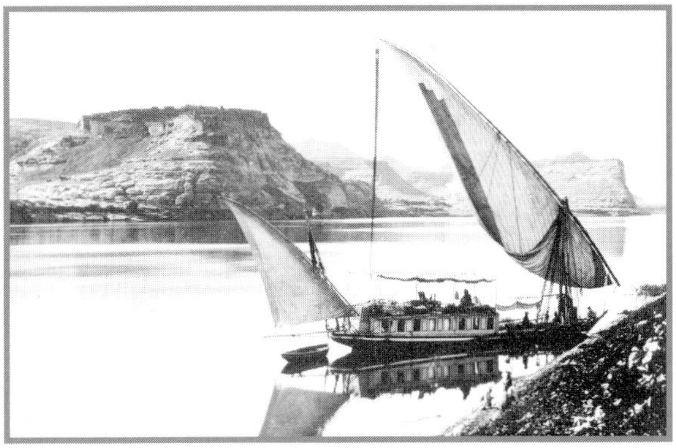

Intrigue and Adventure

He took with him on his travels a specially-designed wicker carriage that acted as both dark-room and sleeping chamber. These far-flung journeys were packed with intrigue and adventure. In his life story, written when he was sixty-three, Frith tells of being held captive by bandits, and of fighting 'an awful midnight battle to the very point of surrender with a deadly pack of hungry, wild dogs'. Sporting flowing Arab costume, Frith arrived at Akaba by camel seventy years before Lawrence, where he encountered 'desert princes and rival sheikhs, blazing with jewel-hilted swords'.

During these extraordinary adventures he was assiduously exploring the desert regions bordering the Nile and patiently recording the antiquities and peoples with his camera. He was the first photographer to venture beyond the sixth cataract. Africa was still the mysterious 'Dark Continent', and Stanley and Livingstone's historic meeting was a decade into the future. The conditions for picture taking confound belief. He laboured for hours in his wicker dark-room in the sweltering heat of the desert, while the volatile chemicals fizzed dangerously in their trays. Often he was forced to work in remote tombs and caves where conditions were cooler. Back in London he exhibited his photographs and was 'rapturously cheered' by members of the Royal Society. His reputation as a photographer was made overnight. An eminent modern historian has likened their impact on the population of the time to that on our own generation of the first photographs taken on the surface of the moon.

Venture of a Life-Time

Characteristically, Frith quickly spotted the opportunity to create a new business as a specialist publisher of photographs. He lived in an era of immense and sometimes violent change. For the poor in the early part of Victoria's reign work was a drudge and the hours long, and people had precious little free time to enjoy themselves. Most had no transport other than a cart or gig at their disposal, and had not travelled far beyond the boundaries of their own town or village. However, by the 1870s, the railways had threaded their way across the country, and Bank Holidays and half-day Saturdays had been made obligatory by Act of Parliament. All of a sudden the ordinary working man and his family were able to enjoy days out and see a little more of the world.

With characteristic business acumen, Francis Frith foresaw that these new tourists would enjoy having souvenirs to commemorate their days out. In 1860 he married Mary Ann Rosling and set out with the intention of photographing every city, town and village in Britain. For the next thirty years he travelled the country by train and by pony and trap, producing fine photographs of seaside resorts and beauty spots that were keenly bought by millions of Victorians. These prints were painstakingly pasted into family albums and pored over during the dark nights of winter, rekindling precious memories of summer excursions.

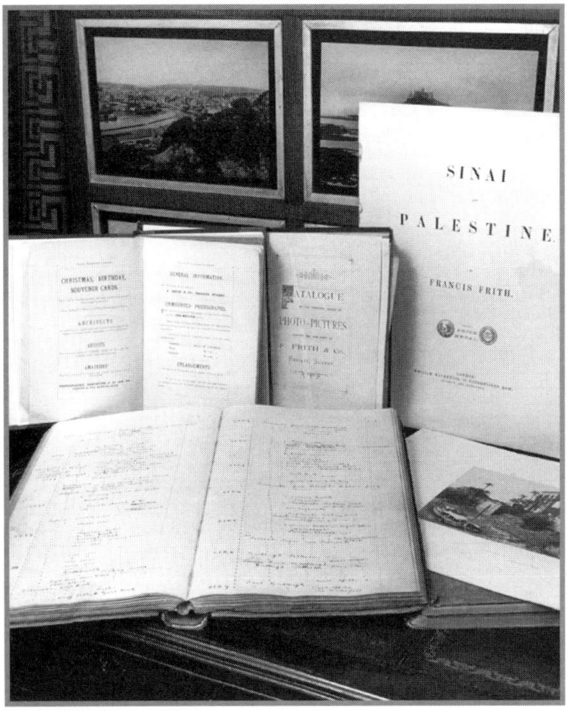

The Rise of Frith & Co

Frith's studio was soon supplying retail shops all over the country. To meet the demand he gathered about him a small team of photographers, and published the work of independent artist-photographers of the calibre of Roger Fenton and Francis Bedford. In order to gain some understanding of the scale of Frith's business one only has to look at the catalogue issued by Frith & Co in 1886: it runs to some 670 pages, listing not only many thousands of views of the British Isles but also many photographs of most European countries, and China, Japan, the USA and

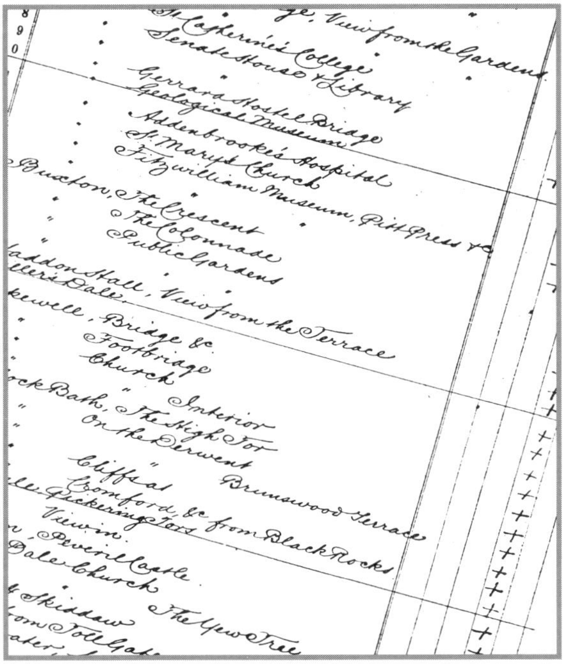
ge, View from the Gardens
St Catherine's College
Senate House & Library
Gerrard Hostel Bridge
Geological Museum
Addenbrooke's Hospital
St Mary's Church
Fitzwilliam Museum, Pitt Press &c
Buxton, The Crescent
The Colonnade
Public Gardens
addon Hall, View from the Terrace
ewell, Bridge &c.
Footbridge
Church
ck Bath, " Interior
The High Tor
On the Derwent
Cliffs at   Brunswood Terrace
Cromford, &c from Black Rocks
View in
Peveril Castle
Dale Church
Skiddaw   The Yew Tree
om Toll Gate

Canada – note the sample page shown above from the hand-written *Frith & Co* ledgers detailing pictures taken. By 1890 Frith had created the greatest specialist photographic publishing company in the world, with over 2,000 outlets – more than the combined number that Boots and WH Smith have today! The picture on the right shows the *Frith & Co* display board at Ingleton in the Yorkshire Dales. Beautifully constructed with mahogany frame and gilt inserts, it could display up to a dozen local scenes.

Postcard Bonanza

The ever-popular holiday postcard we know today took many years to develop. In 1870 the Post Office issued the first plain cards, with a pre-printed stamp on one face. In 1894 they allowed other publishers' cards to be sent through the mail with an attached adhesive halfpenny stamp. Demand grew rapidly, and in 1895 a new size of postcard was permitted called the court card, but there was little room for illustration. In 1899, a year after Frith's death, a new card measuring 5.5 x 3.5 inches became the standard format, but it was not until 1902 that the divided back came into being, with address and message on one face and a full-size illustration on the other. *Frith & Co* were in the vanguard of postcard development, and Frith's sons Eustace and Cyril continued their father's monumental task, expanding the number of views offered to the public and recording more and more places in Britain, as the coasts and countryside were opened up to mass travel.

Francis Frith died in 1898 at his villa in Cannes, his great project still growing. The archive he created continued in business for another seventy years. By 1970 it contained over a third of a million pictures of 7,000 cities, towns and villages. The massive photographic record Frith has left to us stands as a living monument to a special and very remarkable man.

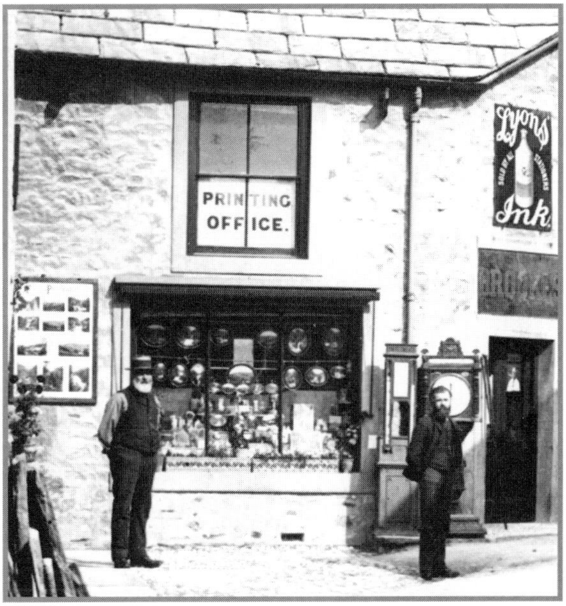

Frith's Archive: *A Unique Legacy*

Francis Frith's legacy to us today is of immense significance and value, for the magnificent archive of evocative photographs he created provides a unique record of change in 7,000 cities, towns and villages throughout Britain over a century and more. Frith and his fellow studio photographers revisited locations many times down the years to update their views, compiling for us an enthralling and colourful pageant of British life and character.

We tend to think of Frith's sepia views of Britain as nostalgic, for most of us use them to conjure up memories of places in our own lives with which we have family associations. It often makes us forget that to Francis Frith they were records of daily life as it was actually being lived in the cities, towns and villages of his day. The Victorian age was one of great and often bewildering change for ordinary people, and though the pictures evoke an impression of slower times, life was as busy and hectic as it is today.

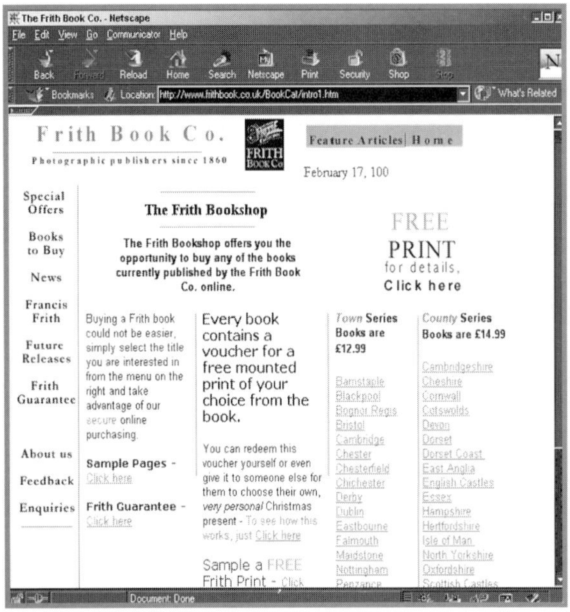

See Frith at www. frithbook.co.uk

We are fortunate that Frith was a photographer of the people, dedicated to recording the minutiae of everyday life. For it is this sheer wealth of visual data, the painstaking chronicle of changes in dress, transport, street layouts, buildings, housing, engineering and landscape that captivates us so much today. His remarkable images offer us a powerful link with the past and with the lives of our ancestors.

Today's Technology

Computers have now made it possible for Frith's many thousands of images to be accessed almost instantly. In the Frith archive today, each photograph is carefully 'digitised' then stored on a CD Rom. Frith archivists can locate a single photograph amongst thousands within seconds. Views can be catalogued and sorted under a variety of categories of place and content to the immediate benefit of researchers.

Inexpensive reference prints can be created for them at the touch of a mouse button, and a wide range of books and other printed materials assembled and published for a wider, more general readership - in the next twelve months over a hundred Frith local history titles will be published! The day-to-day workings of the archive are very different from how they were in Francis Frith's time: imagine the herculean task of sorting through eleven tons of glass negatives as Frith had to do to locate a particular sequence of pictures! Yet the archive still prides itself on maintaining the same high standards of excellence laid down by Francis Frith, including the painstaking cataloguing and indexing of every view.

It is curious to reflect on how the internet now allows researchers in America and elsewhere greater instant access to the archive than Frith himself ever enjoyed. Many thousands of individual views can be called up on screen within seconds on one of the Frith internet sites, enabling people living continents away to revisit the streets of their ancestral home town, or view places in Britain where they have enjoyed holidays. Many overseas researchers welcome the chance to view special theme selections, such as transport, sports, costume and ancient monuments.

We are certain that Francis Frith would have heartily approved of these modern developments in imaging techniques, for he himself was always working at the very limits of Victorian photographic technology.

The Value of the Archive Today

Because of the benefits brought by the computer, Frith's images are increasingly studied by social historians, by researchers into genealogy and ancestory, by architects, town planners, and by teachers and schoolchildren involved in local history projects.

In addition, the archive offers every one of us an opportunity to examine the places where we and our families have lived and worked down the years. Highly successful in Frith's own era, the archive is now, a century and more on, entering a new phase of popularity.

The Past in Tune with the Future

Historians consider the Francis Frith Collection to be of prime national importance. It is the only archive of its kind remaining in private ownership and has been valued at a million pounds. However, this figure is now rapidly increasing as digital technology enables more and more people around the world to enjoy its benefits.

Francis Frith's archive is now housed in an historic timber barn in the beautiful village of Teffont in Wiltshire. Its founder would not recognize the archive office as it is today. In place of the many thousands of dusty boxes containing glass plate negatives and an all-pervading odour of photographic chemicals, there are now ranks of computer screens. He would be amazed to watch his images travelling round the world at unimaginable speeds through network and internet lines.

The archive's future is both bright and exciting. Francis Frith, with his unshakeable belief in making photographs available to the greatest number of people, would undoubtedly approve of what is being done today with his lifetime's work. His photographs, depicting our shared past, are now bringing pleasure and enlightenment to millions around the world a century and more after his death.

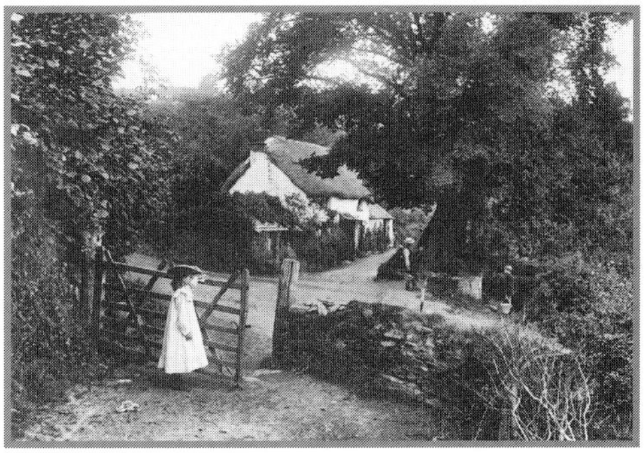

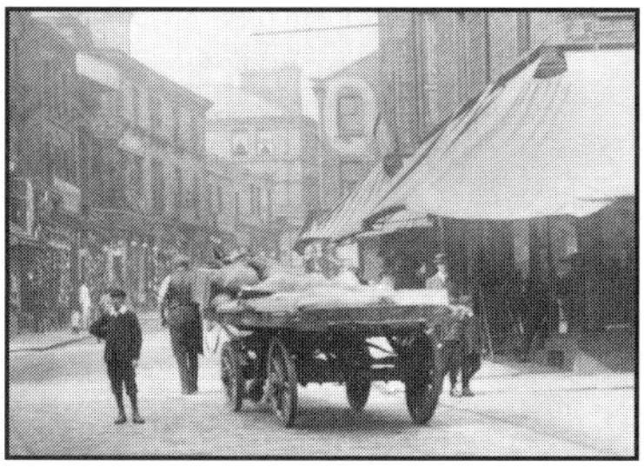

West Yorkshire - *An Introduction*

THE PROSPERITY OF West Yorkshire grew on the back of sheep. The wealth created by the woollen trade allowed factory owners, philanthropists and councils to erect their imposing Victorian architecture. These solid structures were used for civic administration, for religion, for leisure and for commerce.

On his northern excursions, Francis Frith found much of interest for his camera lens. He framed town halls, churches and chapels, bridges, inns and shops - the fabric of life in the last hundred years. Frith's company continued this record, and in the archives we find street scenes right up to the mid 1960s.

The present West Yorkshire is but a third of its former incarnation, the West Riding, which stretched up to Middlesbrough, down to Sheffield, across to Goole and west to Sedbergh. From 1974 the new county has been bounded by the northern Wharfe towns, Ilkley, Otley and Wetherby, with Castleford to the east, Todmorden and Keighley westwards and Wakefield to the south. Even within this truncated topography there is huge variety. Yorkshire people are rightly proud of their individual vistas, and in this book we take in the traditional steep streets of Haworth, the civic triumphs of Leeds, the broad Victorian pleasure parks of Bradford and Huddersfield, and evocative street scenes from towns right across the county.

Looking back in history, we see that the world of agriculture was in a state of change following the Enclosure Act. The increasing population in the towns created extra demands on the countryside, and with the new Act, landowners were able to harness a factory-like system of hardier crops, better fertilisation and more efficient machinery. Gone were the pastoral

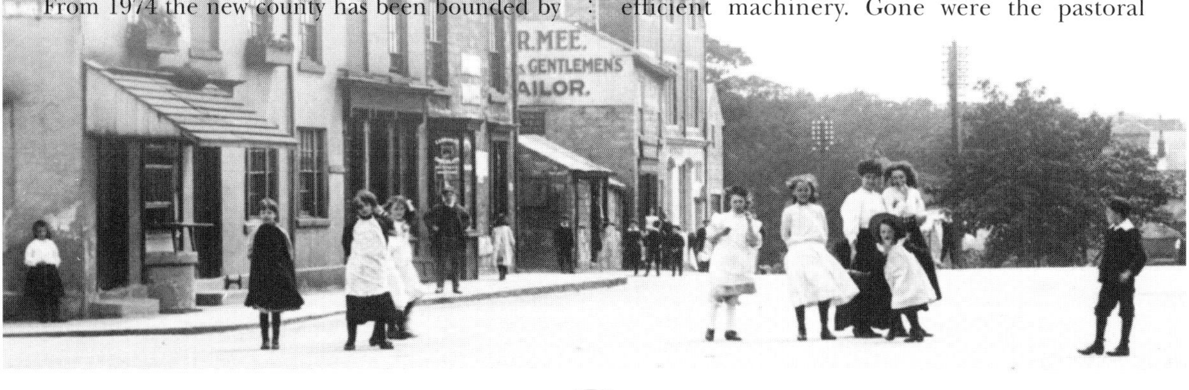

scenes of self-sufficient families using crop rotation and fallow fields. More workers were thrown off the land and forced into the already teeming northern towns. The decline in numbers of agricultural workers began in 1851 and has continued ever since. A hundred years earlier, the market town of Otley was of more economic importance than either Leeds or Bradford.

Coal mining established the West Riding as one of the major industrial powerhouses of the country. From coal developed steam power, which allowed deeper mines to be worked. The steam engine also changed the face of the wool textile industry. Power looms speeded up the manufacturing process, replacing skilled craftsmen. One new shearing frame and gig mill did the work of eight people. Workers in Bingley, Huddersfield, Wakefield and Leeds did attempt to stall the introduction of this new machinery, but the Luddite movement was powerless in the face of increased profits for the mill owners. Factory insurrection led to the hanging of seventeen men, and a further seven were transported to Australia. Steam-powered looms arrived around 1820. A riot of 250 men in Bradford again failed to halt progress, and within nine years the town boasted 378 power looms. This did little, though, to halt the flow of willing workers into the towns and cities.

In Bradford, the population grew from 9,000 in 1790 to 183,000 a hundred years later. In Leeds the increase was even more dramatic - up from 15,000 to 309,000. With this increase came diseases like cholera and tuberculosis; the latter killed half of all children under the age of five. Within West Yorkshire, concerned individuals were starting to see the evils of overcrowding and poor sanitation, and of the long hours worked in dangerous factories. Children as young as five were expected to work 14 hours a day. Richard Oastler of Bradford described this as slavery, and campaigned vigorously for reform. Medical officers in Batley and Dewsbury highlighted the effects of shoddy fever, a bronchial complaint caused by breathing the cloth dust in unventilated factories. In Wetherby a doctor fought long and hard for a universal supply of clean drinking water and the efficient processing of sewage. Gradually these campaigns produced results, and many of the urban ills became the responsibility of the new municipal Borough Councils.

Not surprisingly, the rise of trade unionism was strong in West Yorkshire. The Chartist movement, which campaigned for working class representation in Parliament, had solid roots in the county. Strikes at Manningham Mills in Bradford led in 1893 to the formation of the Independent Labour Party.

This increasing trade in the county demanded better transport. The turnpike roads of the 1700s had opened up the region, but faster links came from the enterprise of two Yorkshire road

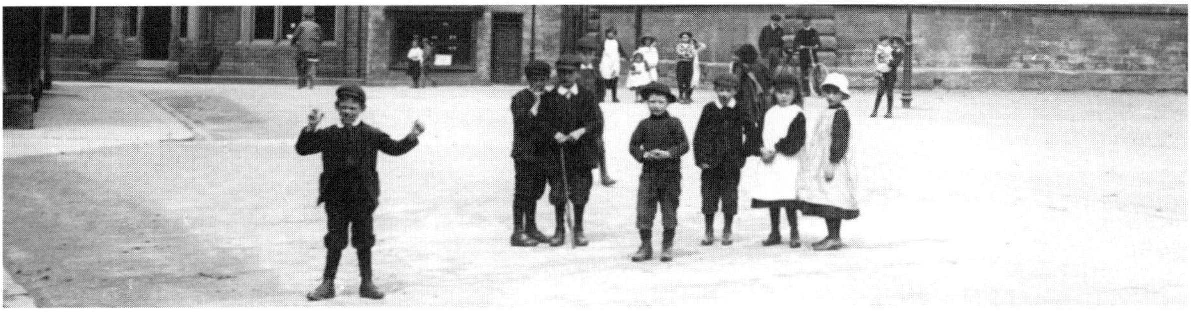

builders, John Metcalf (Blind Jack) and John Macadam. The canal age from 1750 to 1830 saw a direct link from Hull to the west coast, via the River Aire and the Leeds to Liverpool canal. This was rapidly superseded by railway mania, which gave some towns more than one station - Pontefract and Leeds each had three. The tempo of life increased again as the railway timetable began to govern people's lives. After the First World War, motor buses and private cars started to make inroads into the railway trade. Because highways are funded publicly, the apparent cost of road transport was much cheaper. During the decade from 1920 rail traffic was halved, and after nationalisation and the Beeching report the comprehensive network was completely lost.

Entertainment in the 19th century came in many forms. The most bizarre was the interest in public executions. In Leeds in 1864, over 100,000 spectators attended the final hangings.

Francis Frith must also have observed the rapid change in trading within the county. The woollen industry enjoyed its peak years between 1860 and 1874. Foreign competition, complacency in design and trade protection, especially in France and America, led to many depressed periods. Entrepreneurs had to diversify to survive. Bradford held onto wool longer than its neighbour, Leeds, which looked to new ventures such as chemicals, leather, printing and footwear. During the Great War, Dewsbury used its expertise in shoddy by recycling the cloth from the uniforms of soldiers. The aftermath of the Second World War also adversely affected trade in West Yorkshire. Gradually, cheaper foreign production caused massive job losses throughout the region in the knitting, woollen, textile and carpet industries. Coal mining also contracted to a shadow of its previous output; automation, subsidised imports and government policy all added to the collapse. The pioneering industrial processes of the 19th century finally ran out of steam in the face of this huge UK-wide manufacturing downturn.

The majestic buildings born of this industry remain, and Francis Frith reminds us in his well-composed images of this once vibrant and intensely proud industrial heritage.

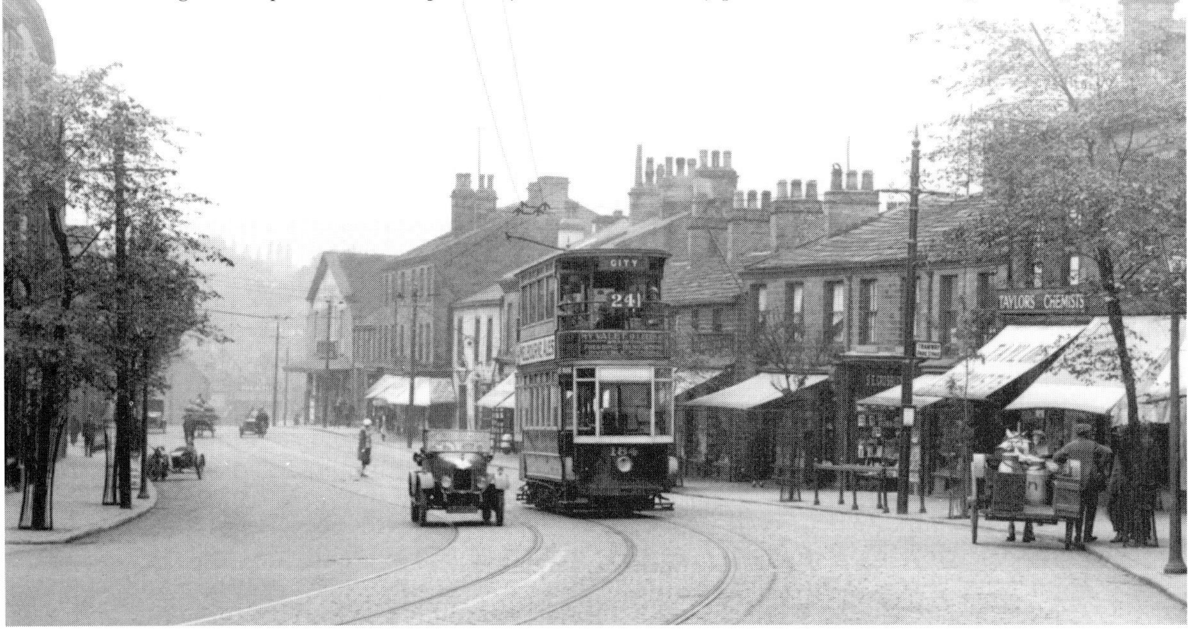

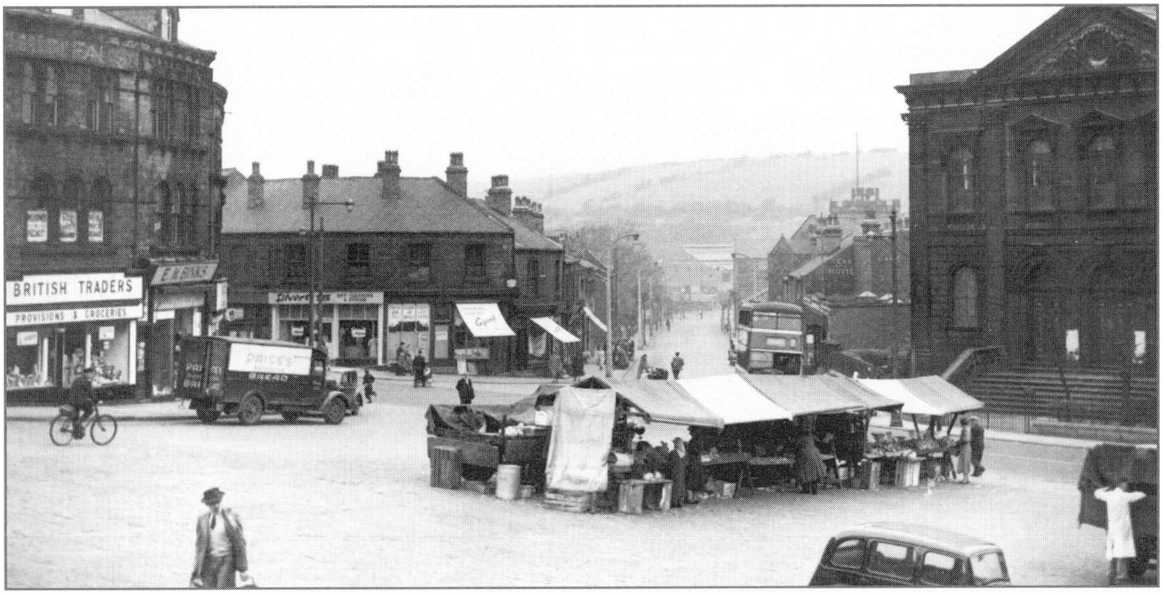

Batley, Market Place and Branch Road c1955 B642015
Batley was the north's shoddy town: its prosperity came from the process of breaking down and reweaving woollen cloth from waste rags. The raw material came from as far afield as Berlin and Rotterdam. Between 1850 and 1880, the population of the town tripled. As it grew, fears were expressed that the local dialect might die out, so in 1860 a glossary was published containing local words and phrases. The Zion Chapel (1869) on the far right seated 600, and the Sunday School catered for 1000 children.

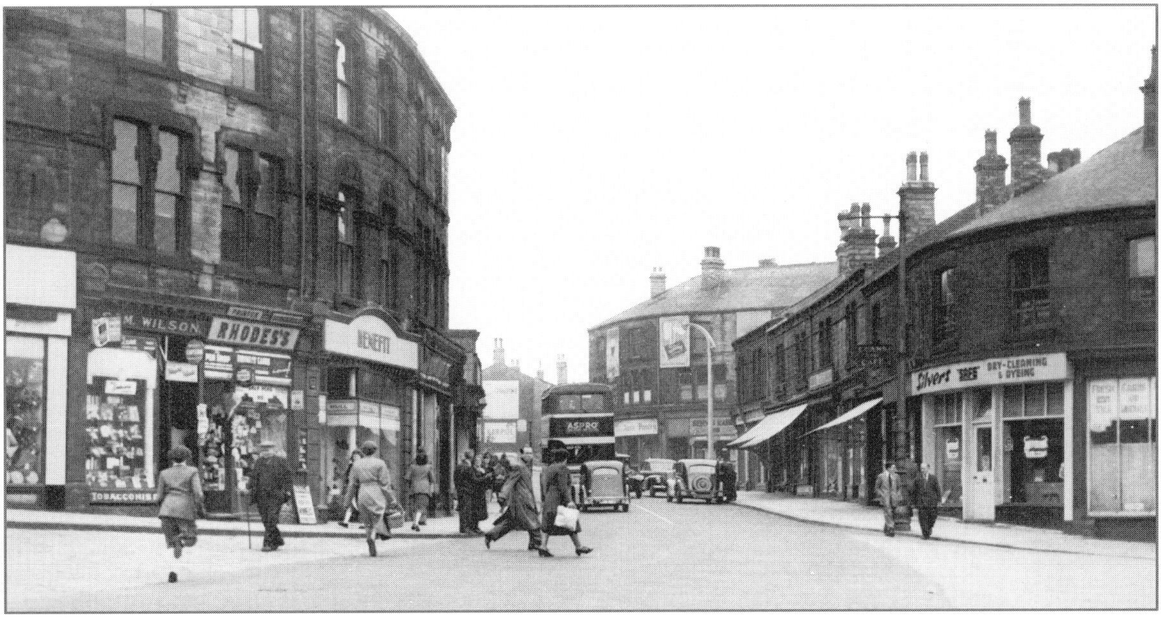

Batley, Commercial Street c1952 B642016
A double-decker bus brings trade to the town's main shopping street. Batley was one of the pioneers of steam trams; they ran from 1874, and the depot in Bradford Road later became Wilson's Mill. The railway came in 1848, and by 1890 the town had links with Bradford, Wakefield and Leeds, giving fast access to major trade markets. Even in 1945, three-quarters of the town's population was employed in the textile trade.

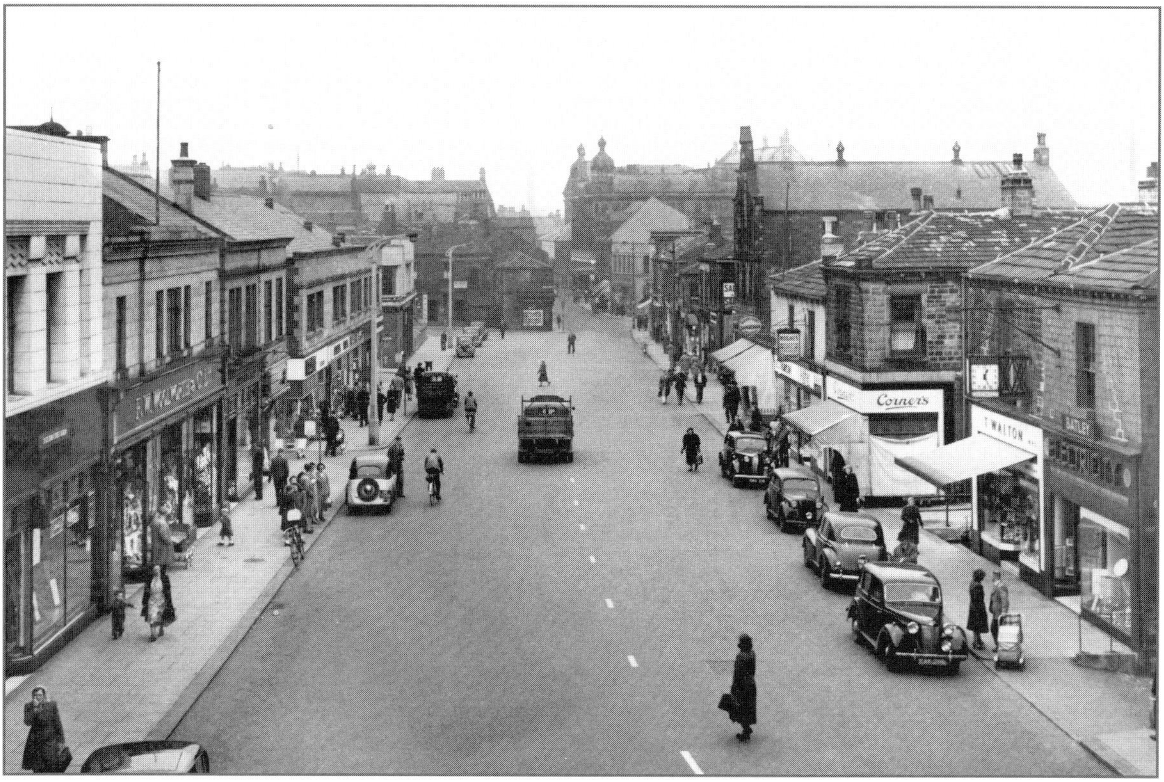

Batley, Commercial Street c1955 B642014
Formerly a dirty, rutted lane, this was changed into a shopping centre from 1872 with the demolition of the Hick Lane cottages. In their place emerged Exchange Buildings, the town's first block of shops. However, by 1881 traders were complaining that Commercial Street was in a disgusting state. It was not improved until 1903, when wooden blocks were used on the roads to keep the noise down. By 1906 the Co-operative store was established in the Market Place; it stayed here until its demolition in 1977. Others stores date from the thirties, including Woolworth's (1931) and Burton's (1937). Many of these were swept away in the next redevelopment of 1964.

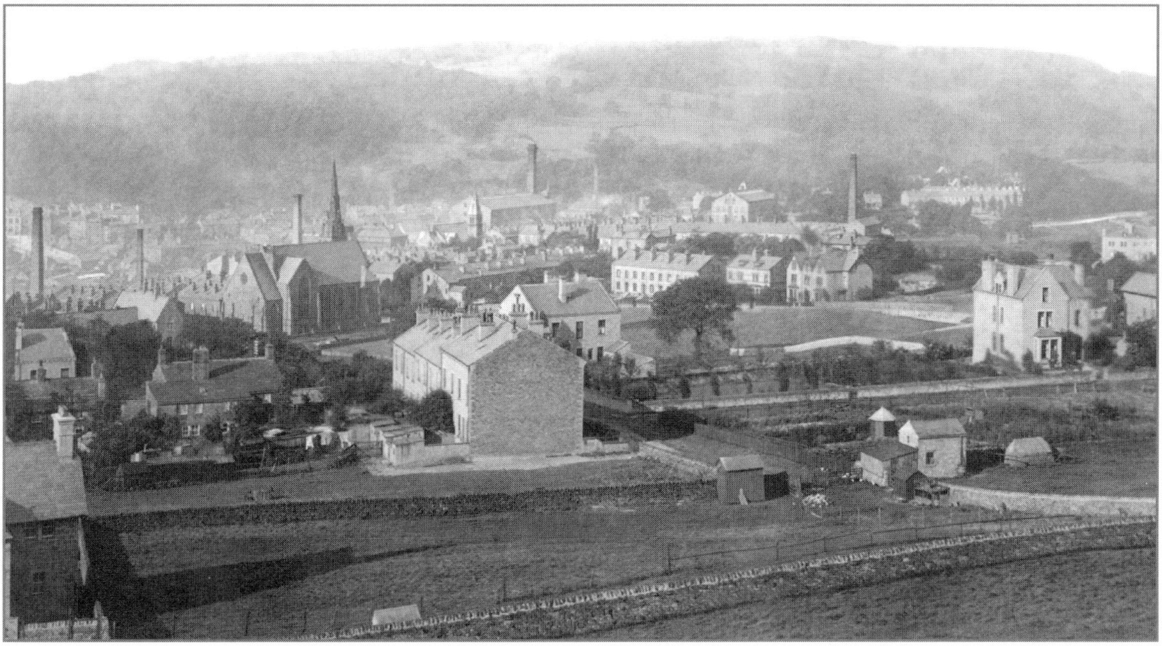

Bingley, From Ferncliff 1894 34744

John Wesley's verdict on Bingley's townspeople was that they were 'genteel'. A century after his visit, the town had been transformed from a quiet village to a vibrant part of the textile industry. The Leeds/Liverpool Canal and the railway both increased access to new markets across the Pennines and down to the south.

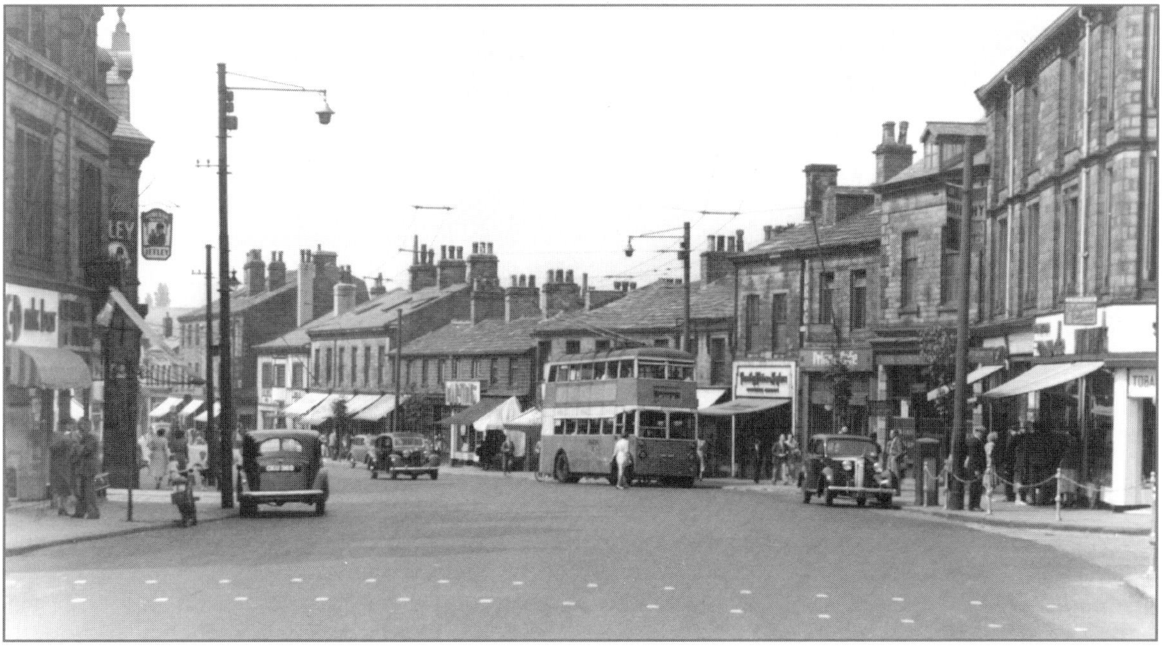

Bingley, Main Street c1955 B98012

Here we see the beginnings of the age of affluence, with black cars starting to compete with public transport, just as the trolley bus had replaced the earlier trams. The Hippodrome Cinema on Main Street replaced an old smithy, which was demolished in 1913.

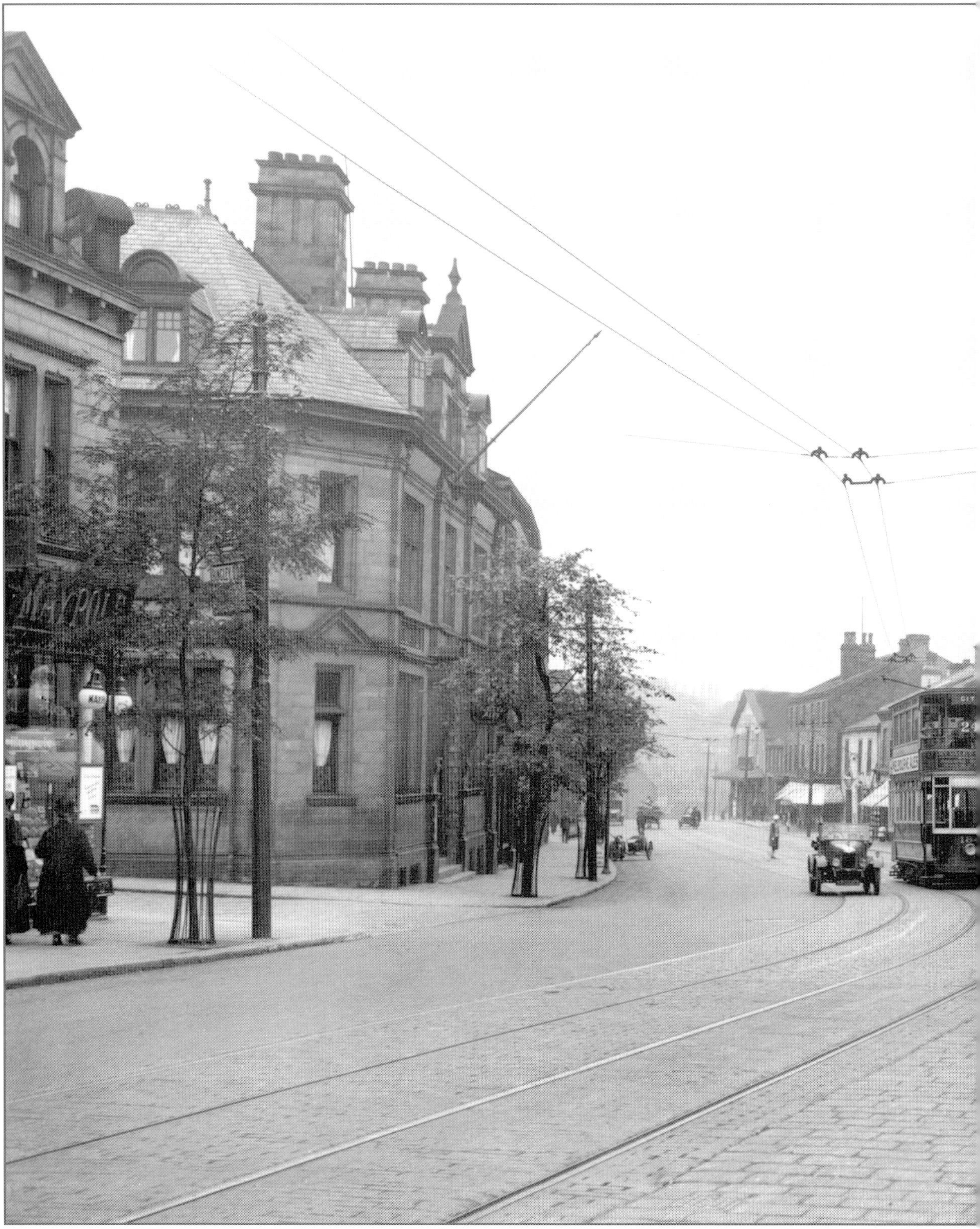
MAYPOLE

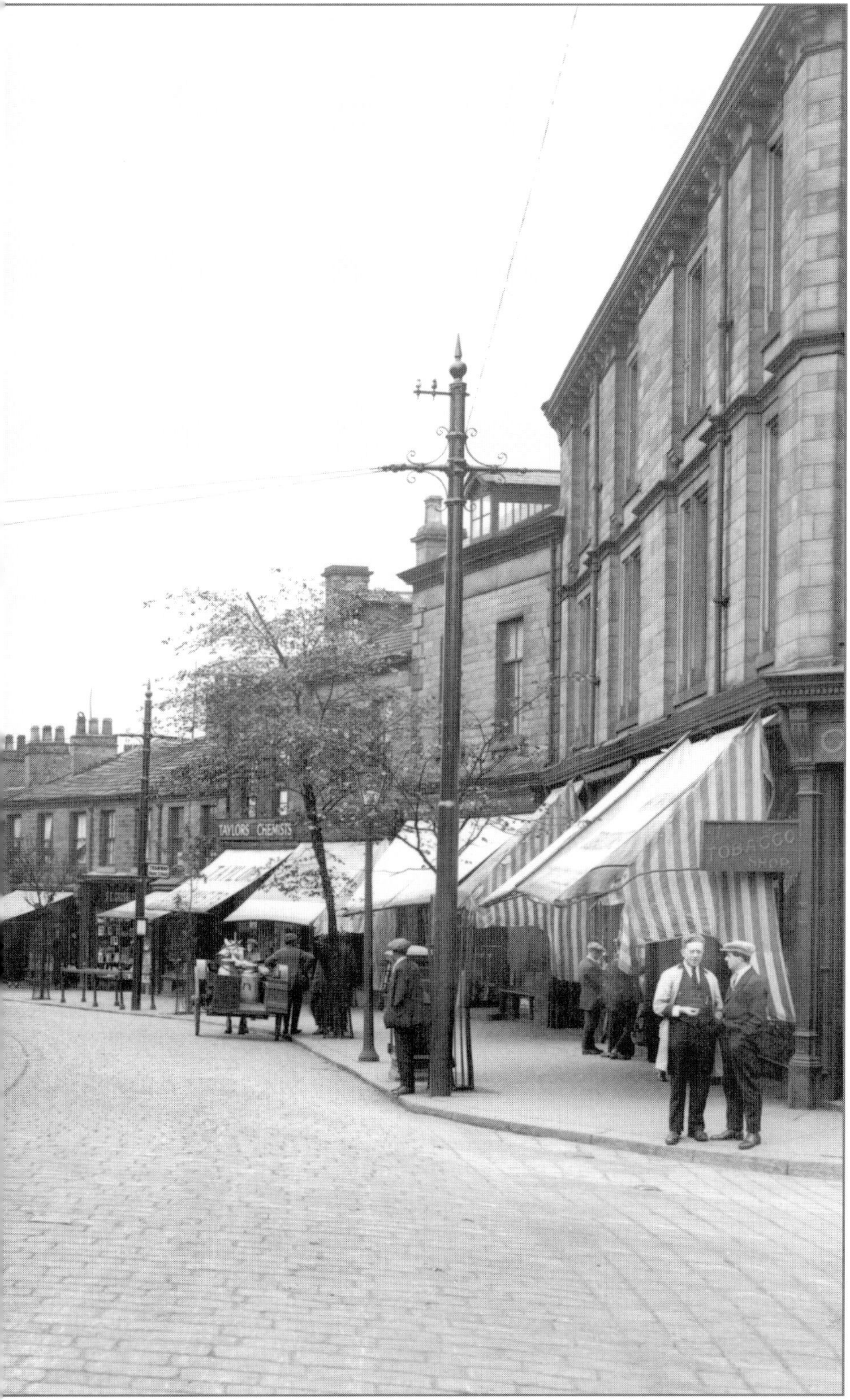

Bingley, Main Street 1926 79084
The ladies of the town used to meet in Main Street at the Loft Café. In 1904, this thoroughfare was straightened - the new route cut through an old graveyard which contained the remains of the poet John Nicholson. The Market Hall and stocks once stood on Main Street opposite Ferrand Lane.

Bingley, The Old Market House 1894 34755
Completed in 1753 at a cost of £12, the Market Hall, Butter Cross and the stocks were removed at a cost of £16 6s from Main Street to the Prince of Wales park in 1888, which is where we see them in this photograph. Trade at the original site was decimated in 1787 by an outbreak of Black Plague. The stocks on the left were still in use in 1870 - they were reputedly the last to be used in Yorkshire. More recently the whole structure has again been moved, this time back to the centre of town near the Arts Centre.

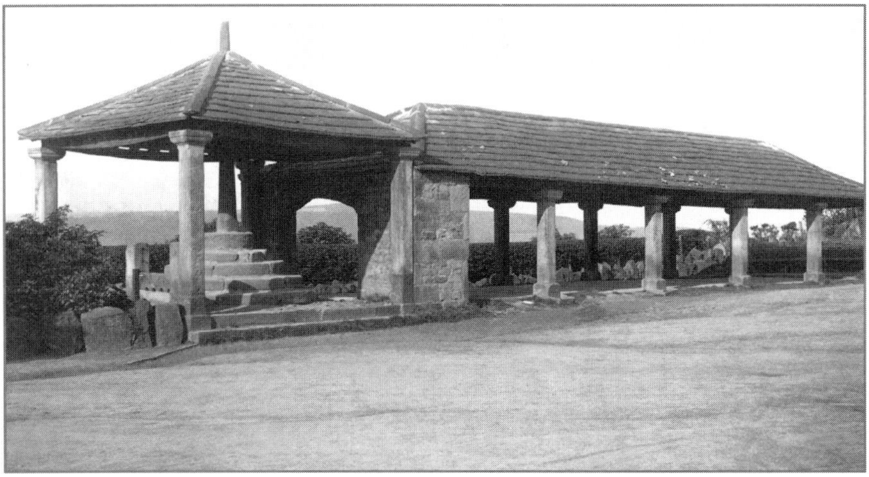

Bingley, Boating on the Aire 1923 74415
The view from this side of the river includes the industrial gasworks, but further down river past the weir is the rather more pleasant Myrtle Park, which opened to the public in 1908. The land was a former country mansion, Springhead. The original Town Hall has been in the grounds from 1770.

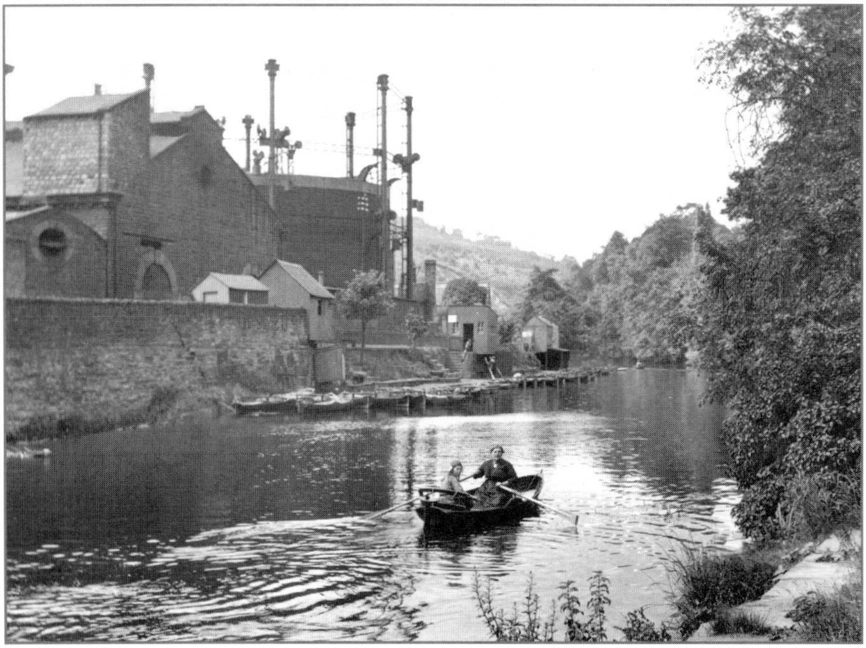

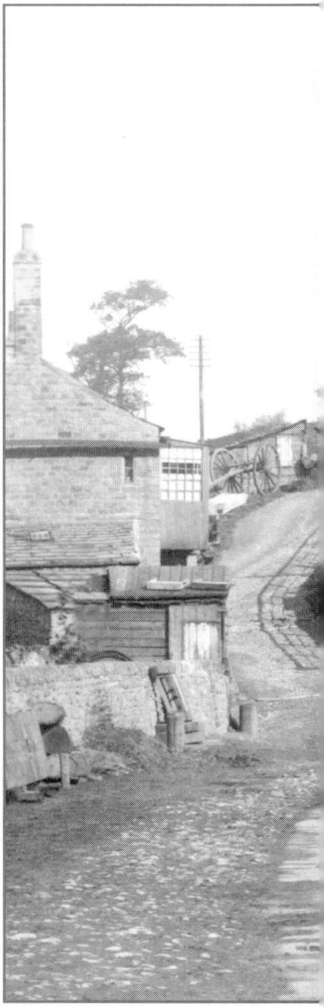

Bingley, Five Rise Locks on the Leeds and Liverpool Canal 1894 34748
These locks were constructed in 1774 on the Leeds/Liverpool canal, which transformed the town of Bingley into an industrial centre. Along the canal are over ninety locks, but this is the most dramatic set, rising an amazing 59 feet. From top to bottom the passage of a barge takes 28 minutes.

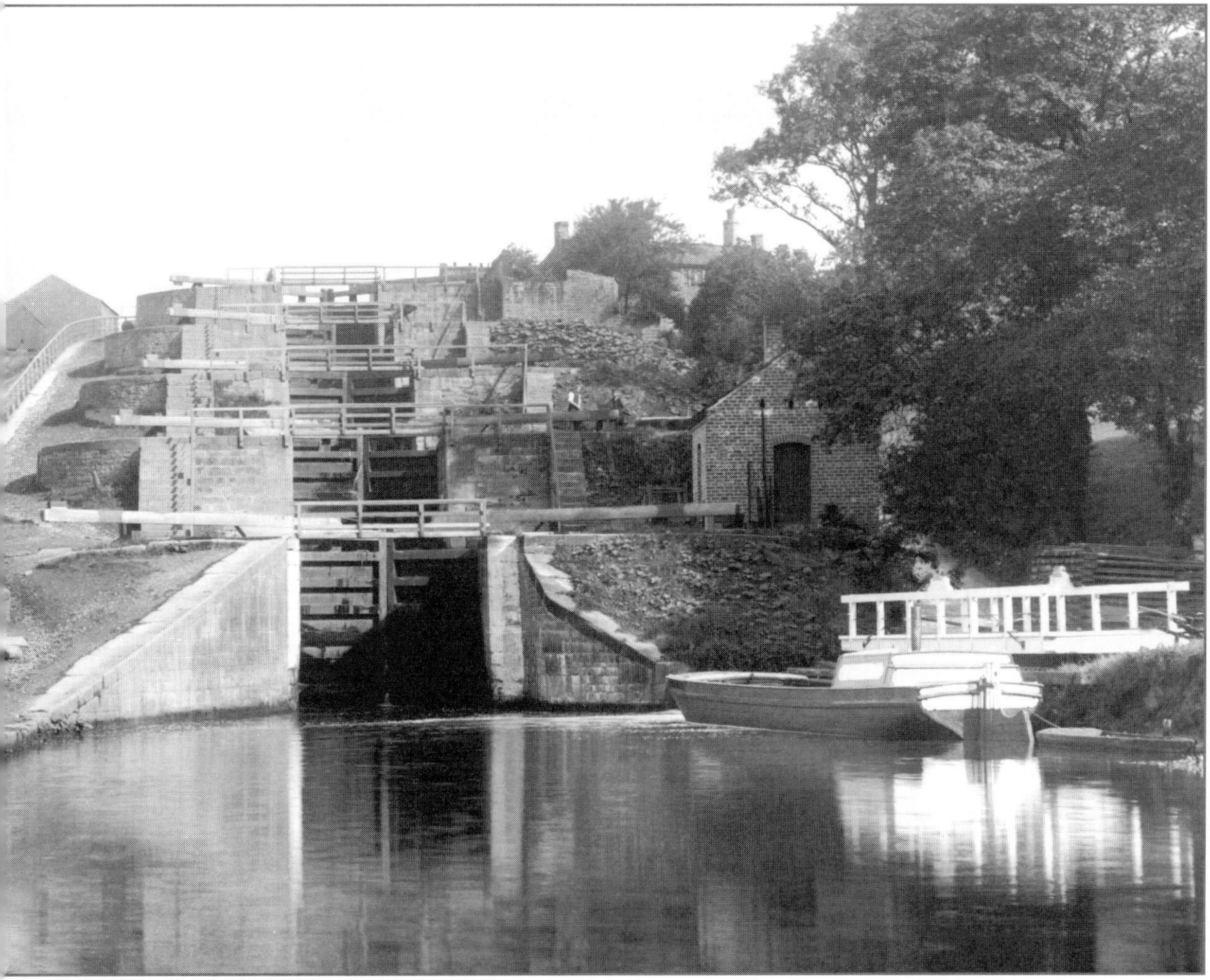

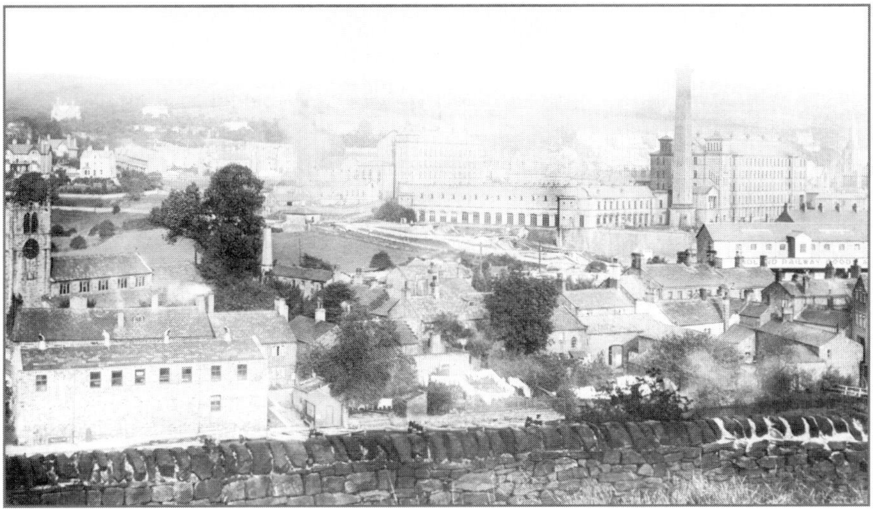

Bingley, From Alter Row 1894 34745
The canal in 1773 and the railway from 1847 brought huge trade and confidence - and pollution - to the small town of Bingley. The massive mill on the right, part of the Bowling Green complex, still stands, and is now used by Damart. Just below the mill is the railway station of 1847, and to the left is the Three Rise canal lock. The famous Five Rise lock is just out of the picture on the left. A total of eleven locks in a three-mile stretch from Shipley give a rise of 120 feet.

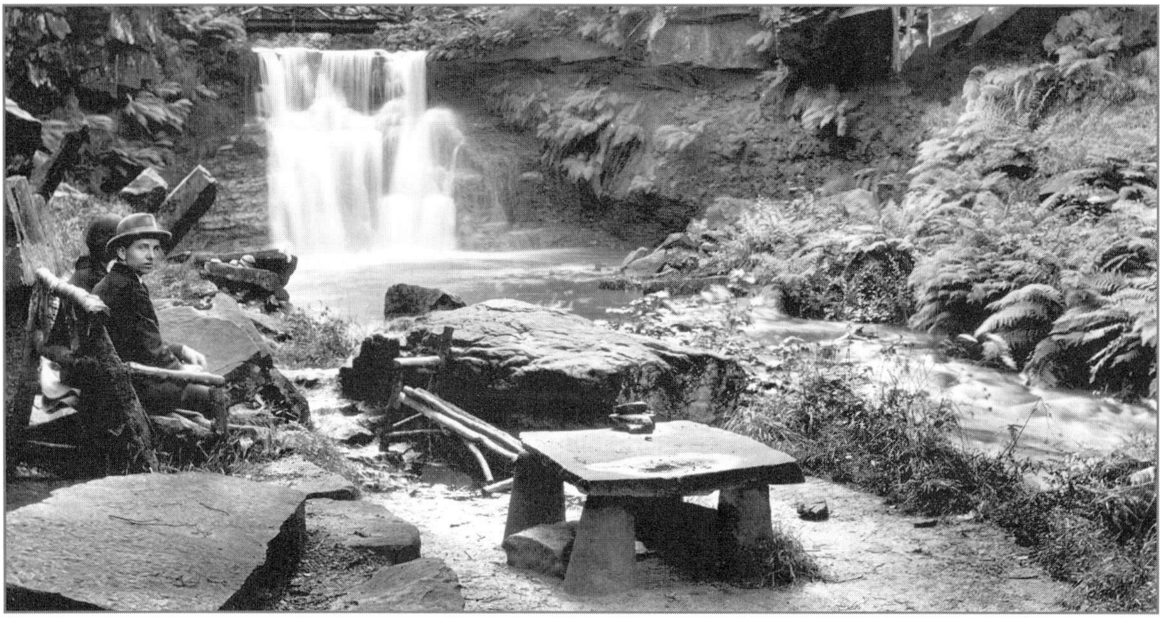

Bingley, Goit Stock Falls 1922 74422
We are a few miles out of Bingley between Harden and Cullingworth. Gone these days are the bridge, the rustic seat and the picnic table, but the tranquillity of this beauty spot remains. Harden Beck, which used to power a cotton-spinning mill up to 1802, is pictured here just below Hallas Bridge. The local poet John Nicholson wrote much of his pastoral work near the 20ft waterfall.

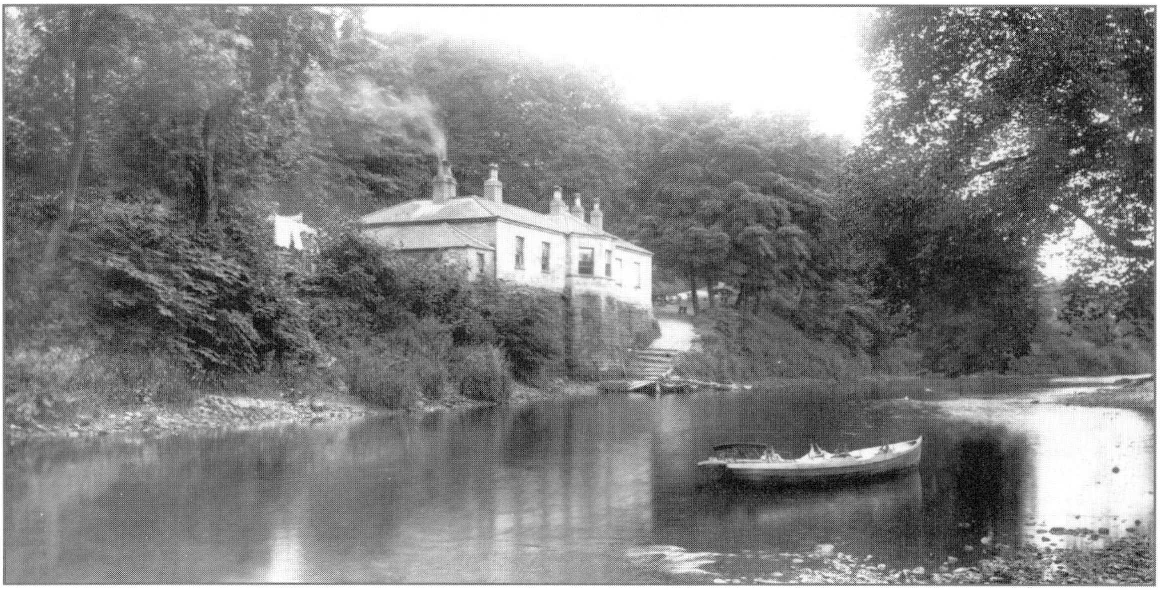

Boston Spa, The Spa Baths 1897 39437
This is an ancient farming settlement. The name derives from bos, Latin for ox, and ton, Anglo-Saxon for township. A Roman villa was here from AD200. The famous spring was discovered on the banks of the Wharfe by labourer John Shires on 4 June 1744. From then on, interest grew in visiting the town for its noted health benefits. The spring issued 36 gallons an hour, and the commercial possibilities were formalised with the building of the Spa Baths between 1810 and 1819.

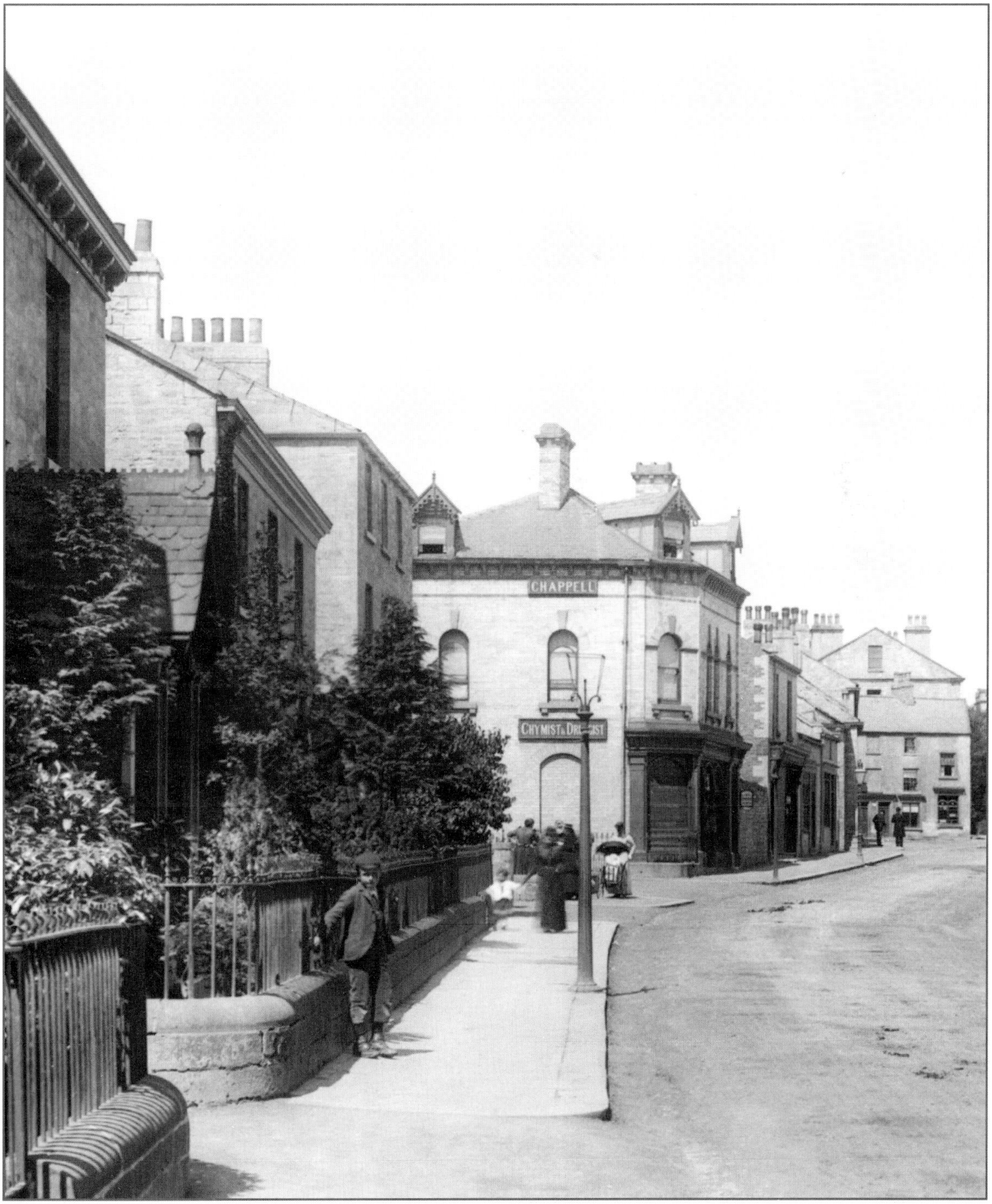

Boston Spa, High Street 1893 32000

This region was originally in the Celtic kingdom of Elmete. The word Spa was added to the town's name in 1840 when the Penny Post began. Boston never achieved the fashionable fame of other Yorkshire spa towns like Ilkley and Harrogate, however, the buildings here on the High Street illustrate the affluence generated by the mere mention of sulphurous, saline water with purgative qualities.

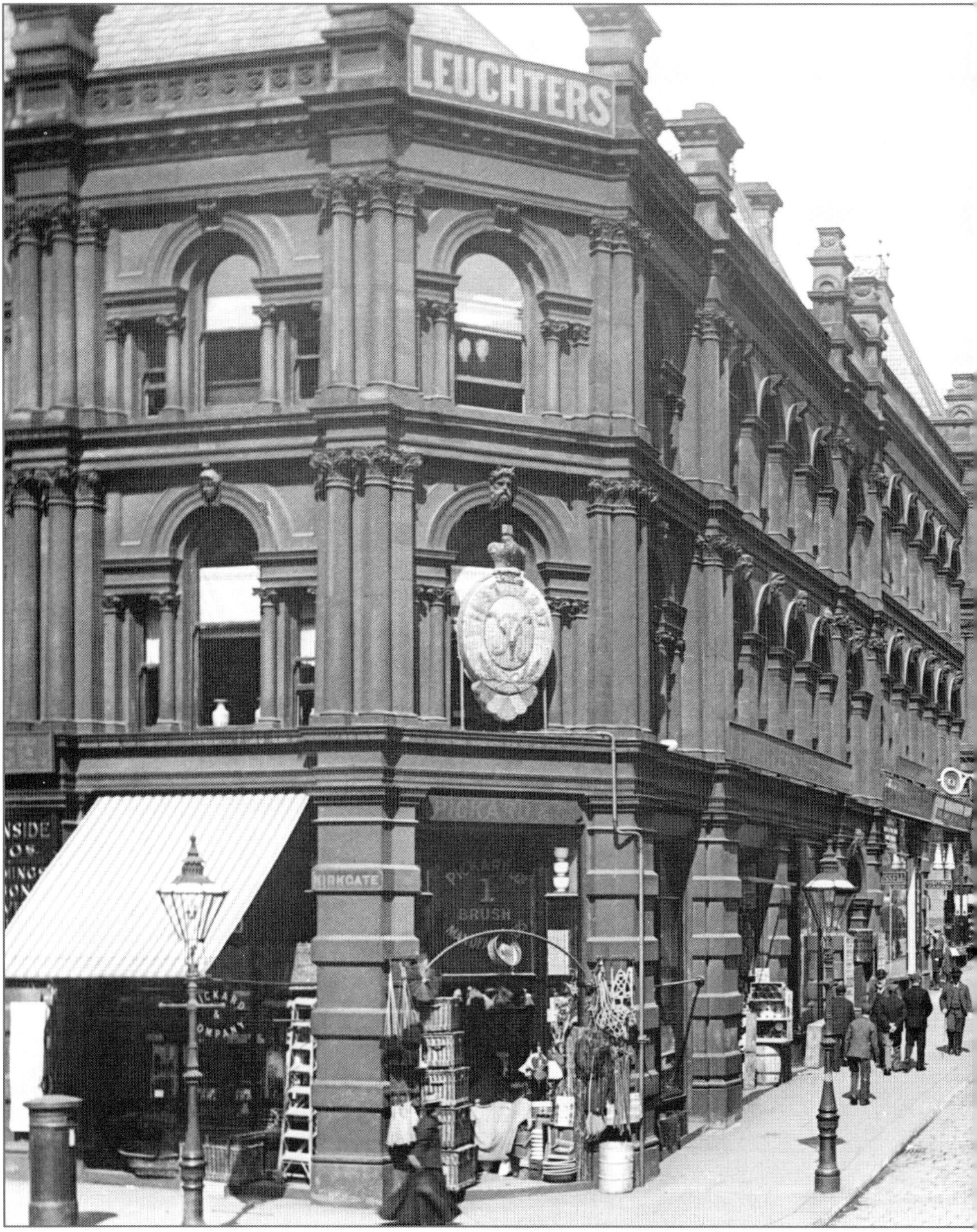
LEUCHTERS
KIRKGATE
BRUSH

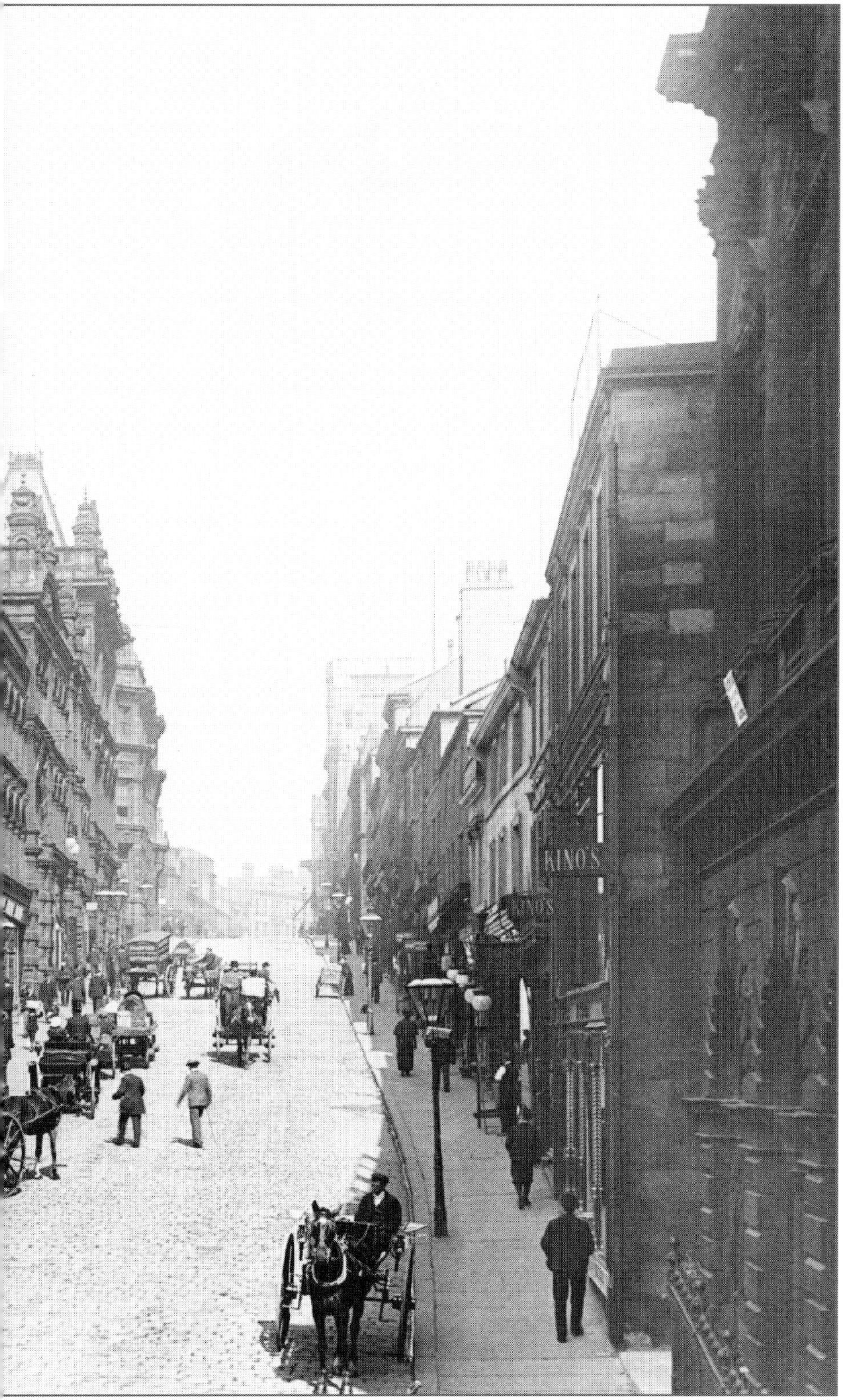

Bradford, Darley Street 1897 39508
In the thirty years from 1880, Bradford's population doubled to nearly 300,000. The quality of life for the inhabitants continued to improve with the provision of many fine public buildings and parks. Darley Street was originally part of the gardens and orchards of the old manorial estate. By 1897 it was a very fashionable shopping area.

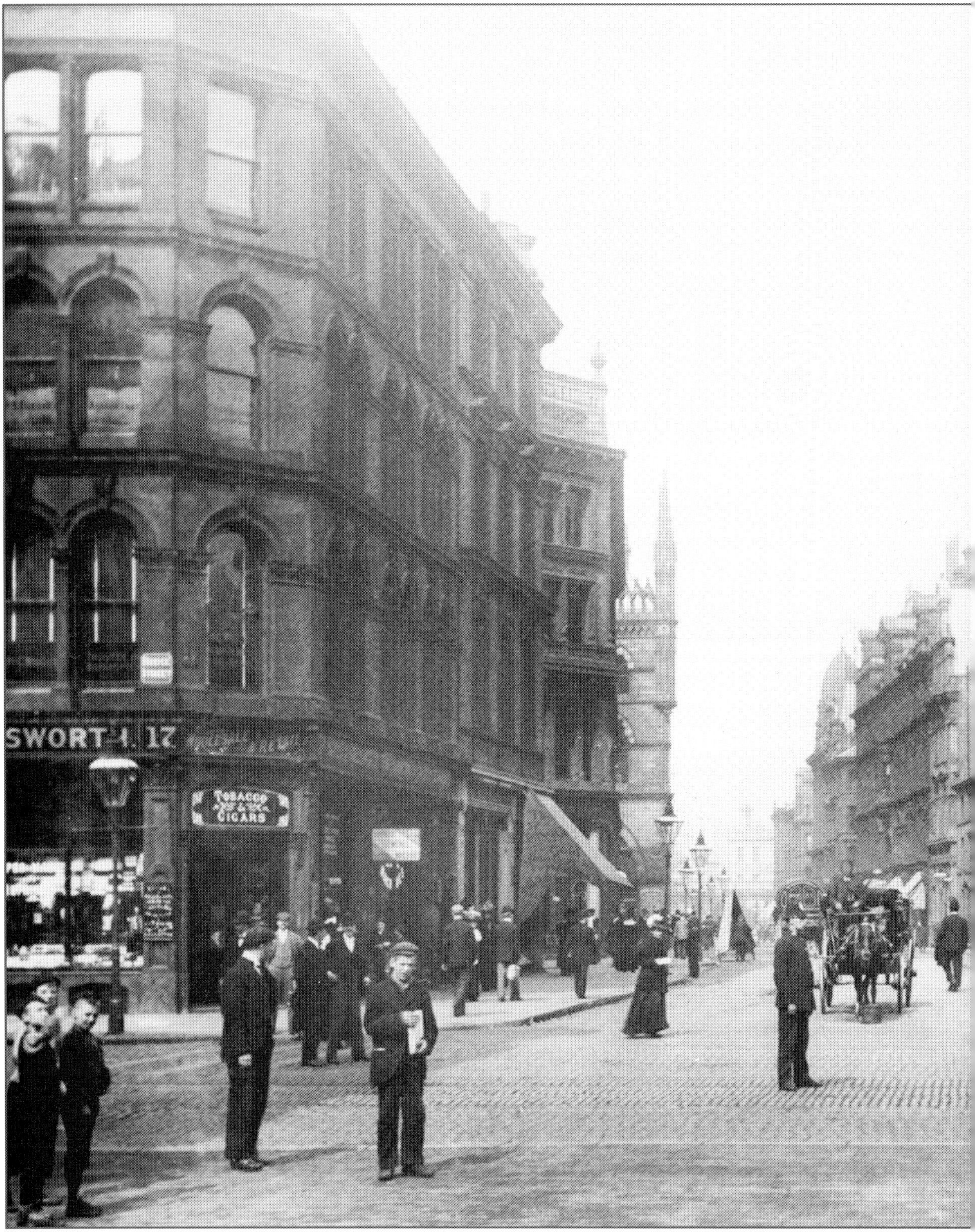
SWORTH 17
TOBACCO
CIGARS

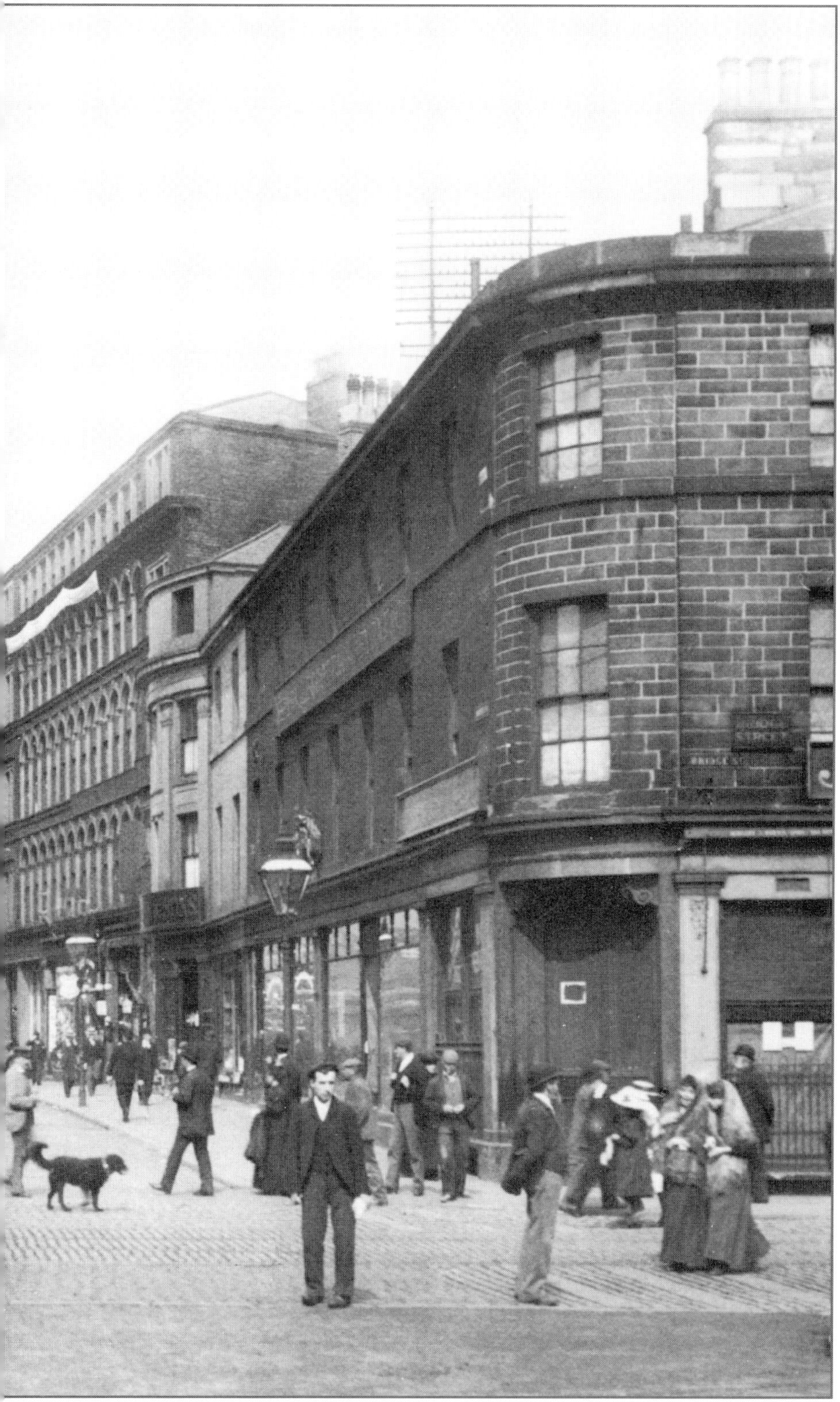

Bradford, Market Street 1897 39509
Market Street was formerly called New Street; it was completely transformed in 1860. To the left is the entrance to Brown and Muff's emporium, which opened in 1871. The Wool Exchange (1867) was a triumphal tribute to the roots of Bradford's prosperity. Market Street also included the Central Free Library.

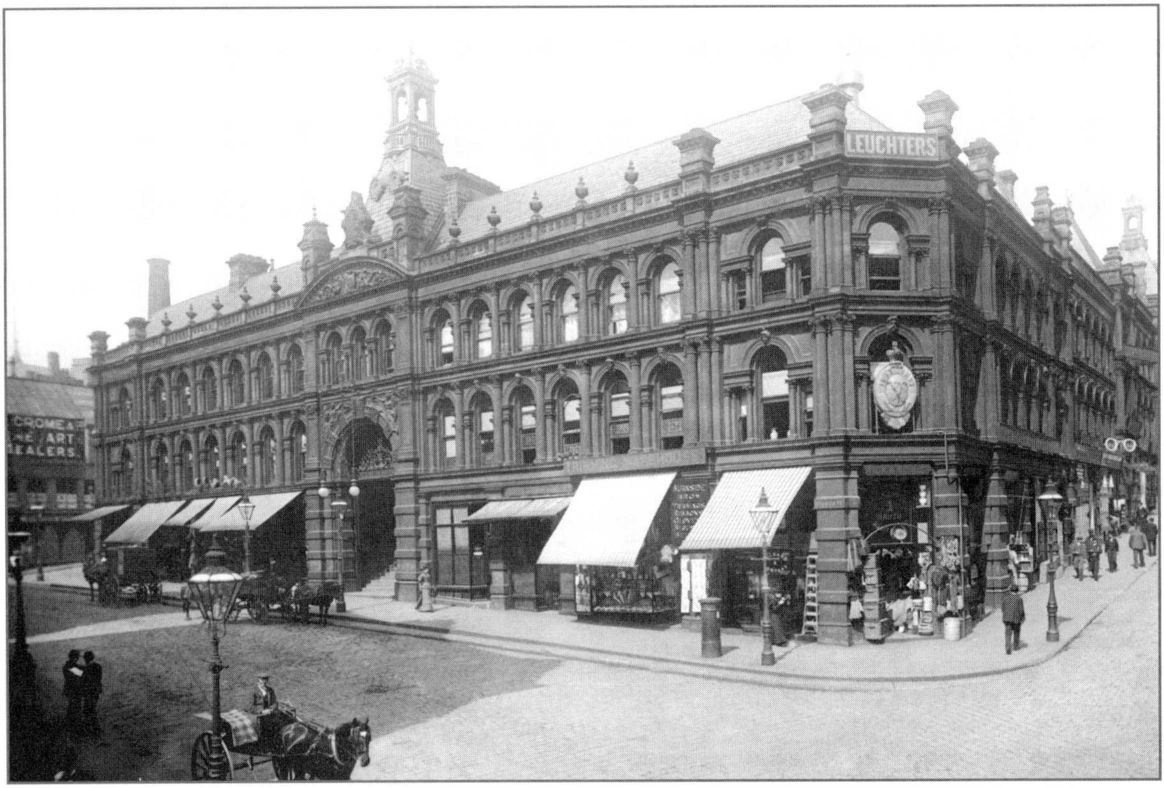

Bradford, Market Buildings 1897 39507
This imposing building of 1878 replaced an earlier market. Here, shoppers were offered an impressive choice of produce right in the centre of the city, just opposite the tram and trolleybus stops outside the town hall. The cast iron frame contained two 60ft-high domes, and huge figures of Pomona and Flora stood over the arched entrance. This market was demolished in 1973.

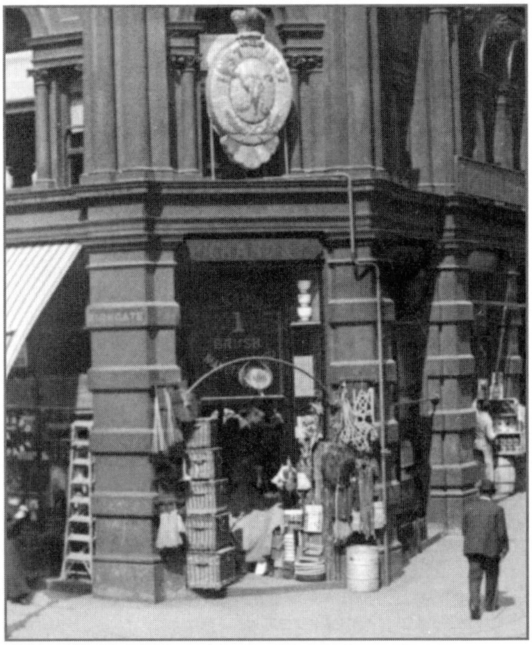

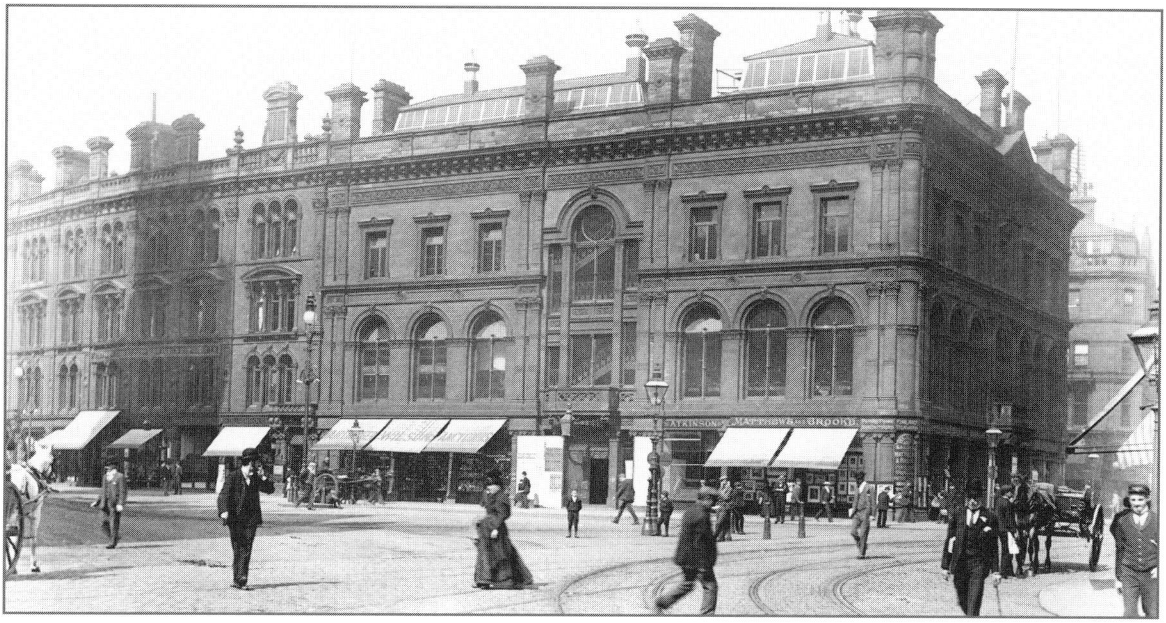

Bradford, The Mechanics' Institute, Market Street 1897 39514
Built in 1870, this was one of the many West Yorkshire institutes to offer working craftsmen the opportunity to study new skills and learn more about the world. A very well-stocked library would have been illuminating to many of the new workers pouring into the vibrant city. The elongated Venetian window added a continental look to the street. The building is now demolished.

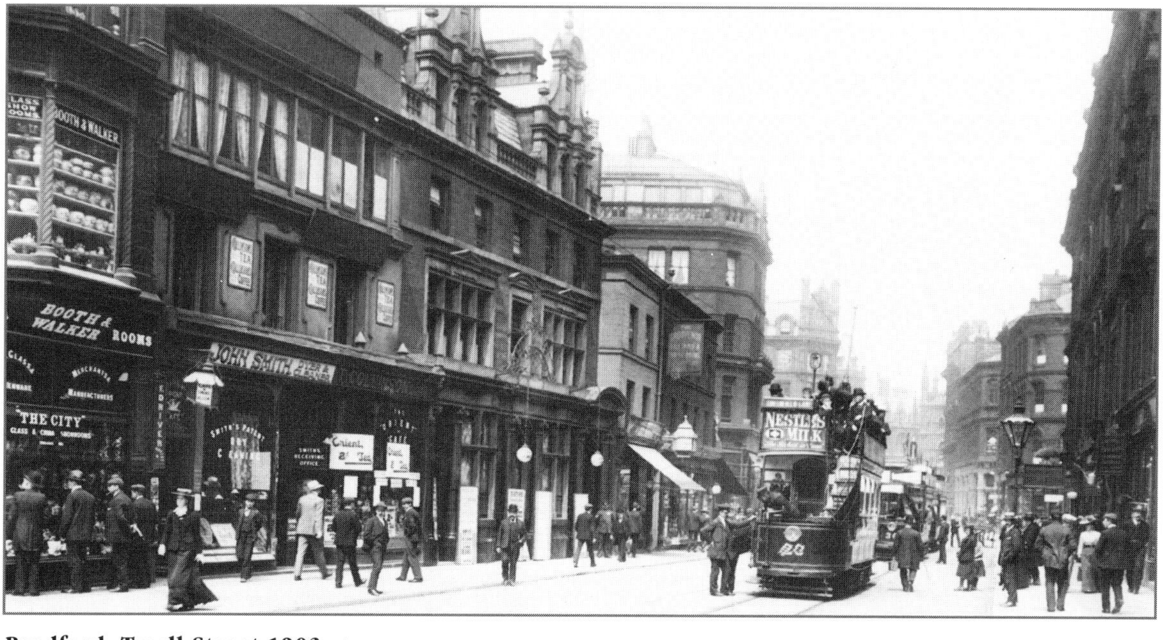

Bradford, Tyrell Street 1903 49713
The aroma of freshly-ground coffee used to drift down this street in the heart of the city. Collinson's Café, above John Smith's on the left, also offered a three-piece orchestra. Transport into this part of Bradford progressed from horse trams in 1882 to steam trams by 1884, and electric ones from 1897. By 1911 the Corporation could boast a transport profit of £52,000.

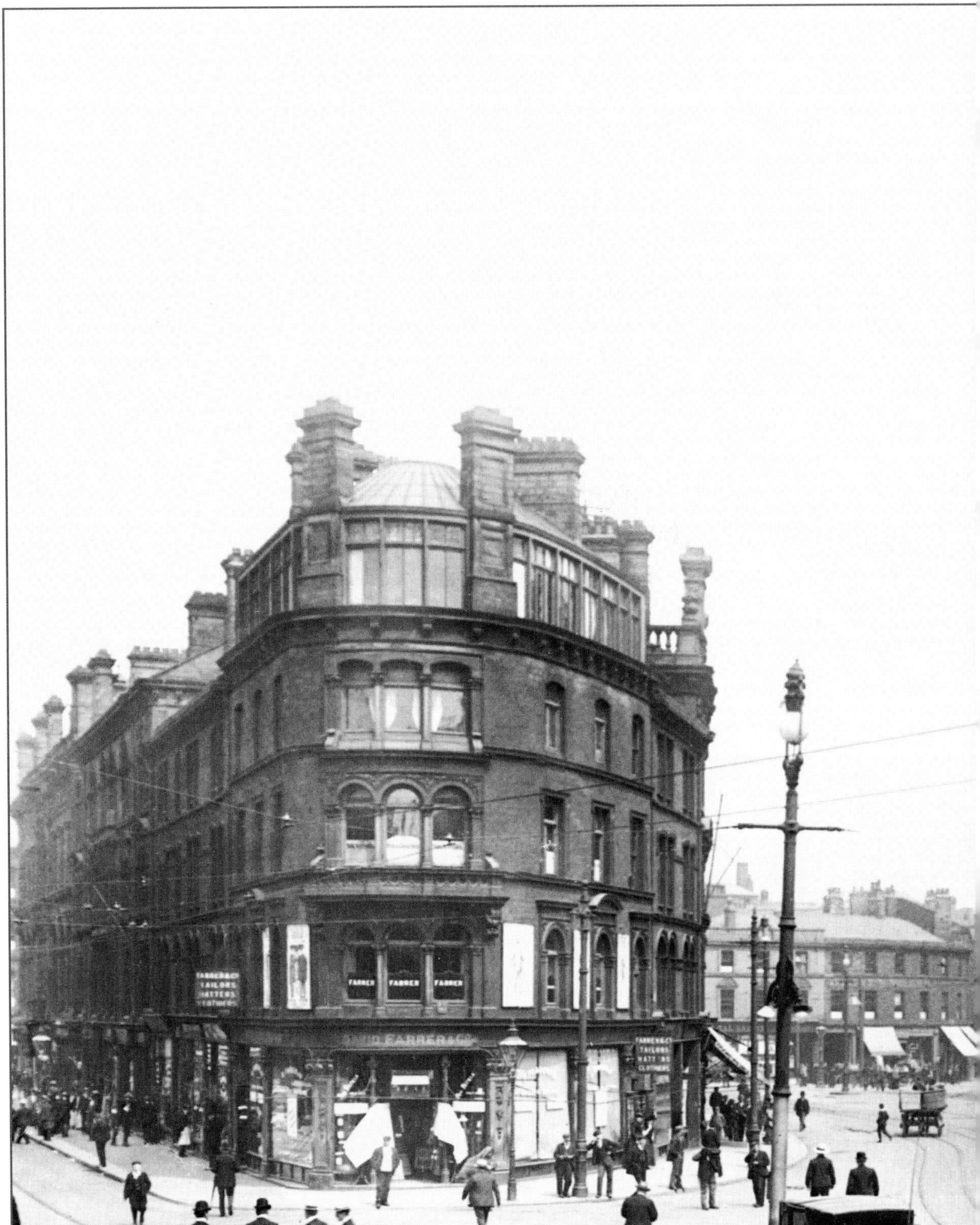

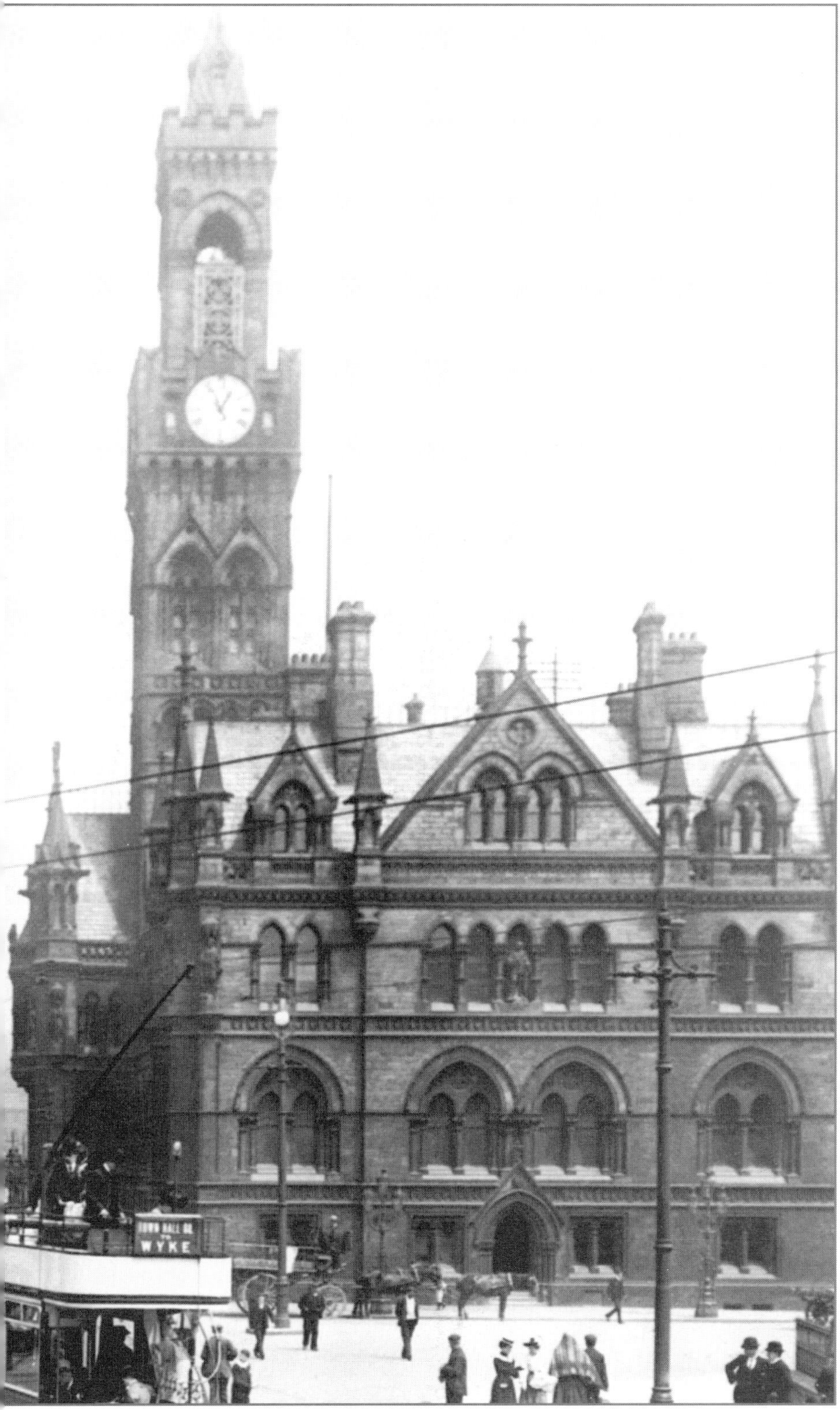

Bradford, Town Hall Square 1903 49712
The opening of this municipal building took place in September 1873 amid jubilant celebrations, and despite the torrential rain. The 200ft tower was modelled on the Palazzo Vecchio in Florence. The nearby St George's Hall (1853) was an earlier design by the same architects.

▼ **Bradford, Victoria Square c1955** B173030
The statue of Queen Victoria graced the square from May 1904. A crowd of 70,000 cheered the Prince and Princess of Wales, who were also here to open the Bradford Exhibition at Lister Park.

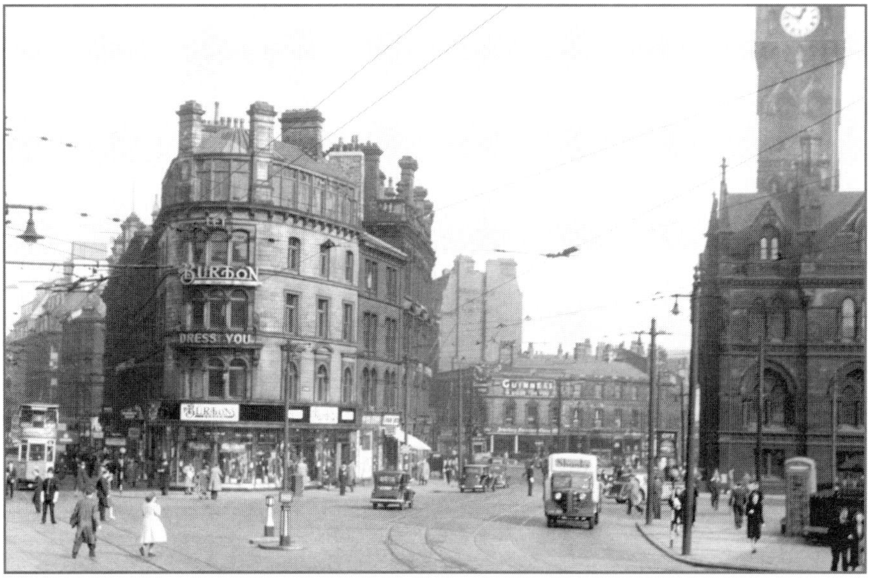

▼ **Bradford, The Post Office c1950** B173029
Now used as offices, the Post Office in Forster Square was erected in 1887. The fine open square also housed the nearby Midland Station and warehouses. The square was named after the Bradford MP for 25 years, W E Forster, who was responsible for the momentous 1870 Education Act.

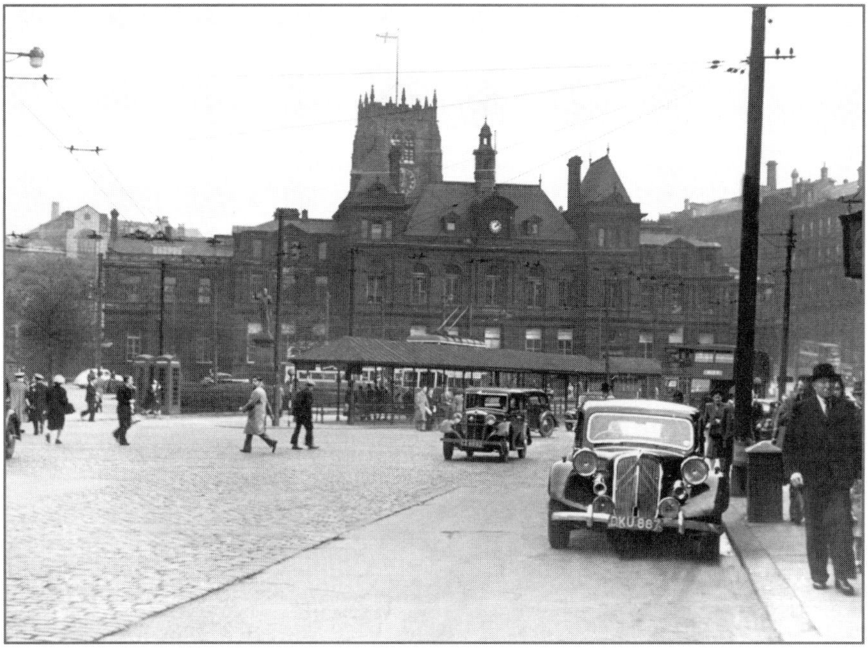

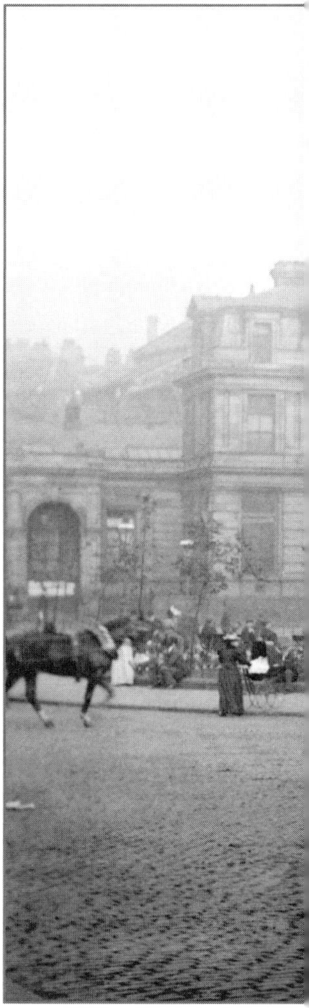

▲ **Bradford, Forster Square 1897** 39506
The statue of Richard Oastler and two children was unveiled in May 1869 at what was then the end of Market Street - Forster Square had yet to be laid out. Although Oastler was from Huddersfield, Bradford was chosen for the site of his statue as his campaign to reduce working hours for factory children was centred in the city.

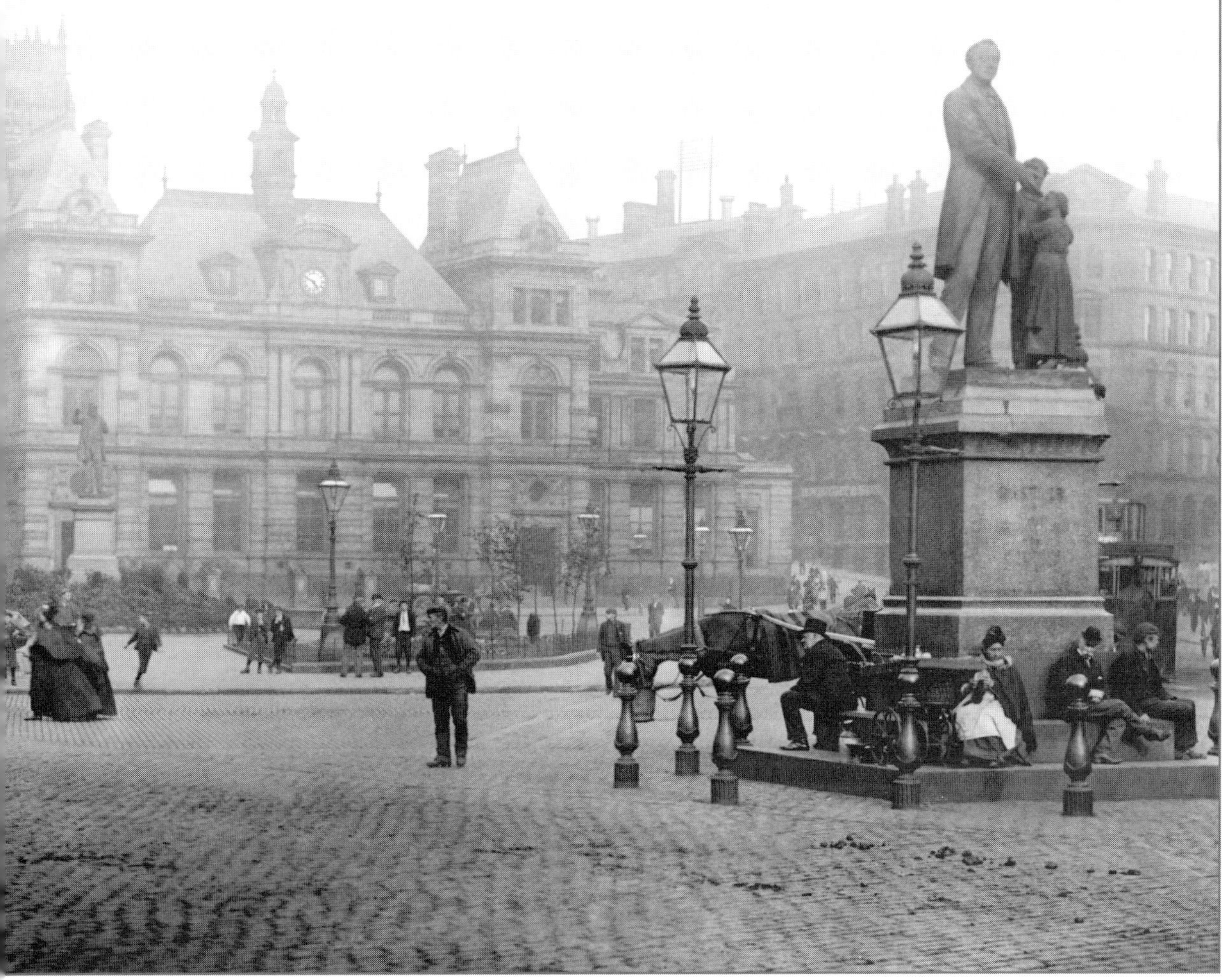

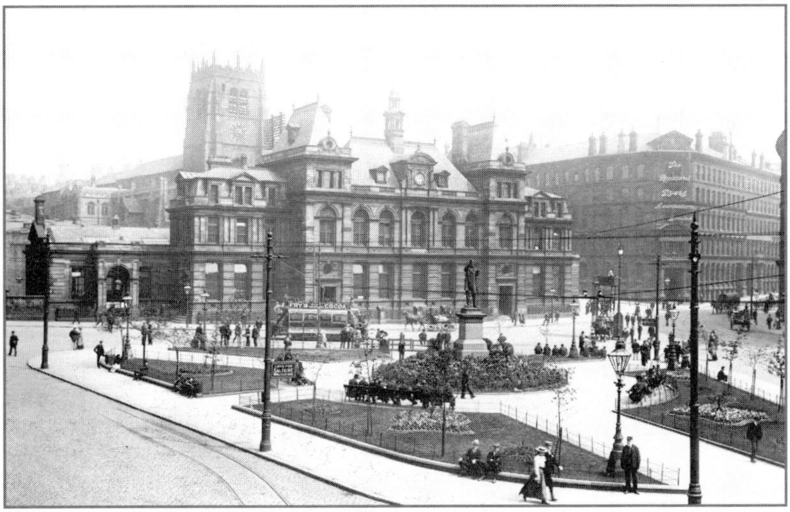

◄ **Bradford, Forster Square 1903**

49711

W E Forster's statue was unveiled on 17 May 1890, and remained here until after the Second World War. It was re-erected here on 30 November 1957. Behind the Post Office is the Parish Church with its 16th-century tower - it became a cathedral in 1918. To the right is part of Little Germany, a warehouse complex built by German traders who came to the city as cloth merchants in the 1820s and after the 1870 Franco-Prussian war. The area has recently been renovated, and is a major tourist attraction in the city. A German church remains in the city, up behind the Alhambra.

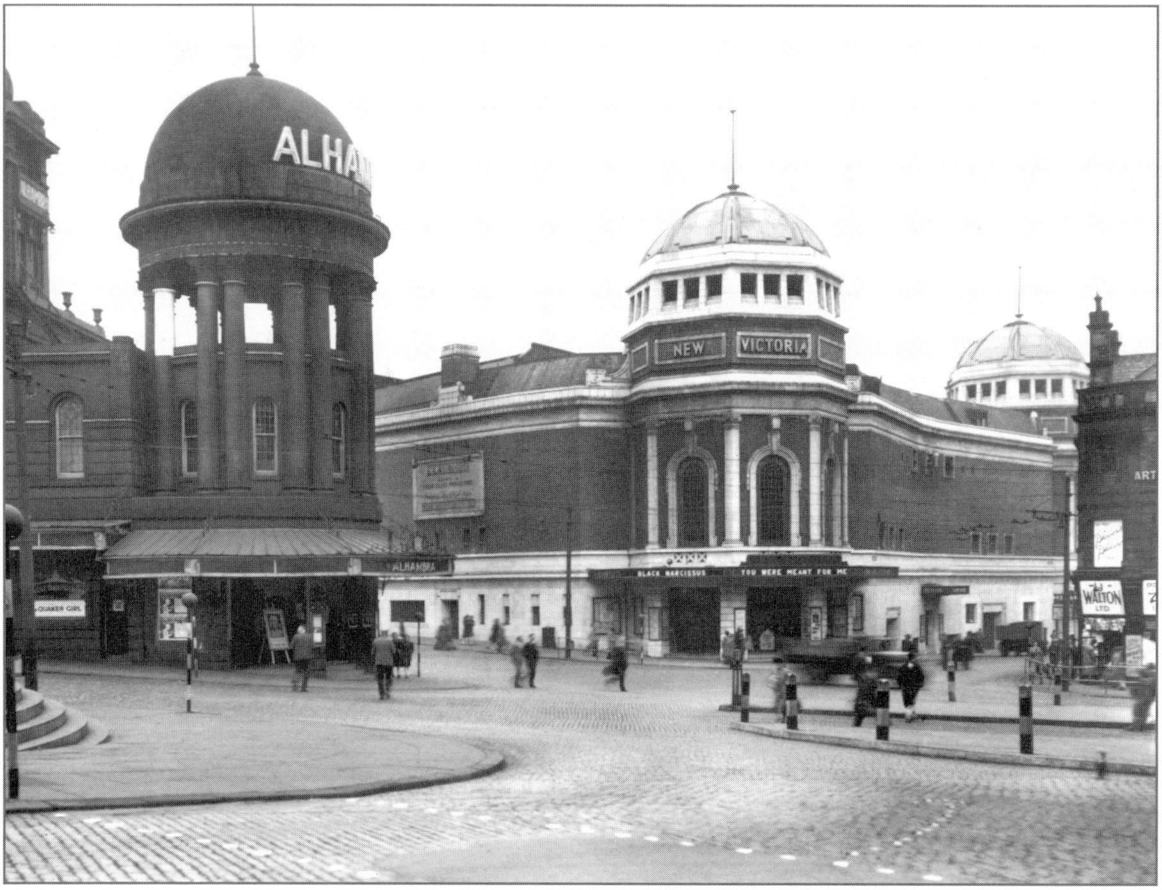

Bradford
The Alhambra and the New Victoria Theatre c1955 B173009
The 1800-seat Alhambra was built in 1914 by the pantomime impresario Francis Laidler, who also ran the nearby Prince's Theatre. The Alhambra was extensively renovated in 1986, and attracts major touring shows. Two million bricks went into the New Victoria Theatre, which opened on 22 September 1930 with the film 'Rookery Nook'. It was the city's supercinema, complete with ballroom and café. It later became the Gaumont/Odeon Cinemas and bingo social club. It has recently been eclipsed by a new Odeon multiplex on the outskirts.

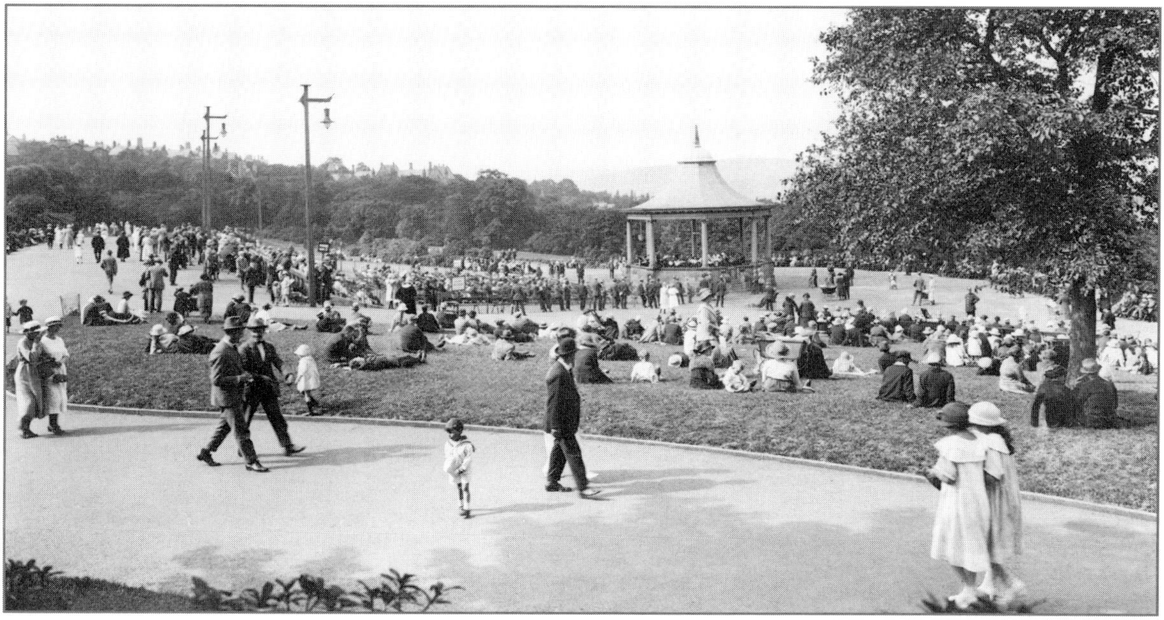

Bradford, Lister Park 1923 74400
The park occupies the original site of Manningham Hall, which was demolished; the land was given to the city by its owner, Samuel Cunliffe Lister. The Cartwright Art Gallery was built here in 1904; the gallery is a tribute to Edmund Cartwright, inventor of the power loom. The statue of Sir Titus Salt was moved here from outside the Town Hall in 1896.

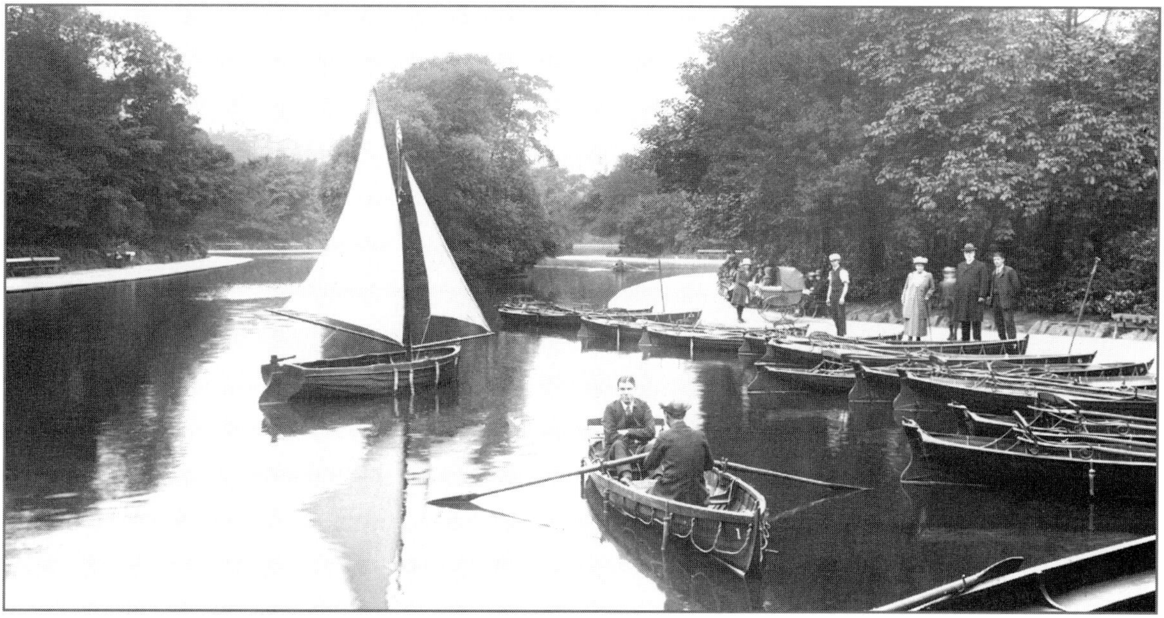

Bradford, Boating at Lister Park Lake 1921 71629
The Bradford Exhibition of 1904 stimulated the laying-out of this former country estate. As well as a Somali Village, the Exhibition also contained a switchback railway and also a water chute, which cascaded into this lake. These fairground rides had previously been used at three other exhibitions; they later went to the 1907 exhibition in Dublin. Today, the park is a wonderful oasis away from busy Manningham Lane.

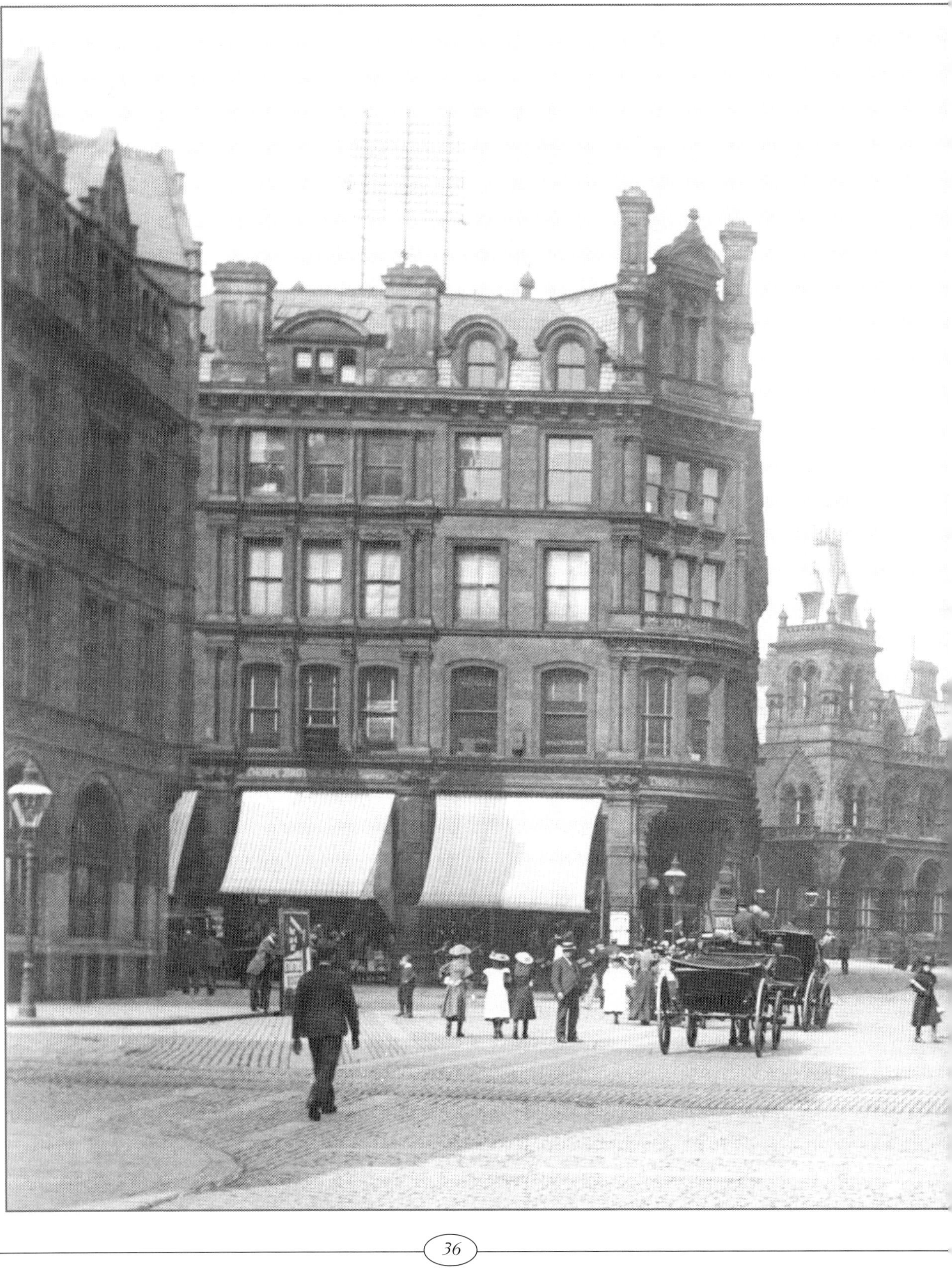

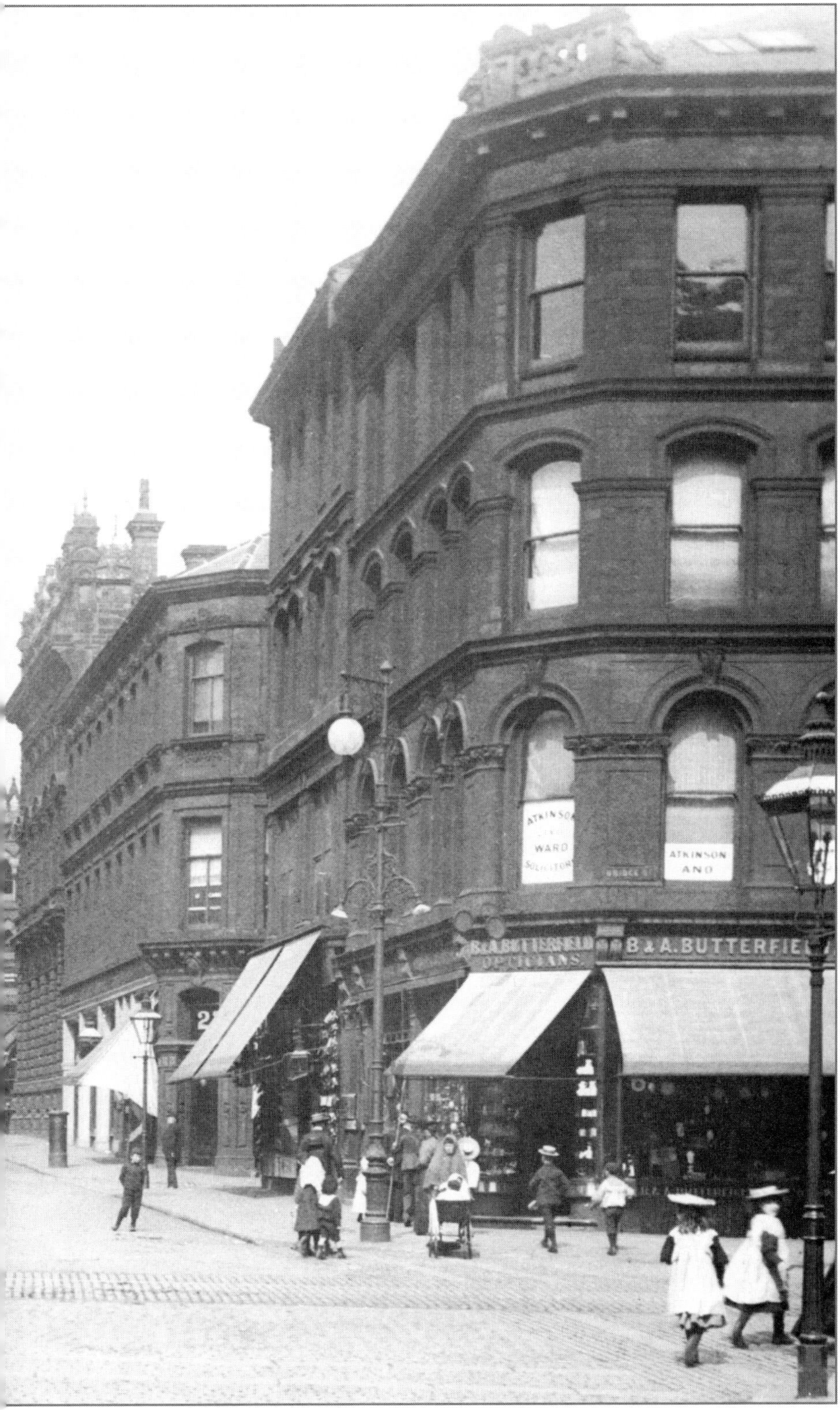

Bradford, Tyrell Street 1897 39510
One year after this photograph was taken, lines were laid for the new electric tramcars. These continued to run through Tyrell Street until 5 November 1949. Bradford's complete tram system closed on 6 May 1950 when trolleybuses took over - they lasted until 26 March 1972. On the final day of the trams, crowds came out to mourn their passing. Many placed pennies on the tracks to be clipped as a souvenir.

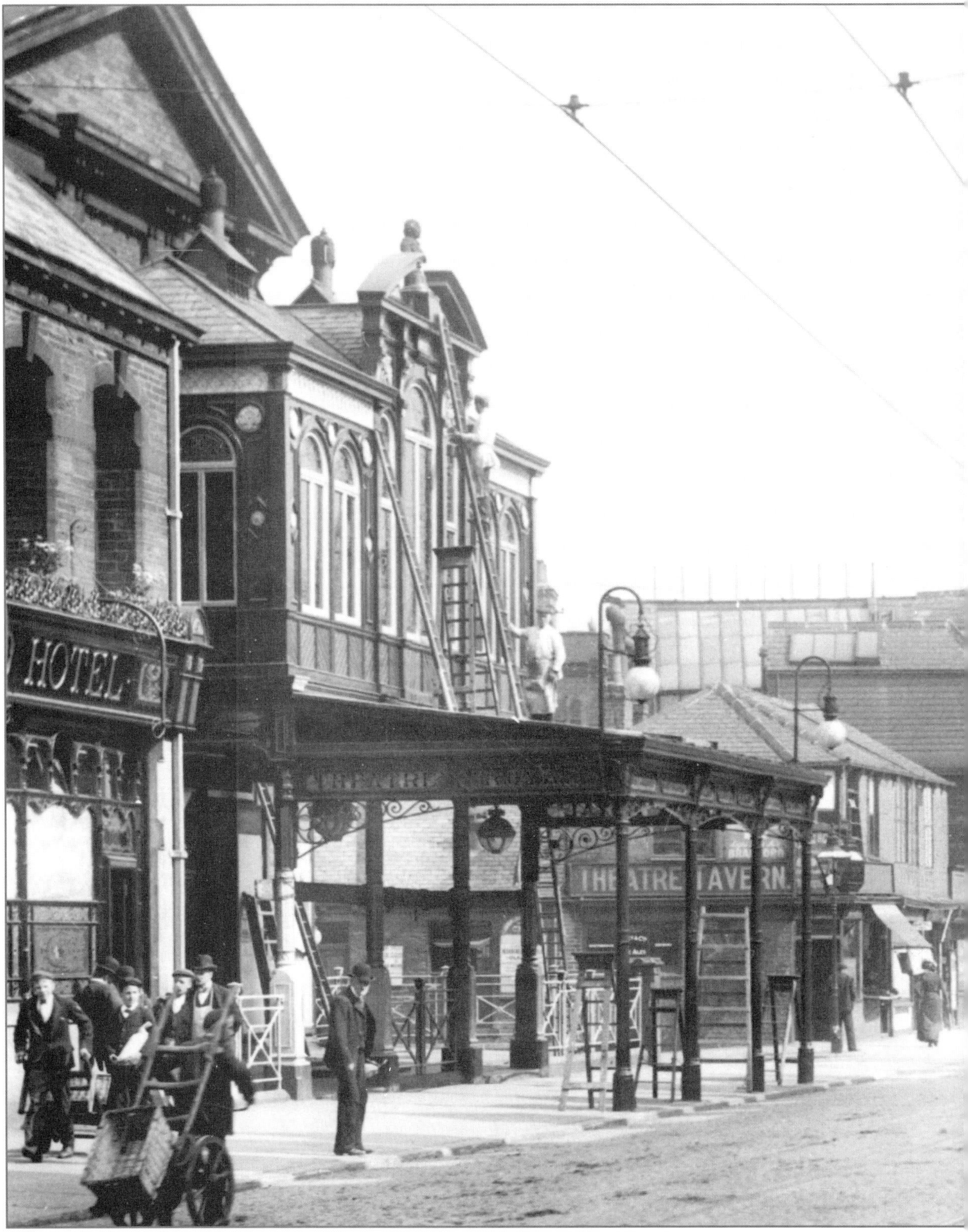
HOTEL
THEATRE TAVERN

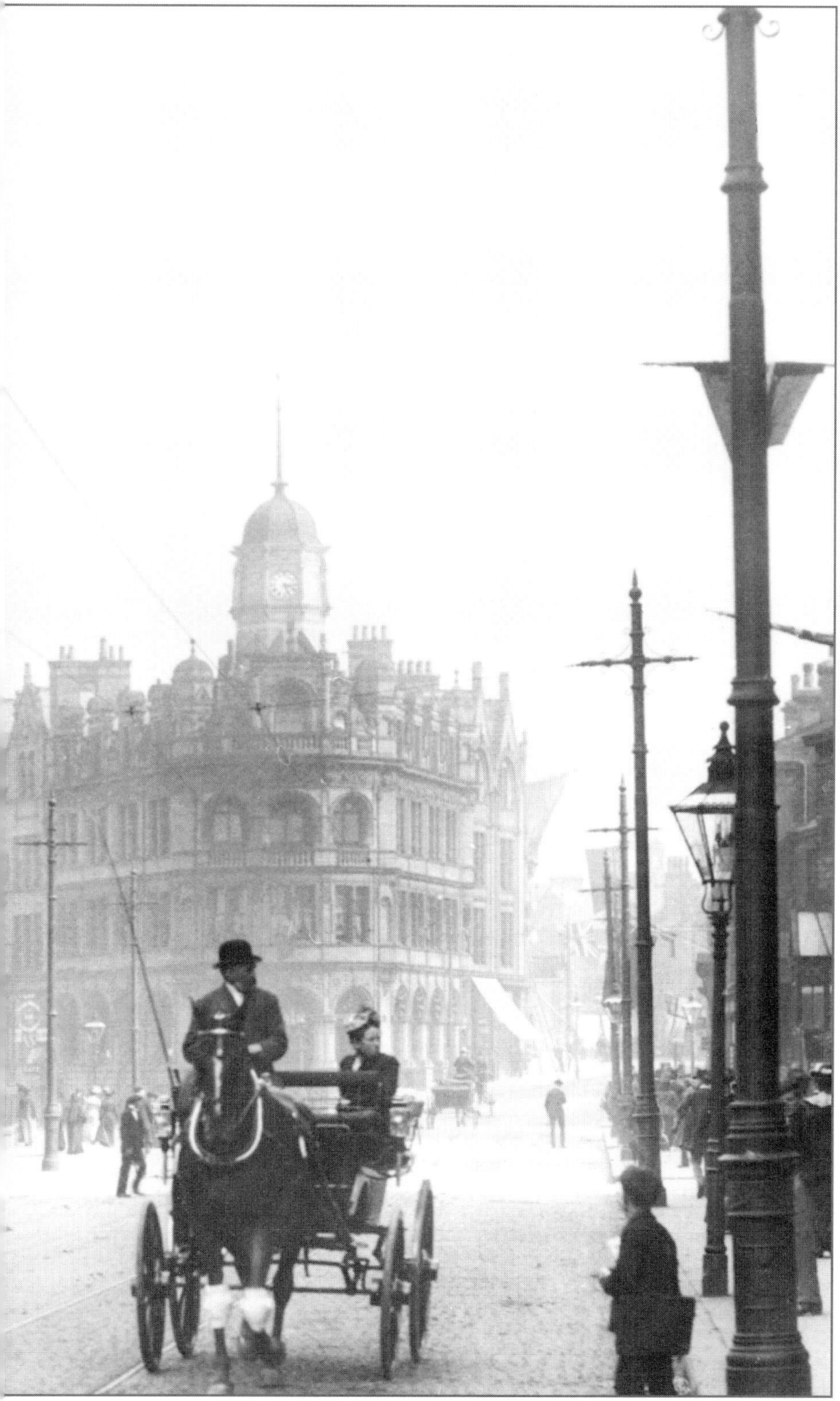

Bradford Manningham Lane 1902 48570

This is one of the main routes out of the city. Behind the horse and carriage is the old Yorkshire Penny Bank (1895). On the left is the Theatre Royal (1864), originally the Royal Alexandra Theatre. This was a cinema from 1921 to 1976, when it closed and was demolished. In 1905 Sir Henry Irving was on stage as Becket. His final words in the play were 'Into thy hands, O Lord'. He died that same evening at the Midland Hotel where he was staying with his manager, Bram Stoker, author of 'Dracula'.

▼ **Castleford, The Bus Station c1965** C257027

When the new bus station opened in May 1963 on the site of two former glass works, it was during a period of massive redevelopment in the town centre. One side was modernised, while Victorian Castleford remains on the right. Opposite the bus station was the 980-seat Theatre Royal (1873-1955), which was remodelled by Frank Matcham in 1913. Listed buildings remaining in the town are the Rising Sun inn (a former village institute built in 1905), and a nearby row of miners' cottages.

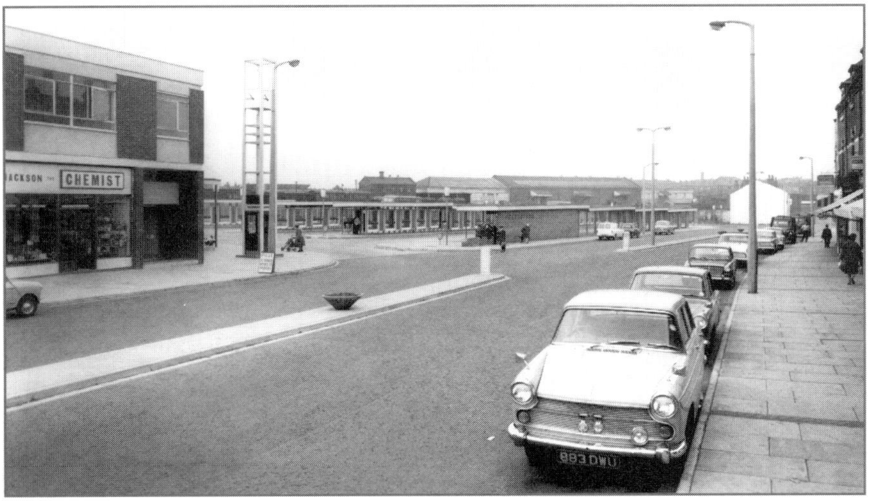

▼ **Castleford, Valley Gardens c1965** C257019

Described as a new lung for the town, these recreation grounds and ornamental gardens were constructed from derelict land next to the railway embankment. The opening by Lady and Sir Percy Jackson took place on Saturday afternoon 7th October 1933. The much larger Queen's Park (1897) gives splendid views right over the town.

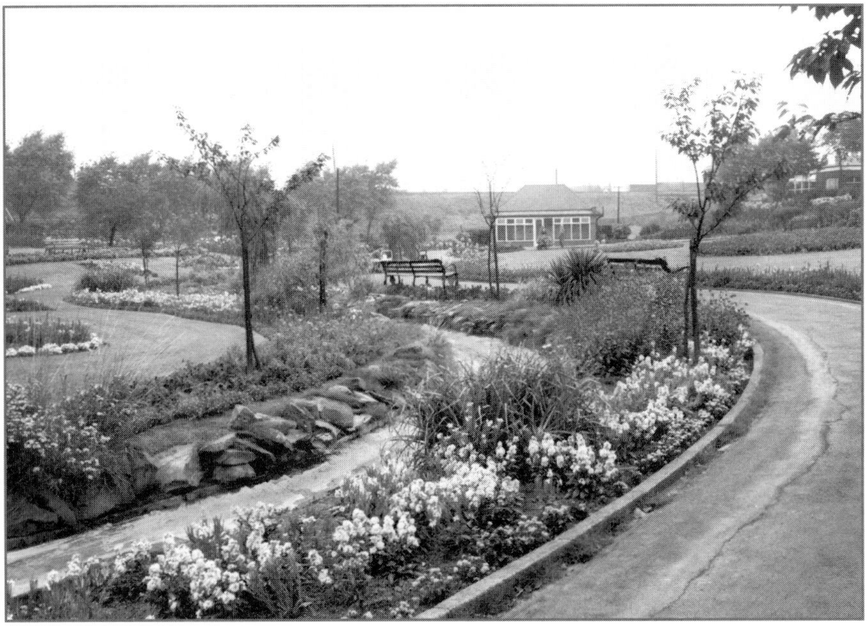

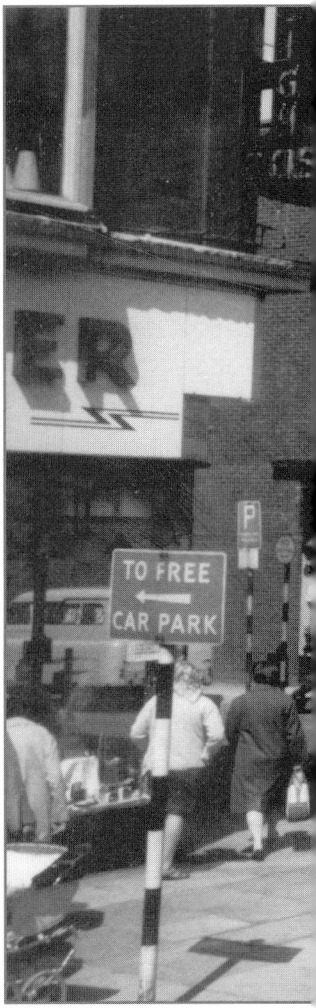

▲ **Castleford, Carlton Street c1965** C257044

This is the main shopping parade in the town. M & S proudly displayed their new frontage from 1964. At the end of the street were the swimming baths, which opened in May 1911. By 1901, the Castleford bottling industry was producing 16 million items per year; however, glass production ceased here in 1983. The world-famous sculptor Henry Moore was born in Castleford in 1898.

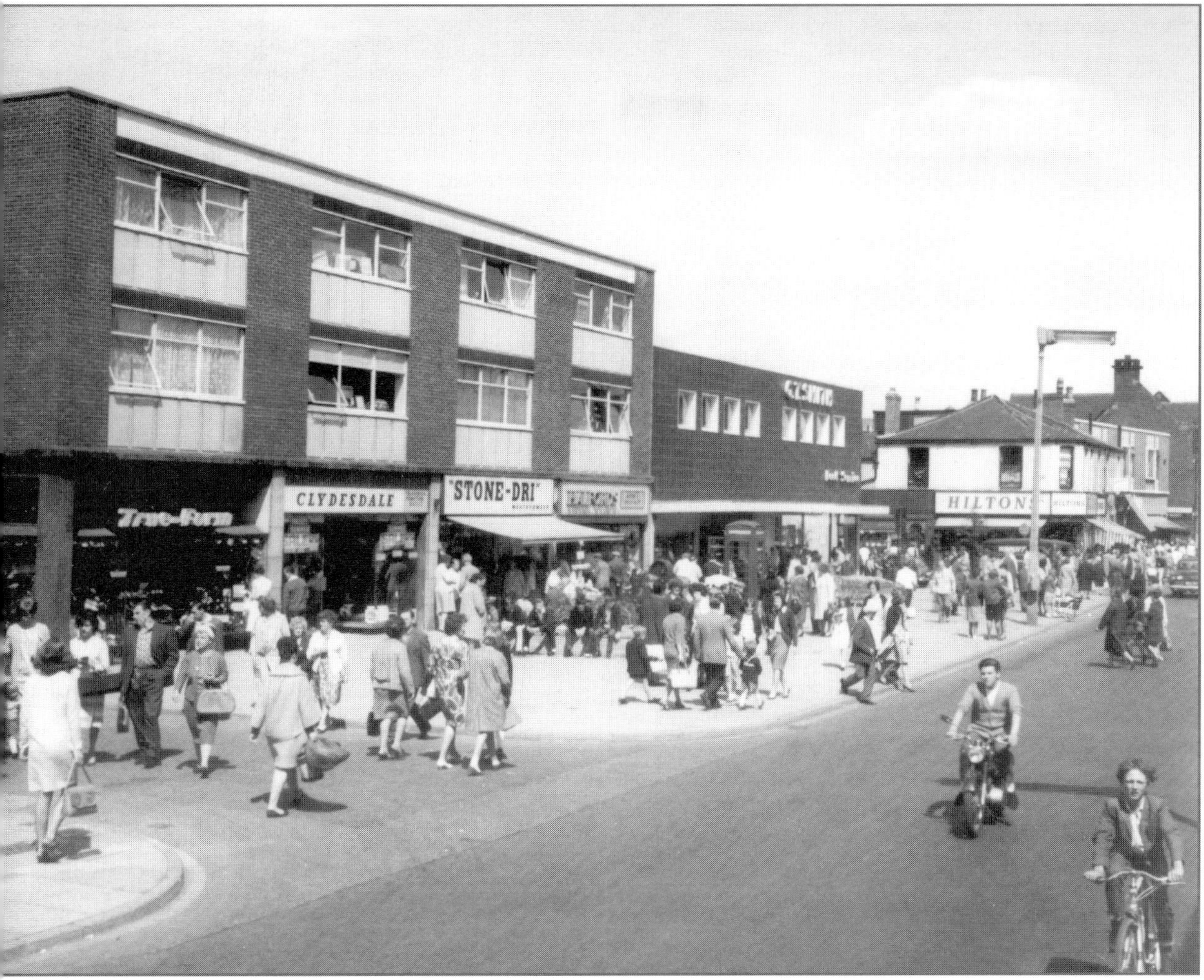

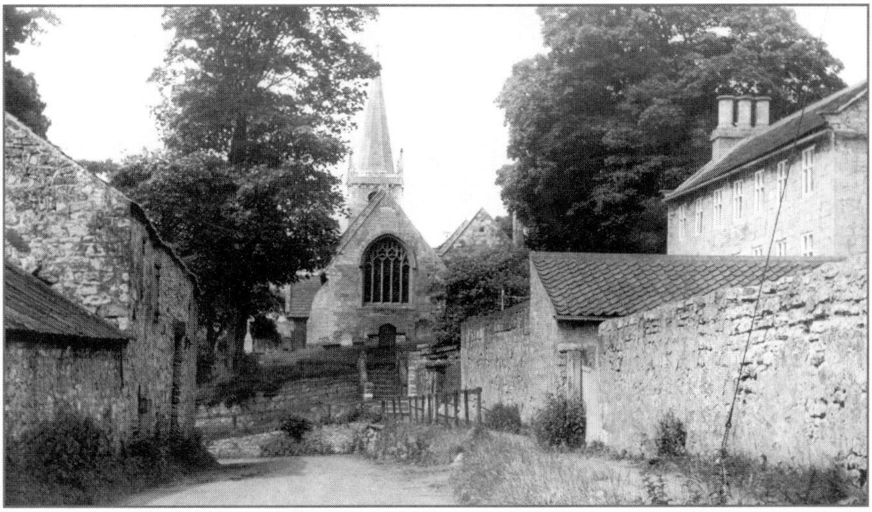

◄ **Castleford, Ledsham Village c1965** C257015
This charming village contains one of the most perfect examples of a Saxon church. Dating from the 8th century, All Saints also has a 15th-century tower; the church was restored in 1871. The nearby vicarage was built in 1821. Despite being close to the coalfields, Ledsham escaped any industrial activity.

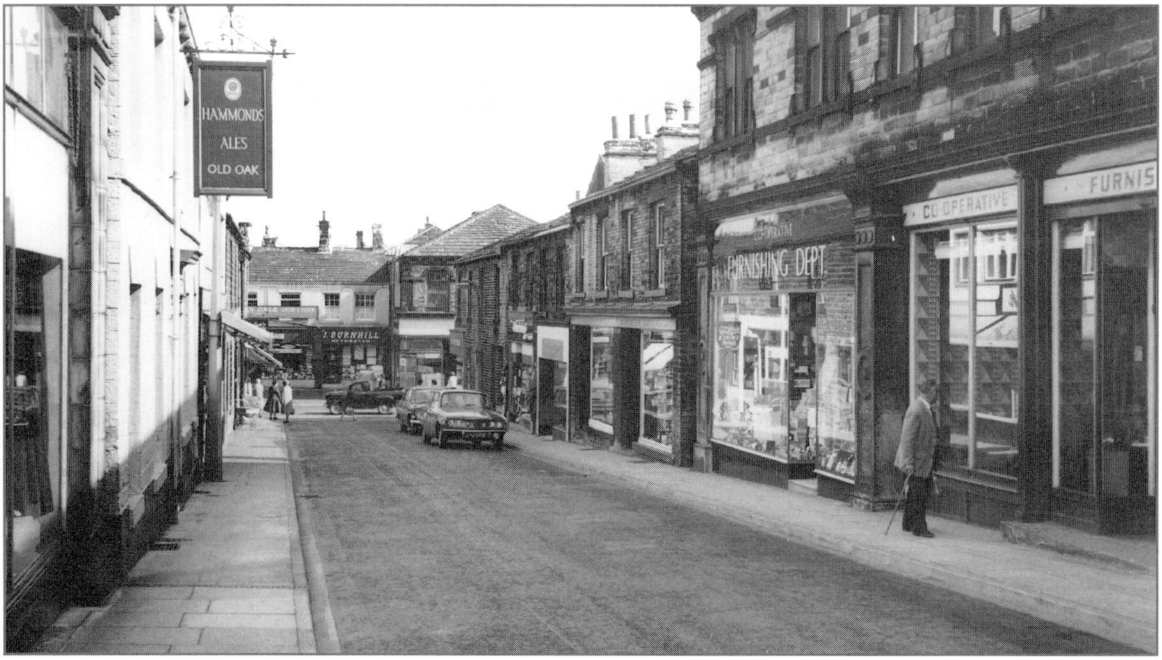

Cleckheaton, Cheapside c1965 C263016
In 1800, this was a small village bisected by one turnpike road. Within a few decades, the face of Cleckheaton had changed beyond recognition with the establishment of machine manufacturing. New streets began to be laid out as the town's population increased with the influx of new workers. By 1890, the town was the world centre of card clothing, the making of a device (a sheet of leather inset with wire teeth) to comb wool prior to being spun. Before the machines were invented, women and children as young as four set the wire teeth and were paid half a penny for every 1400 teeth carded.

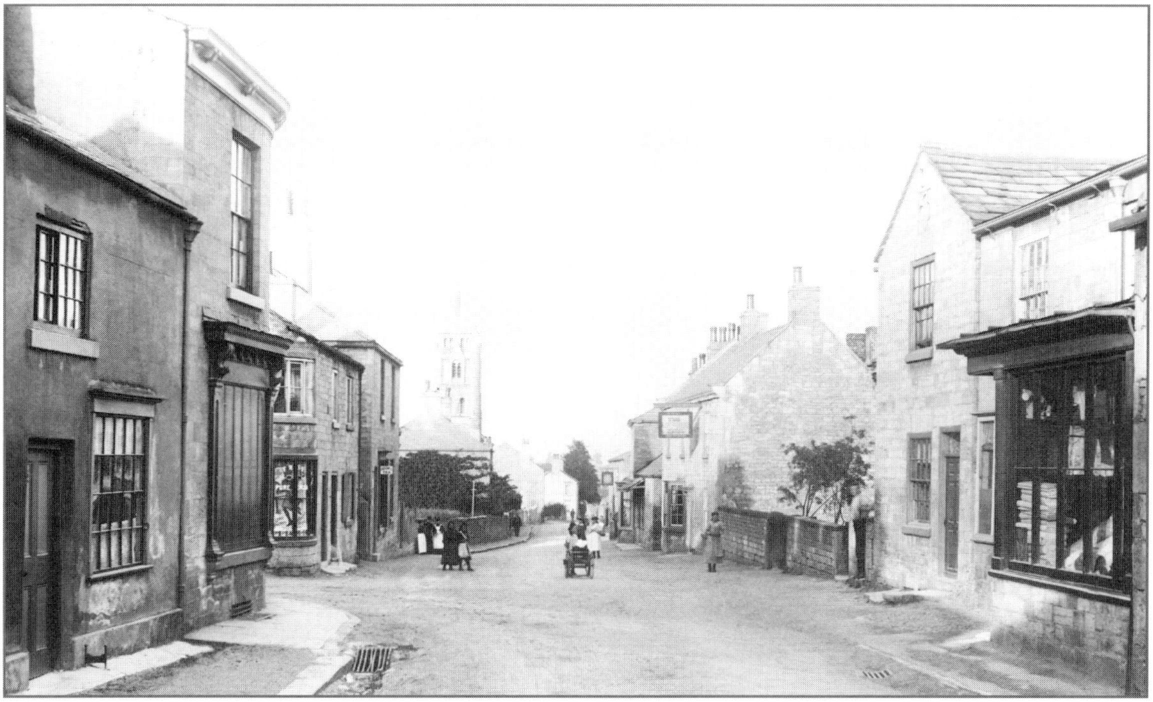

Clifford, The Village 1897 39445
Originally sited on a ford over Firgreen Beck, Clifford was at one time the manor that included all of nearby Boston Spa. People from Clifford used to collect the money for the rights to use the spa water. Irish linen workers settled here in the mid 1800s. The Catholic church in the background is the stunning St Edward, King and Confessor, which was completed in 1848. The tower is modelled on Angouleme Cathedral. The builder, Joseph Aloysius Hansom, had earlier in 1836 patented the new safety cab bearing his name.

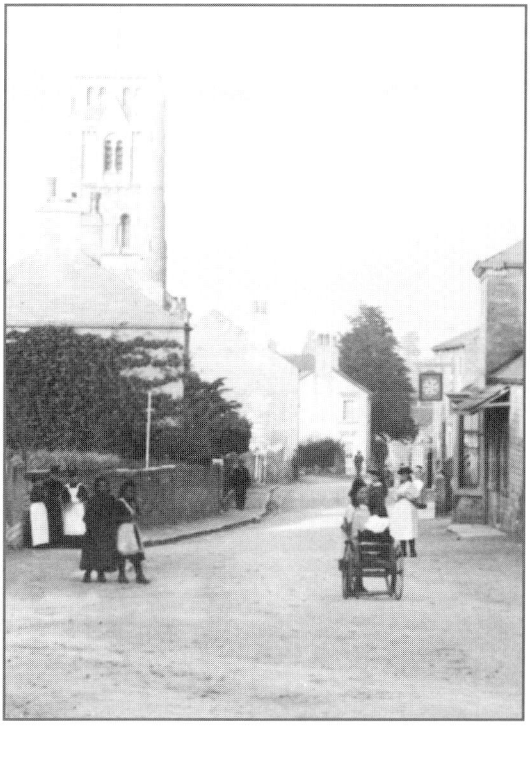

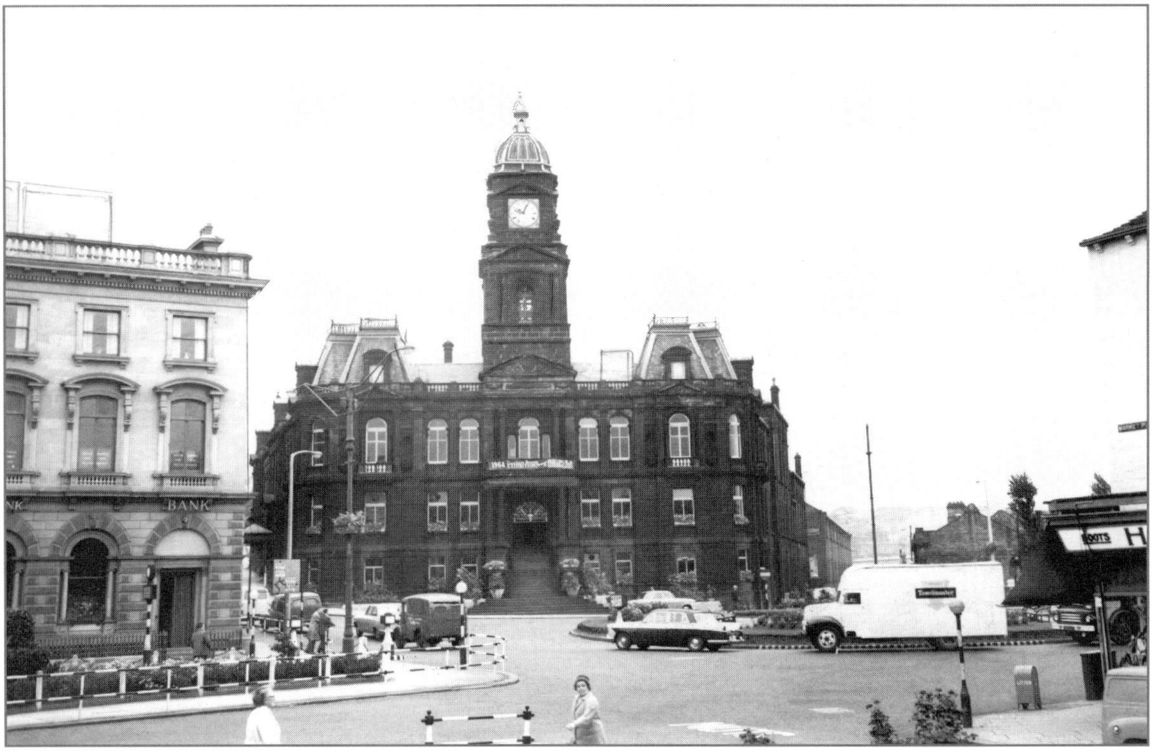

Dewsbury, The Town Hall c1960 D100001

Three years in the building, the Town Hall opened on 17 April 1889, and this day was proclaimed a public holiday in the town. The Italianate style reflected the prosperity of this weaving community. The Albion Hotel and a beer house, the Cross Keys, were previously on the Town Hall site. To the right is the site of the Lancashire and Yorkshire line Market Place railway station, which was here from 1867 to 1930. The West Riding Union Bank on the left (later Barclays) replaced the Royal Hotel. In the middle on their own island site was Fletchers the grocers. Behind the bank was the Post Office (1907-1988) and the magnificent Empire Theatre (3rd July 1909 to 24th April 1955) whose closure, caused by TV and cinema, was so sudden that the stars booked for the following week were not even aware that their performances had been cancelled. Anthony Newley was a resident actor here for a number of years.

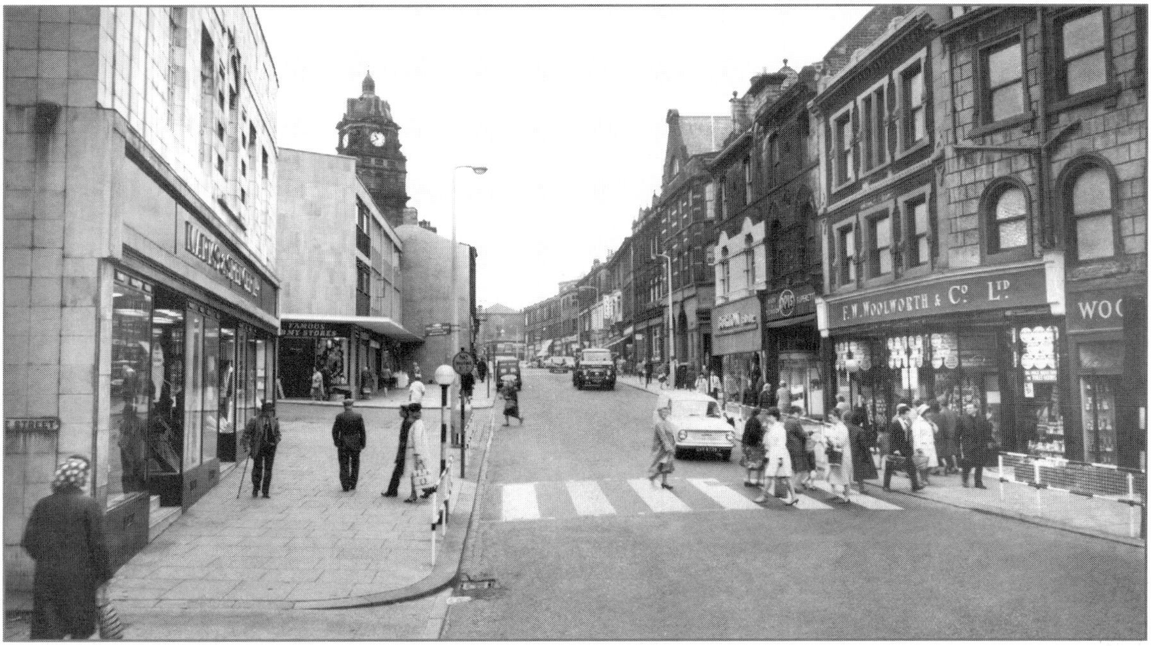

Dewsbury, Northgate c1965 D100012
The eastern end of Market Place was opened up in the 1830s as the Dewsbury and Gomersal turnpike road. The clocktower, top left, is part of the Co-operative building, which was opened in 1880 at a cost of £7,000 on the site of the old Cottage Hospital.

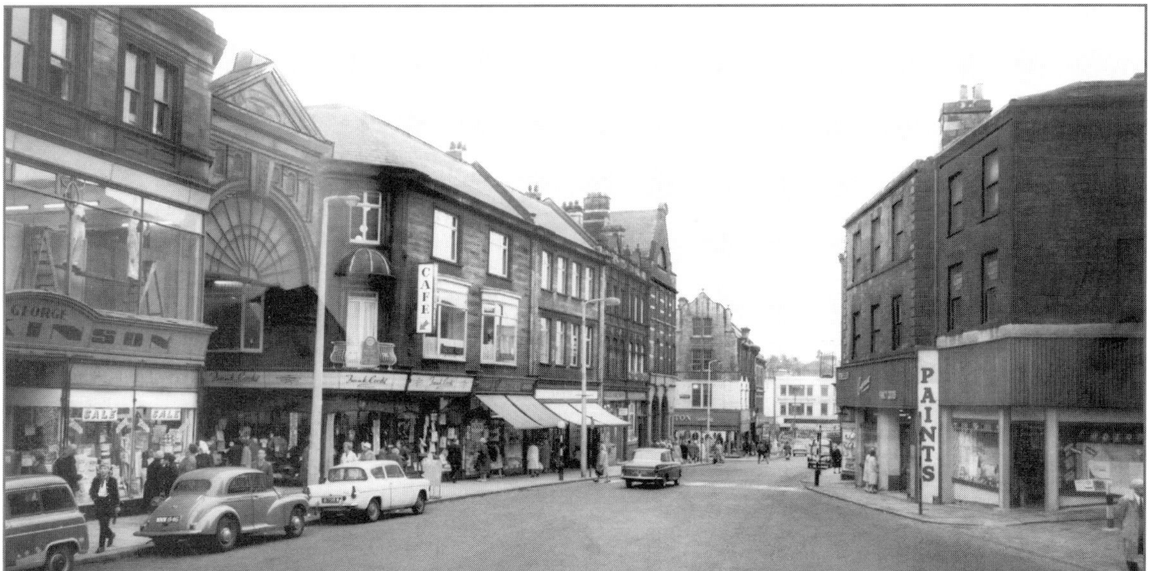

Dewsbury, Northgate c1965 D100014
The Kingsway Arcade (1916) is on the left. King George V and Queen Mary visited the town in July 1912, but they spent only fifteen minutes here for a reception at the Town Hall. Their second and somewhat longer visit in 1918 was spent at the army ordnance depot; here they met the workers who, during the war, had processed 36 million items of clothing reclaimed from the battlefields.

Dewsbury, The Town Centre c1965 D100013

The town achieved nation-wide fame in 1941 when a wartime radio show was broadcast from the Empire Theatre. On stage was Roy Barbour's comedy revue, 'Great Stuff This'. Another national figure was Dewsbury's only MP to become a Cabinet Minister. Walter Runciman, the Liberal MP, headed the Education Board in 1908 and was at the Board of Trade in 1914.

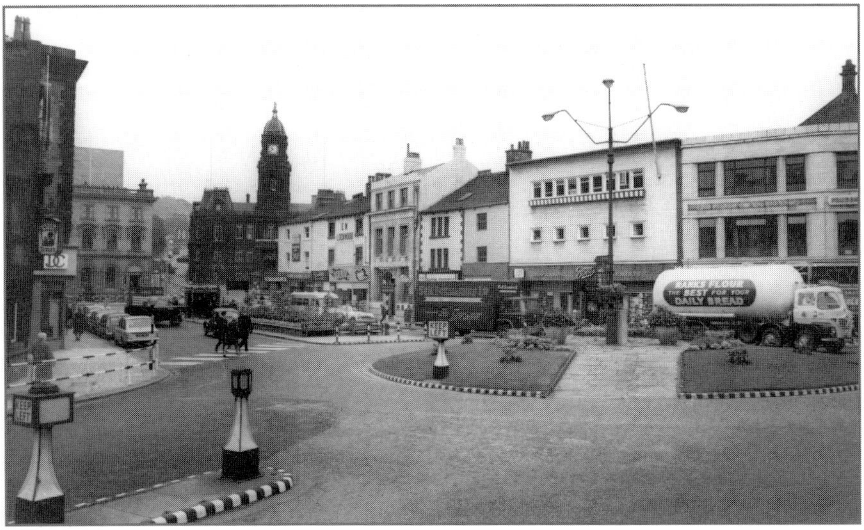

Ferrybridge, The Old Bridge over the Aire c1955 F166001

It is hard to believe that the arched bridge, built in 1797 by John Carr of York, used to carry all the main Great North road traffic. It also gave access to Fryston Hall nearby, which was demolished in 1931 when the power station was extended. Each year the generating station consumes 5 million tons of coal.

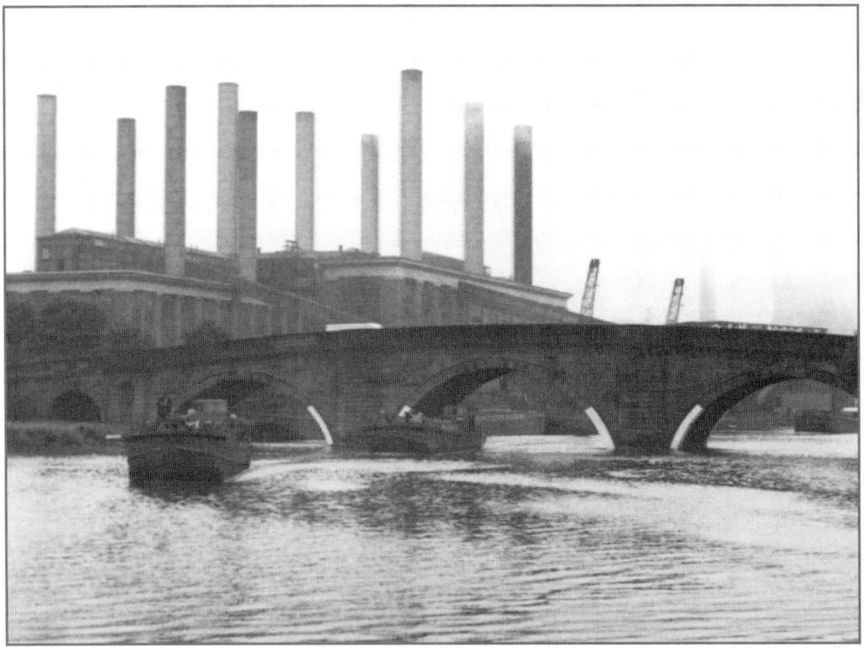

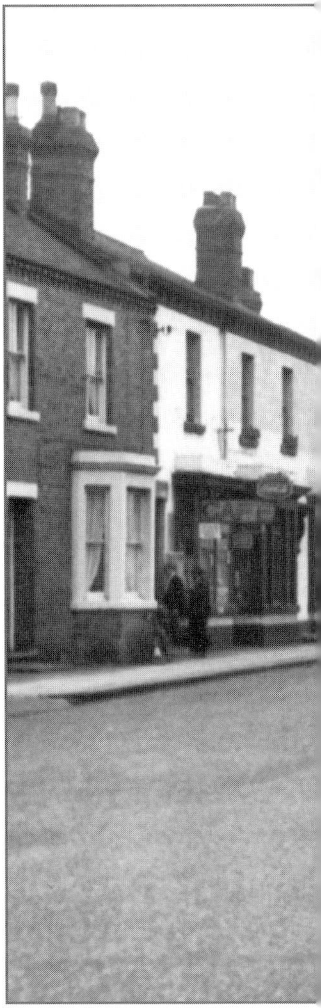

Ferrybridge The Power Station c1955 F166011

Ferrybridge was a rendezvous point for the gentry travelling up the Great North Road. Ferrybridge had Yorkshire's largest pottery, which was founded in 1792 and was part-owned by Ralph Wedgwood. The power station that dominates the town was established in 1927. The bulk of the station was demolished in 1968 and rebuilt with massive cooling towers.

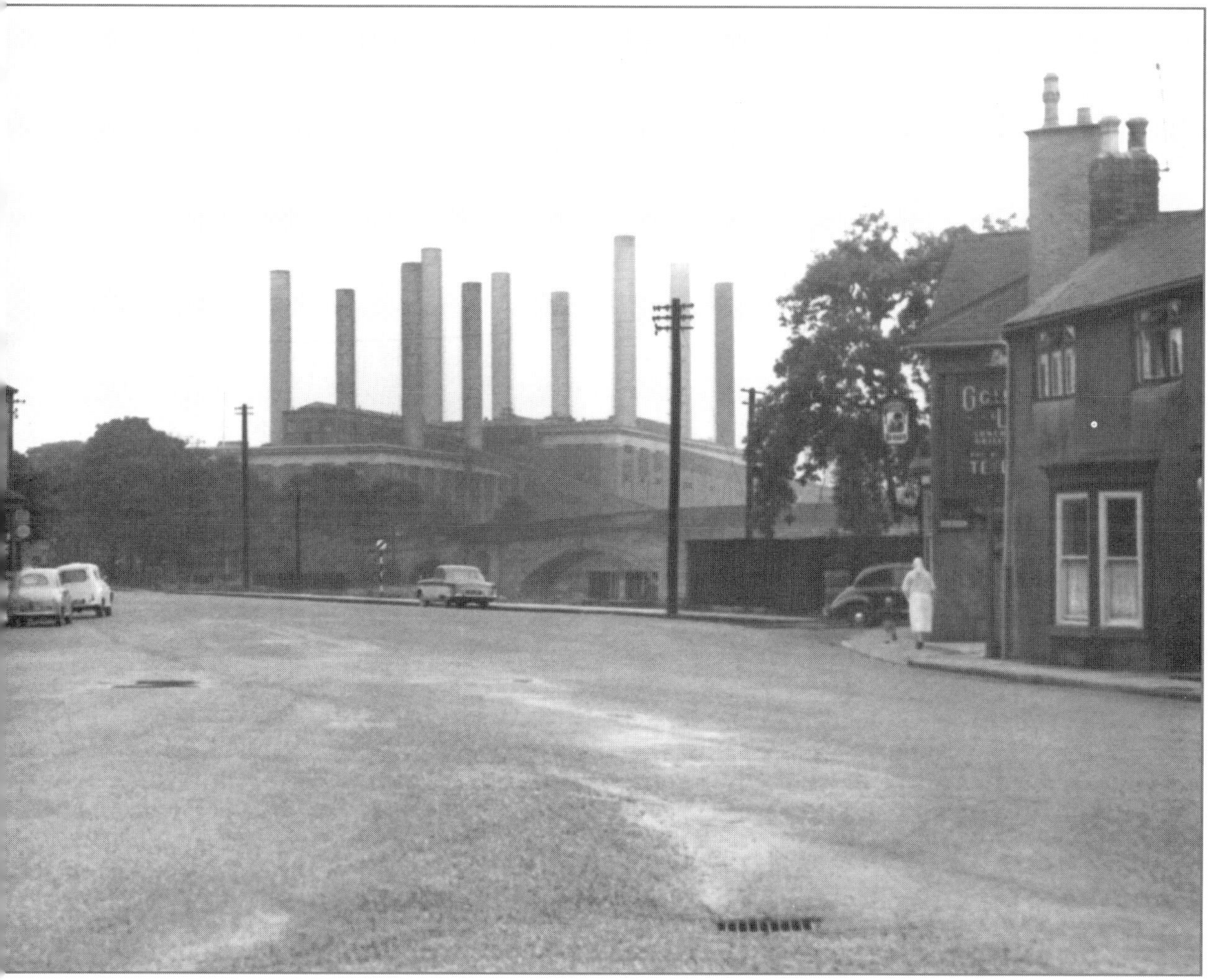

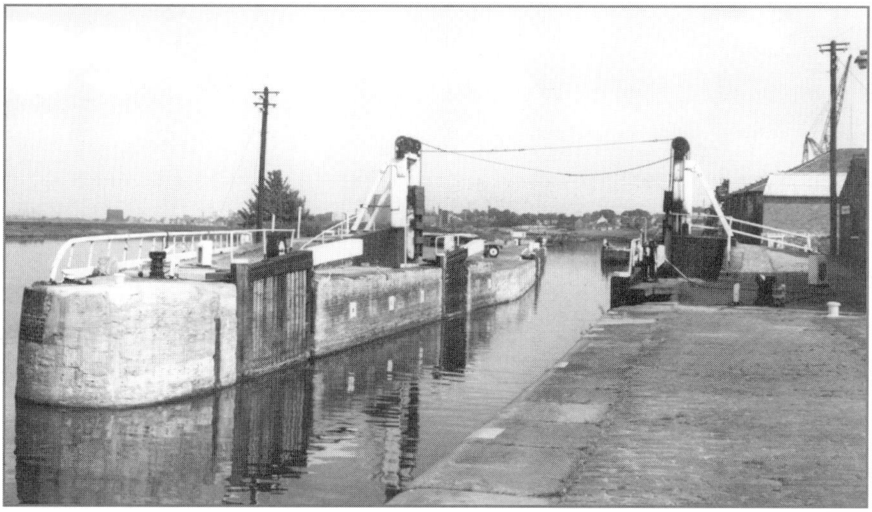

Ferrybridge, The Canal Locks c1955 F166025
The Aire and Calder Navigation of the late 18th century opened up trade between West Yorkshire and the Humber, and thence to the rest of Europe. Coal from Kellingley Colliery also travelled this route up to the power station, which has been on the riverside since 1927.

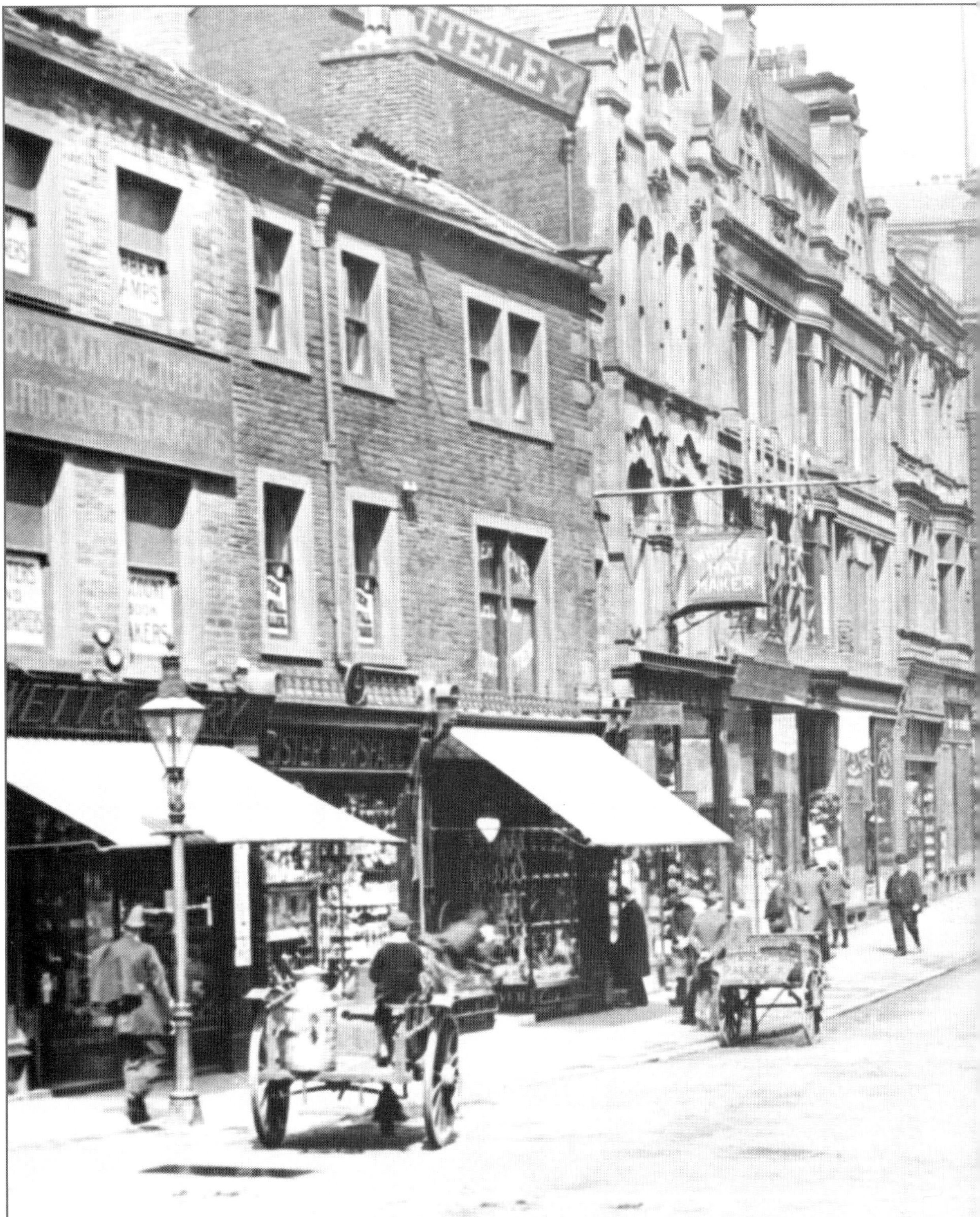
BOOK MANUFACTURERS
HAT MAKER

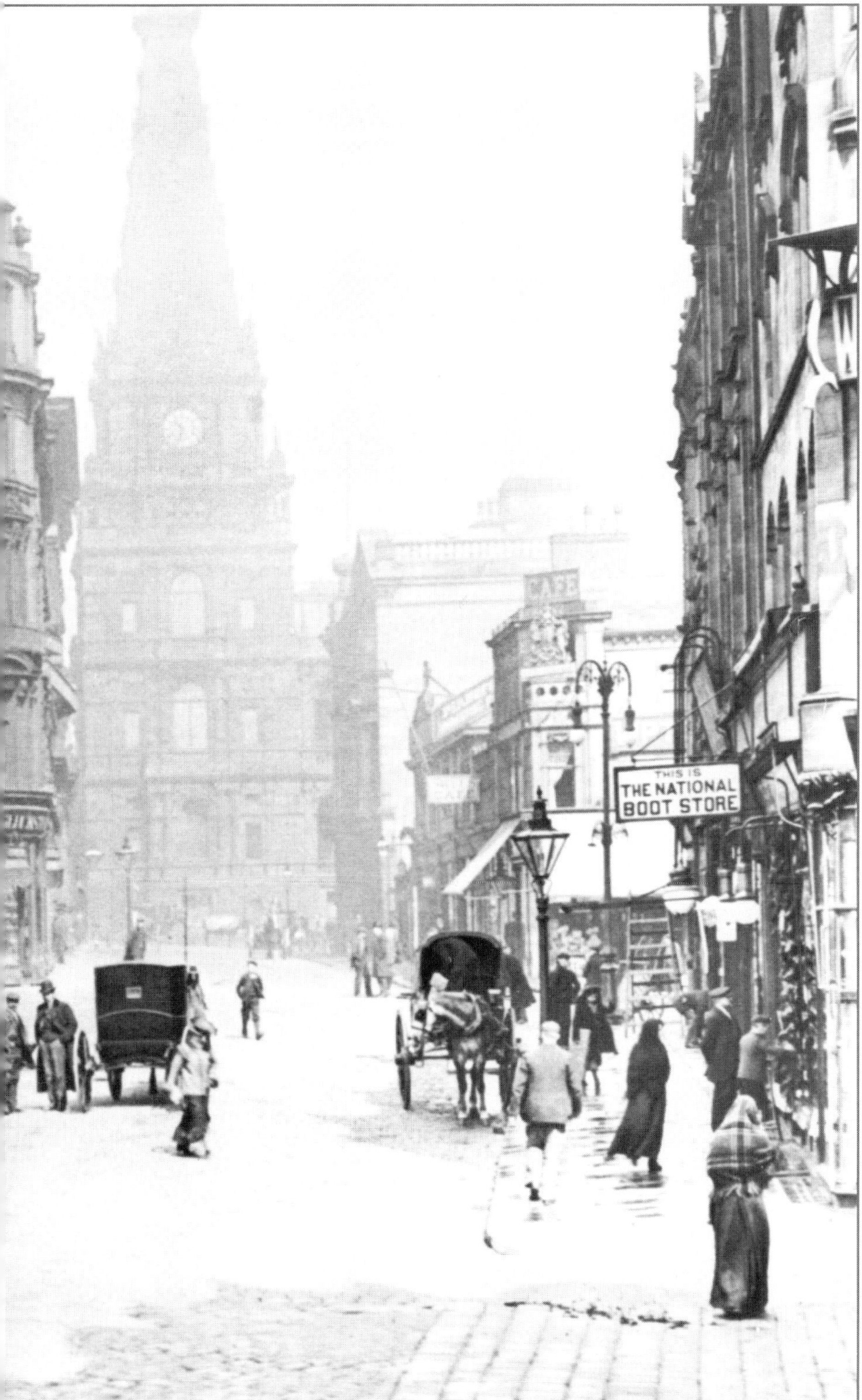

Halifax, The Town Hall 1900 H9001
Described as a cross between a Renaissance palace and a medieval cathedral, the Town Hall opened at the head of Princess Street in 1863. The builder also worked on sculptures at the Houses of Parliament and Harewood House. The central Victoria Hall had a splendid stone and marble floor covered in a tasteful Crossley carpet provided by the one-time Mayor John Crossley, the town's biggest carpet manufacturer.

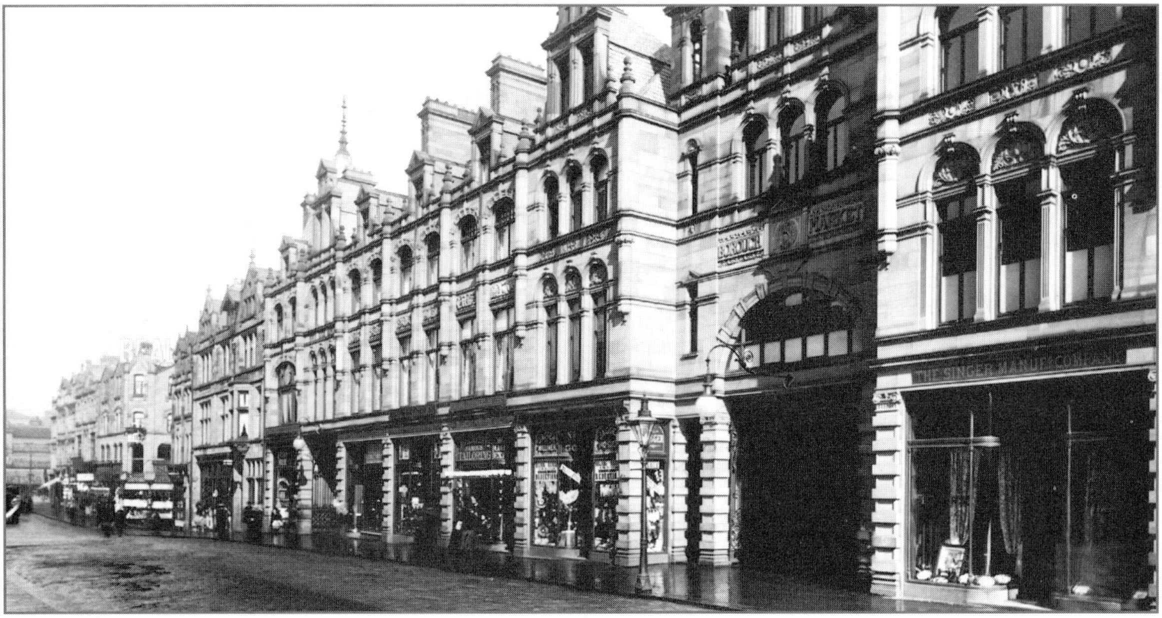

Halifax, The Market Building 1896 38776
The Market was newly-opened in the year of this photograph. It was designed by the local firm Leeming and Leeming of Northgate, with a lofty roof supported by richly-decorated ironwork. The official opening was conducted by the Duke and Duchess of York, whose arrival was met by a 21-gun salute. On the same day, they lunched at Belle Vue before opening the new Infirmary building in Free School Lane.

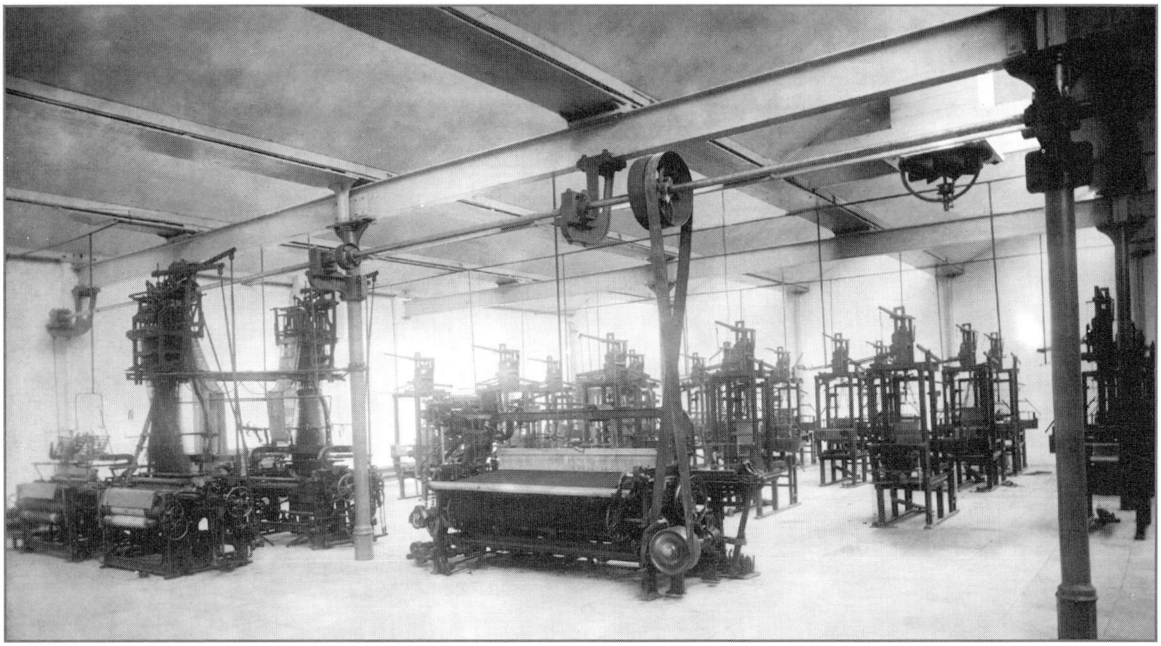

Halifax, The Technical School 1896 38781
Following the passing of the Technical Act of 1889, the Corporation began this fine building in Hopwood Lane; it was completed in 1895. Here, technical education could be carried out away from the pressures of the workplace. Further education remains on the site: the Calderdale College now occupies the building.

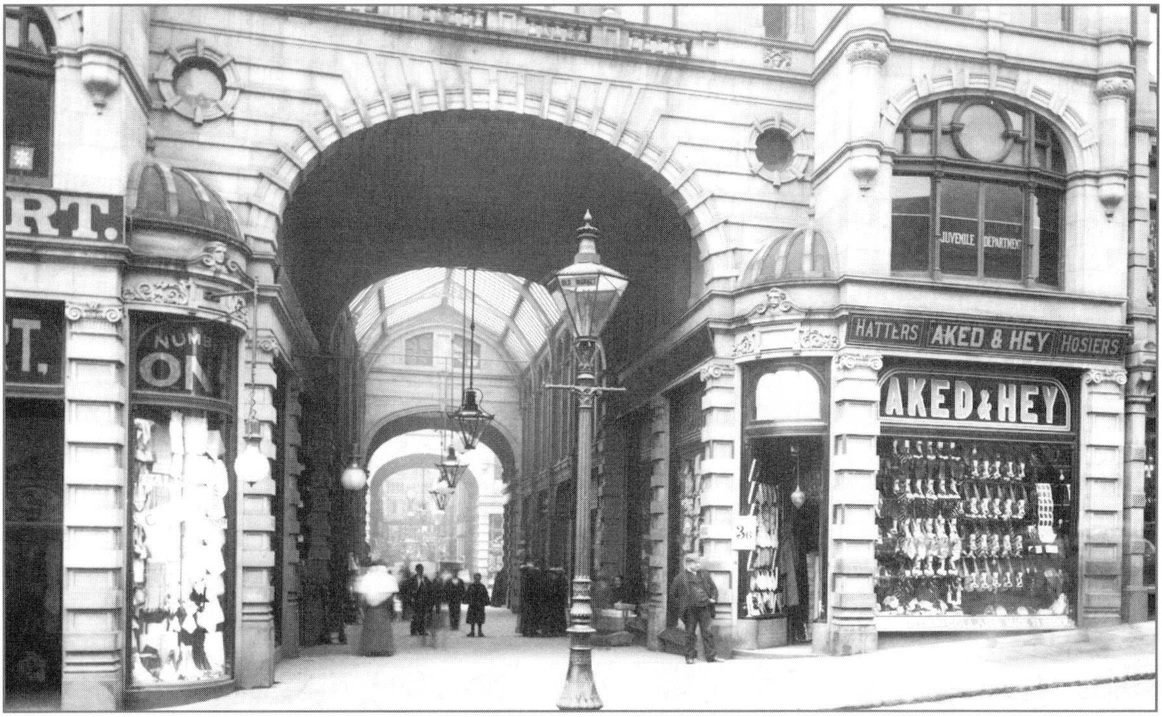

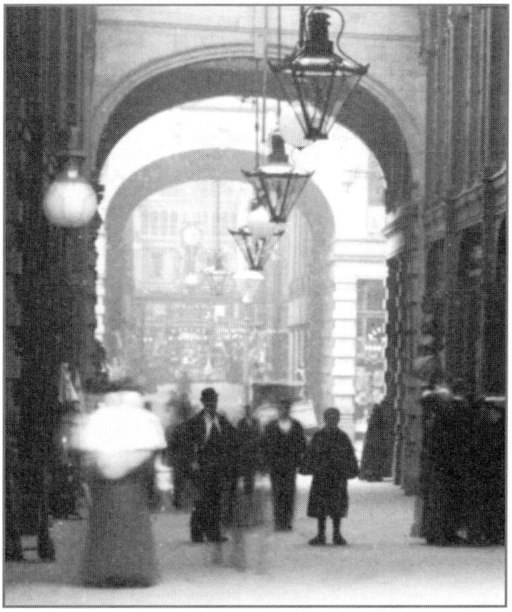

Halifax

Entrance to the Arcade 1896 38777

Building commenced on the site of the former red brick market in 1891 to the designs of the local architects Joseph and John Leeming. Inside the entrance were many tempting shops, including a confectioners and refreshment rooms. The Arcade opened somewhat before the main entrance, and gave residents a taster of the fine interior to come.

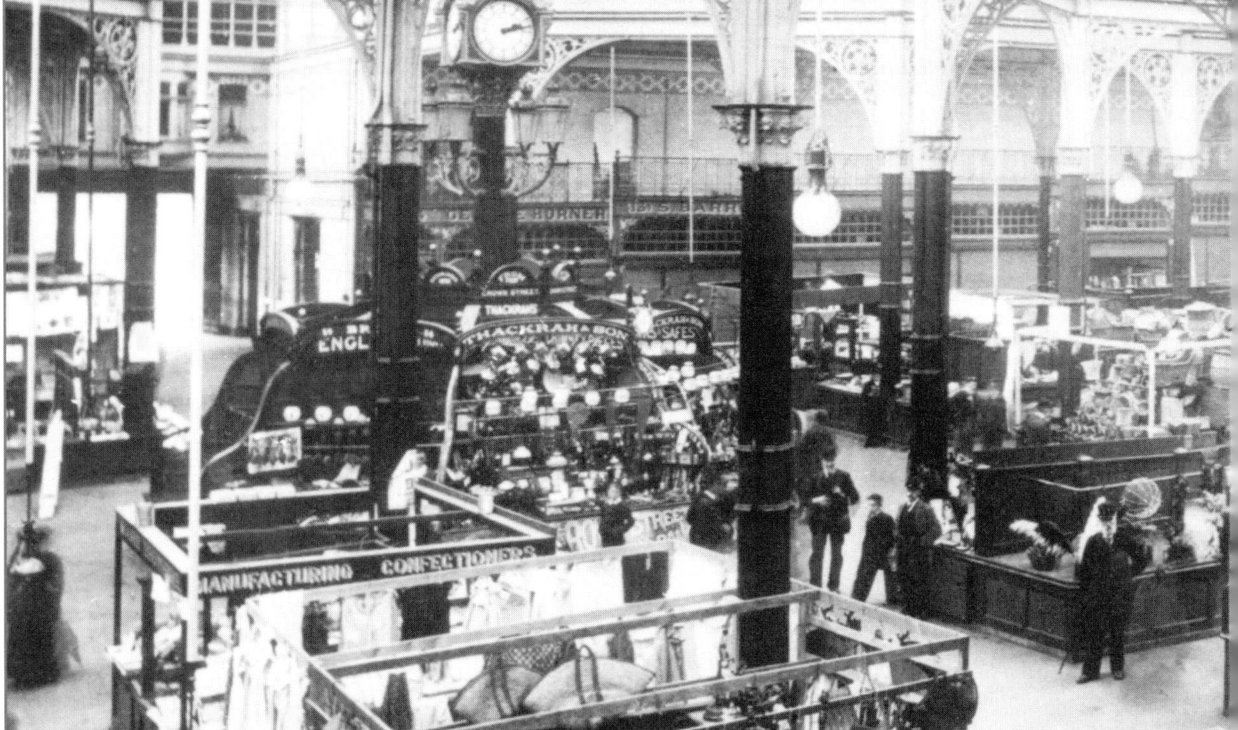
CONFECTIONERS
THACKRAH

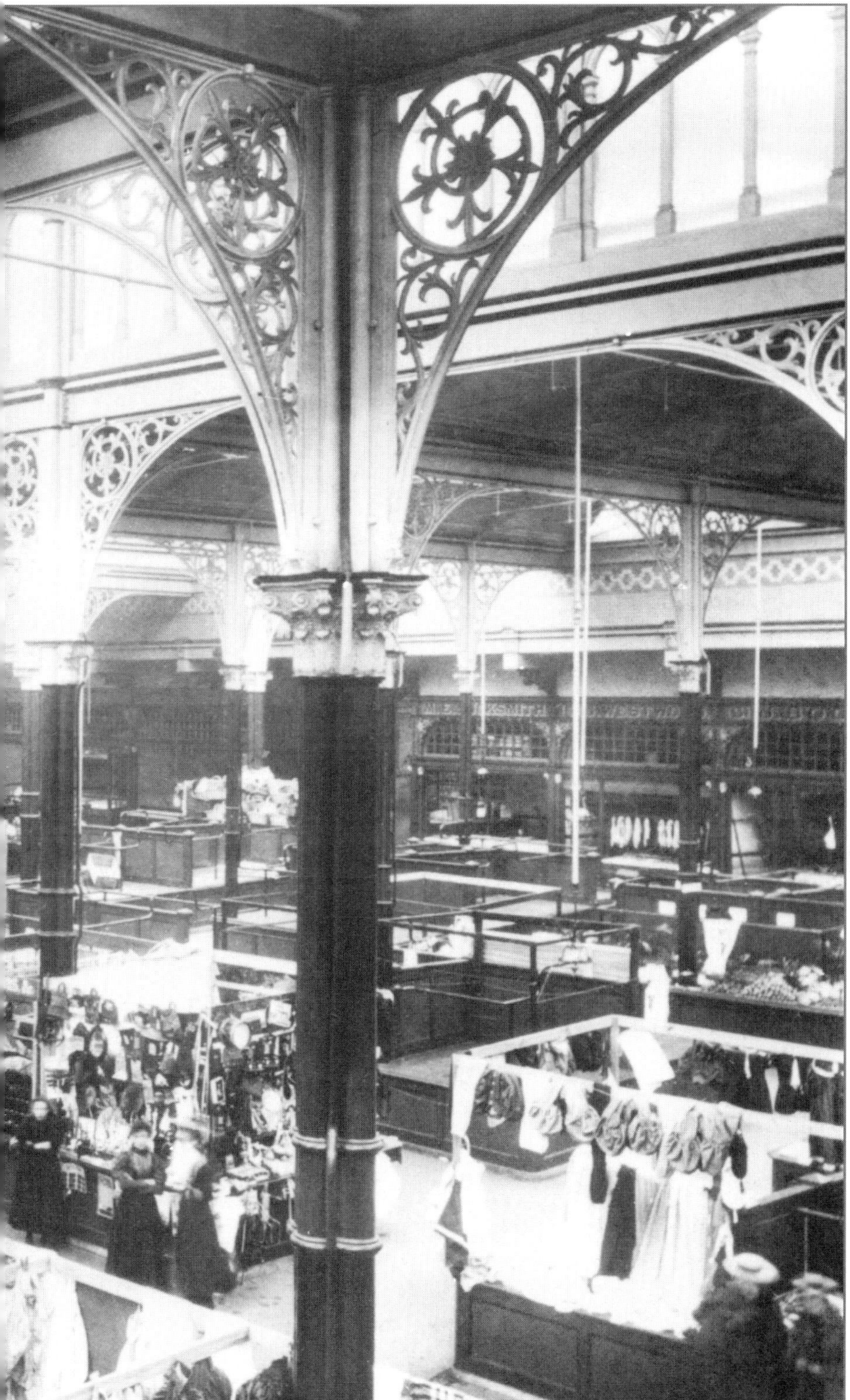

Halifax, Inside the Market Hall 1892

38782

Here there was space for forty-three shops and over 100 stalls. In addition, a fish market offered sixteen choice counters. Shoppers could purchase all their weekly goods here, from hardware to the freshest vegetables. The magnificent cast iron pillars held up the glass roof, giving welcome natural light to the interior of the busy Borough Market.

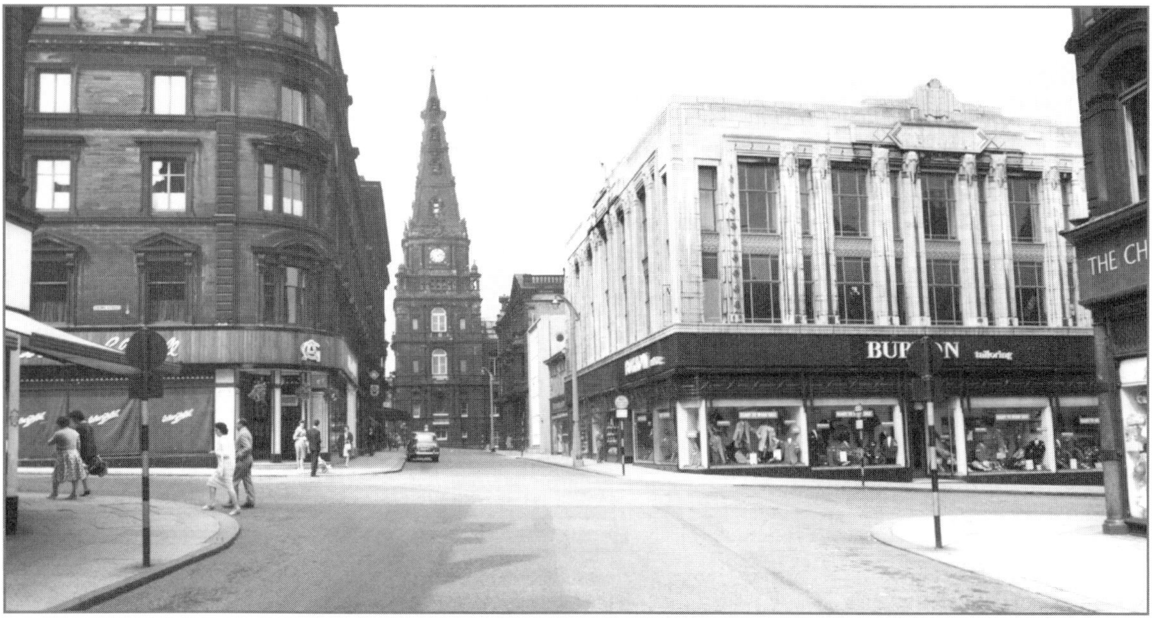

Halifax, Southgate c1965 H9086
This stylish Burton's tailoring shop was built in 1932; it replaced many small shops along Old Market and Princess Street. Originally, the upper floors contained a billiard hall and a skating rink. Later, the top floor became the Empress Ballroom. These days, the building houses McDonald's fast food restaurant, who gave the site a much-needed facelift.

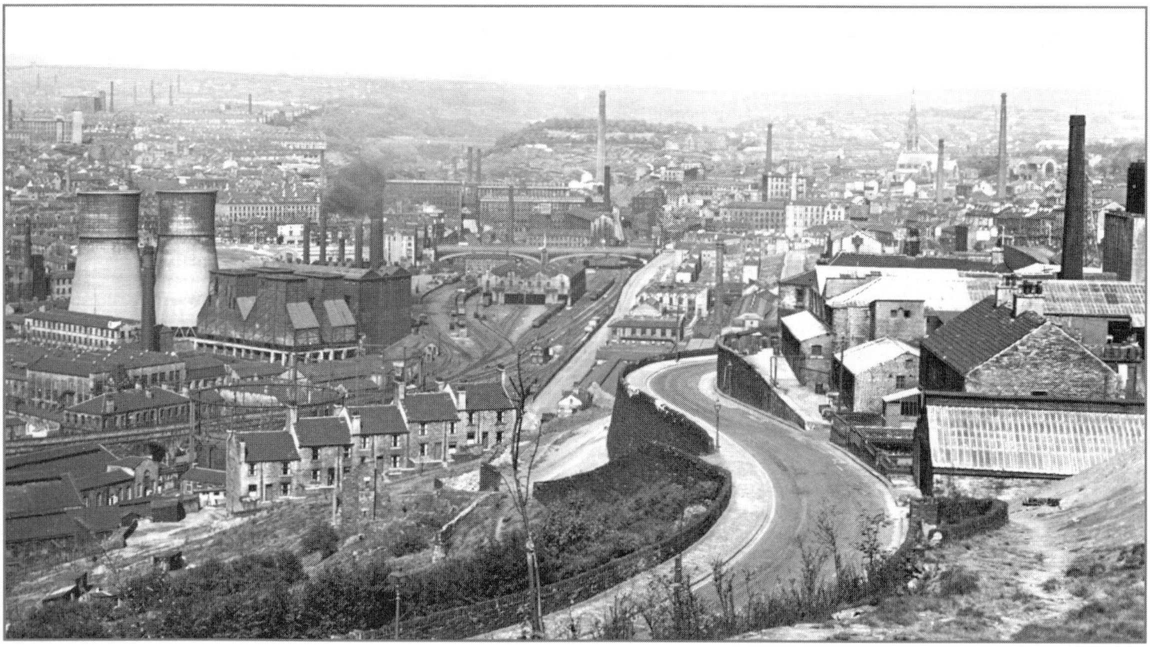

Halifax, General View c1965 H9070
Although the Manchester and Leeds railway opened in 1841, Halifax was bypassed; the nearest station was at Elland. The Halifax station eventually opened in 1855, and was designed in a Baroque Palladian style by Thomas Butterworth.

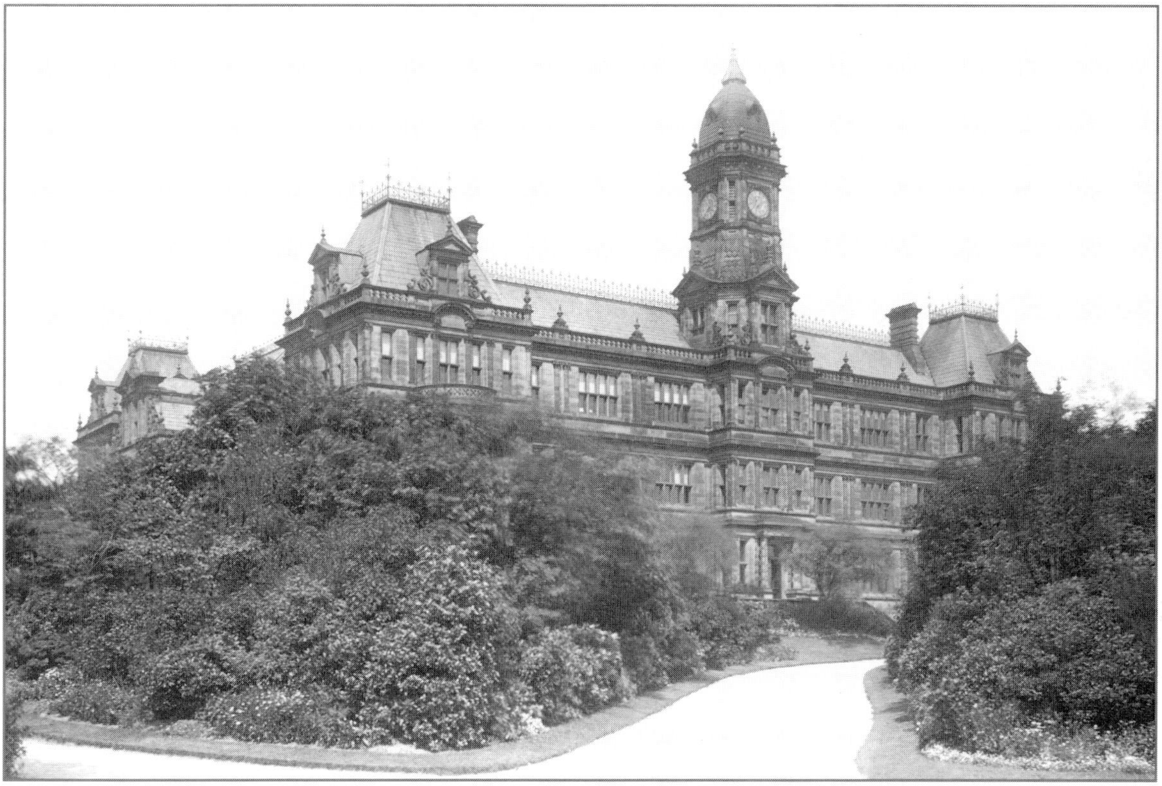

Halifax, The Orphanage 1893 33210

The Crossley family, Halifax carpet manufacturers, contributed £56,000 to build and establish this orphanage for between 200 and 300 youngsters from right across the county. It was designed by local architect John Hogg, and was built in 1864. Three years later a Manchester yarn merchant, Thomas Porter, offered an endowment fund of £50,000 to facilitate feeding and educating the children. Boys stayed here until aged 15, girls until the age of 17. The orphanage closed in 1909 to become a secondary school, which merged in 1985 with Heath School.

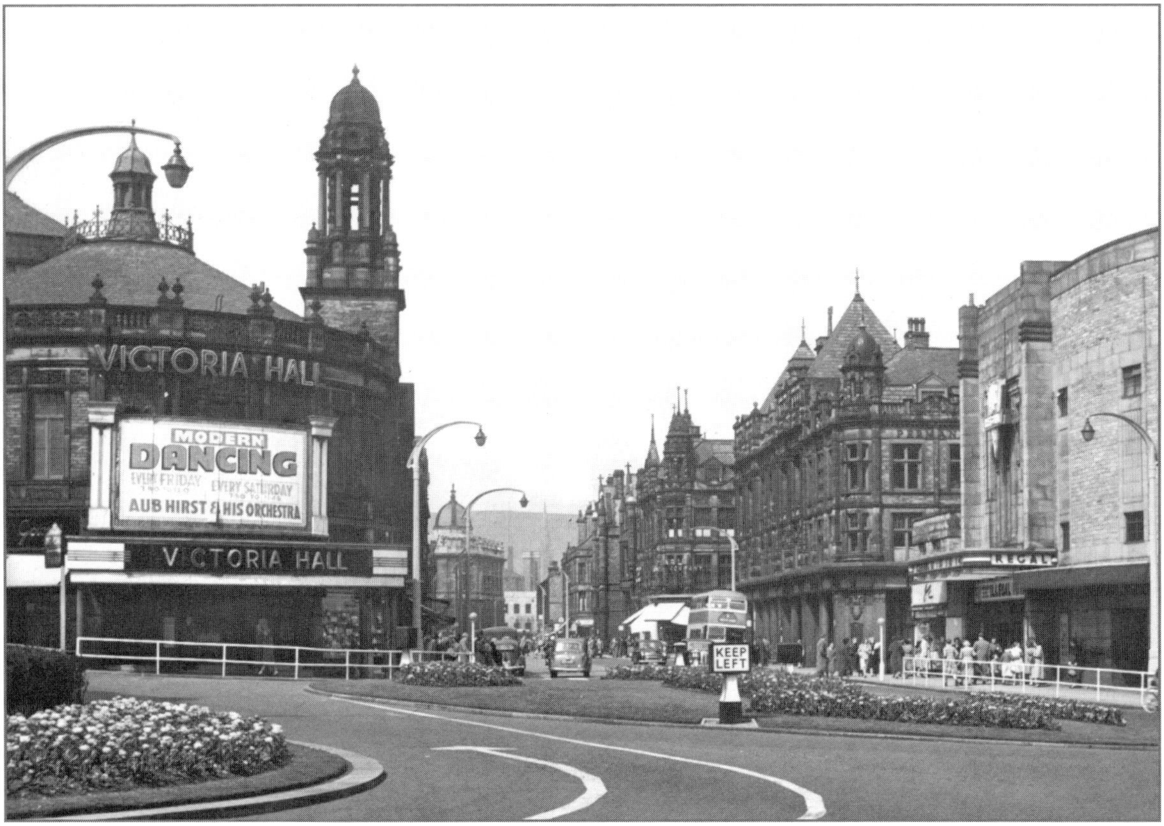

Halifax, Town Centre c1965 H9051
This was the entertainment centre of the town. Around Ward's End were many cinemas and theatres. The Electric Theatre opened as early as 1910, the Coliseum (now a dance hall) some ten years later. The Victoria Hall was an early concert hall, which is now used as the civic theatre. The Regal Cinema on the right was the town's supercinema; it opened in 1938 and seated 1,918; in 1976 this capacity was tripled. Behind this cinema is the magnificent Theatre Royal of 1905. Bingo was played here in its latter years, but it now lies vacant, forlorn and awaiting a new use.

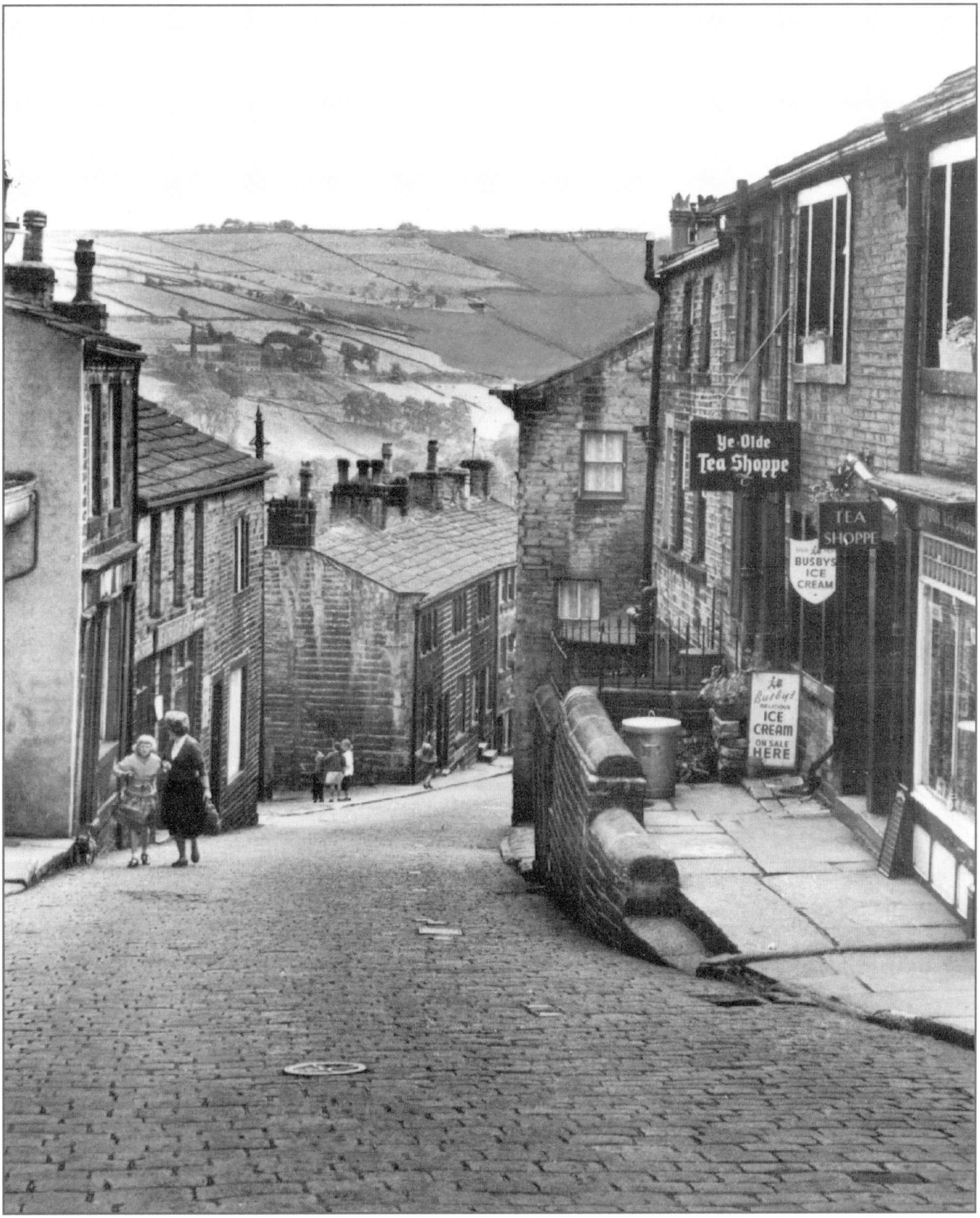

Haworth, Main Street c1955 H194050
The old cobbled street still remains, and views of the brooding Yorkshire moors are still enchanting visitors from around the world. The Parsonage Museum provides a fascinating insight into the bleak and often solitary life led by the Bronte family. Half a century ago, Ye Old Tea Shoppe was the only concession to tourism.

▼ **Haworth, Main Street 1955** H194028

A walk up the hill takes the visitor back a hundred years. The older corner shops, at one time serving locals with groceries and hardware, are even in 1955 being used for tourist attractions such as antiques. The antiques shop was previously used by the Bronte Society as a museum from 1895. Books and postcards of the literary sisters are on sale at the Haworth Post Office.

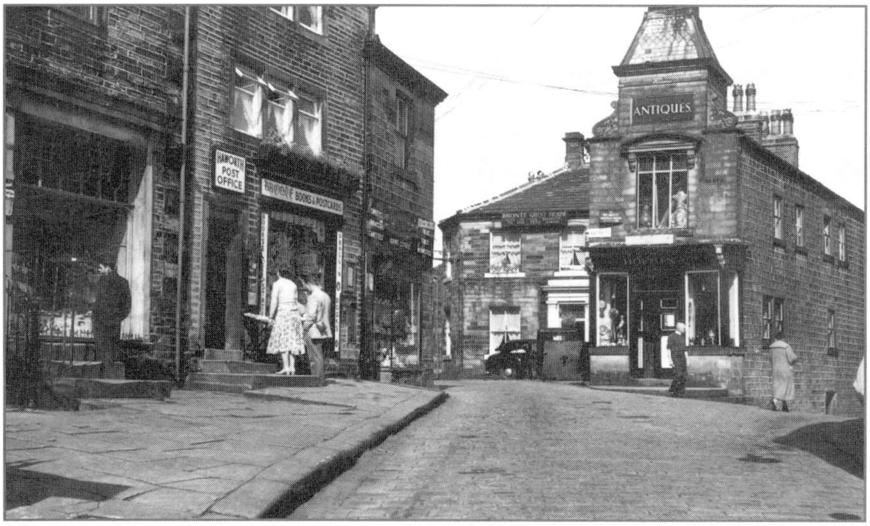

▼ **Haworth, The Black Bull Hotel c1955** H194024

A pub and a church always seem to be intertwined in village life. Members of the Bronte family are certain to have imbibed here, and the 17th-century hotel traded heavily on this association. The church to the right is St Michael's.

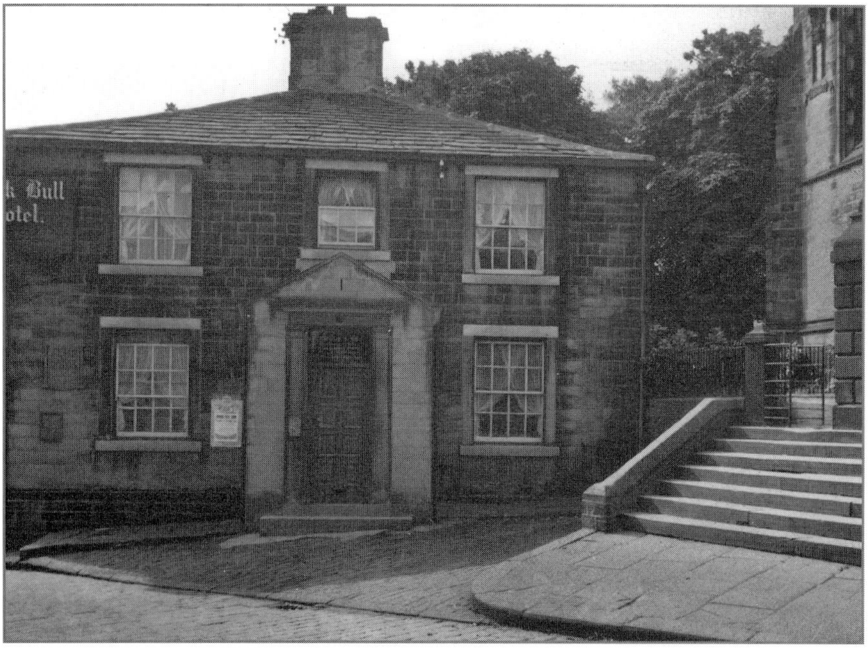

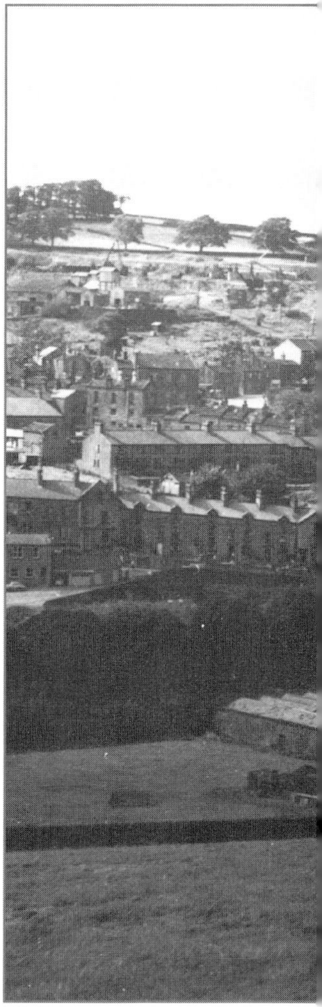

▲ **Haworth, View over Haworth c1955** H194052

This view of the village on the hill from Hebden Road is dominated by the two big mills, the Ivy Bank Mills on the left and Bridgehouse Mill in the foreground. The rectangular building on the left was the Drill Hall, around which beetroot boiling took place. Over to the right are the railway station and the old corn mill.

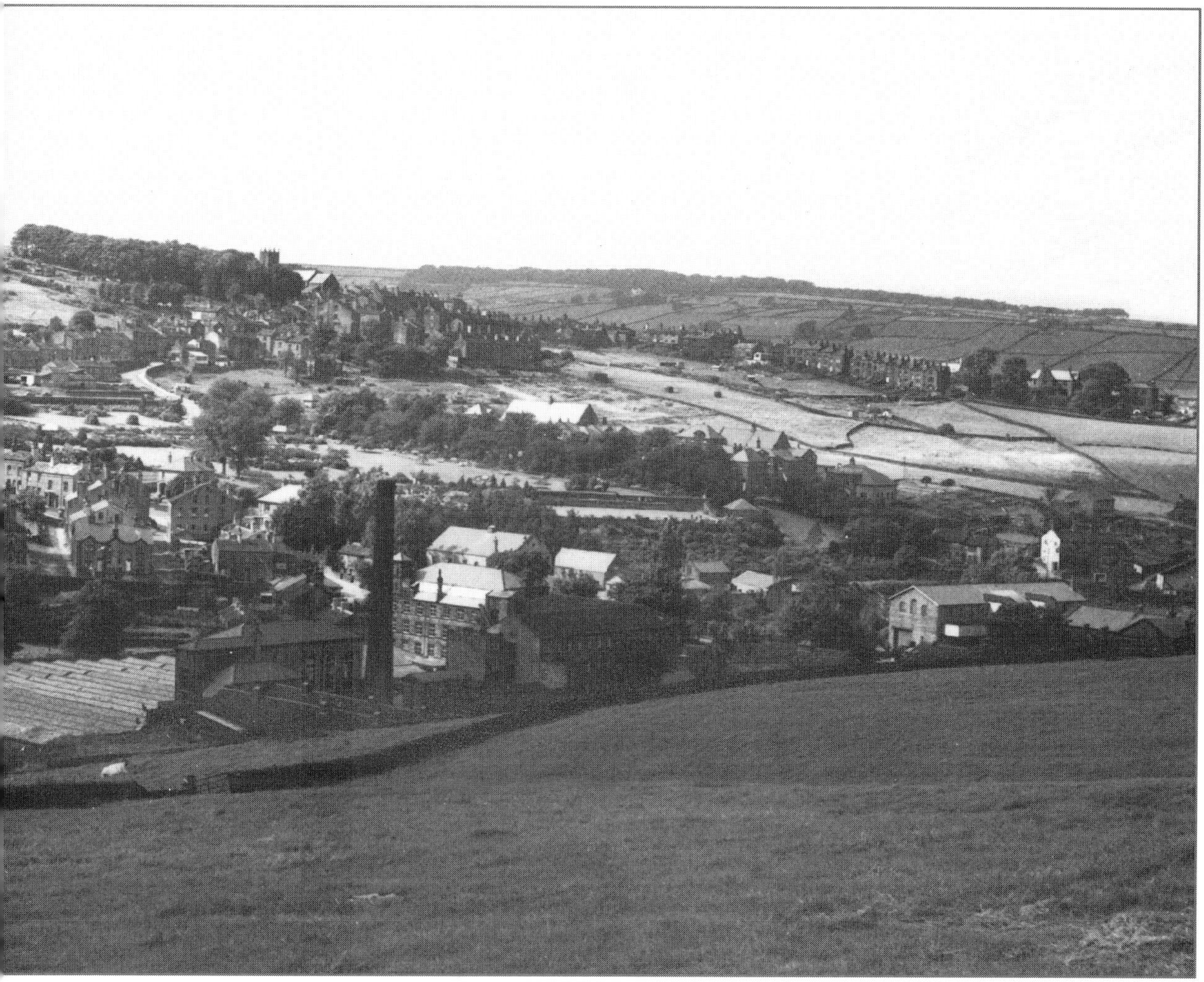

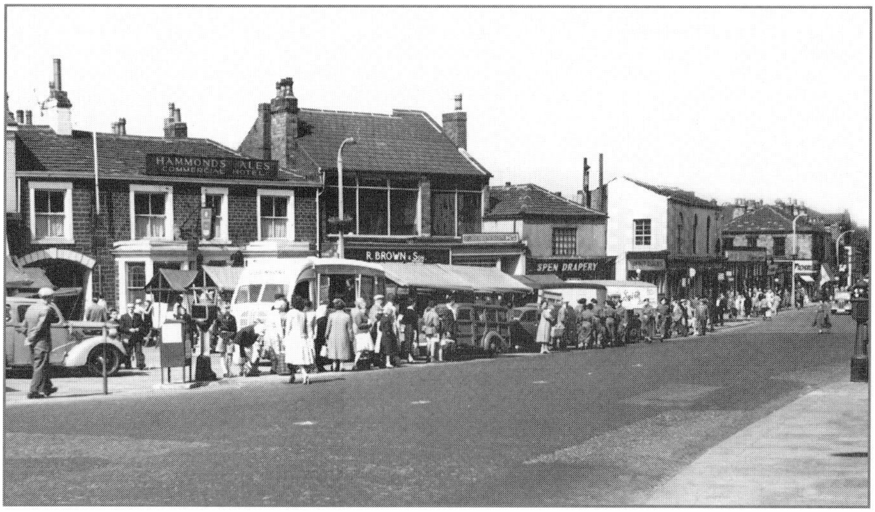

Heckmondwike, Market Place and Westgate c1960 H199016
Heckmondwike lies just two miles from Dewsbury in the heart of the heavy woollen district; its speciality was blanket making. Two market halls were built exclusively for this trade, the first in the 17th century and the second in 1840. The original hall was behind the George and Dragon Inn, and part of it still stands.

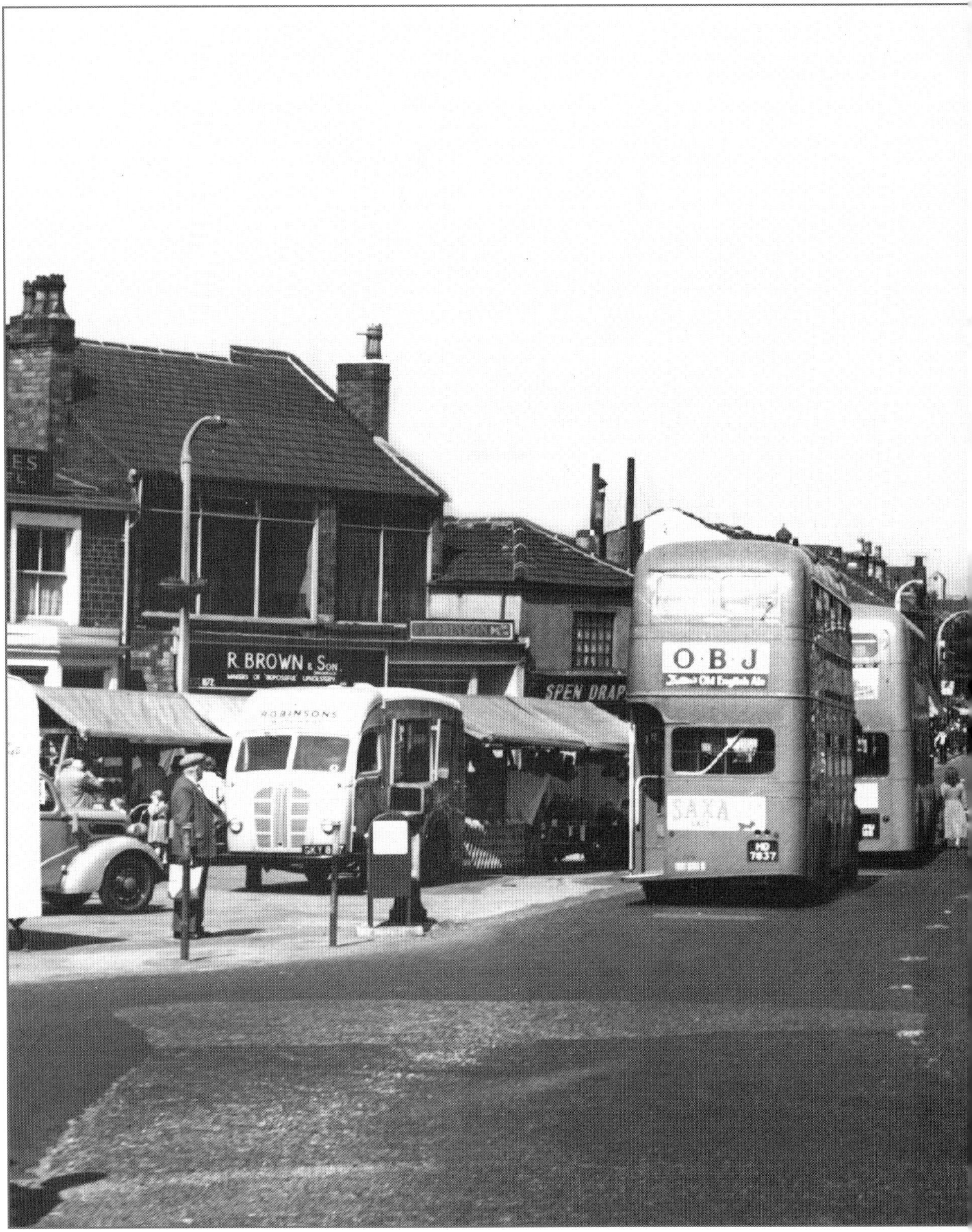
R. BROWN & SON
ROBINSONS
SPEN DRAP
O·B·J
SAXA

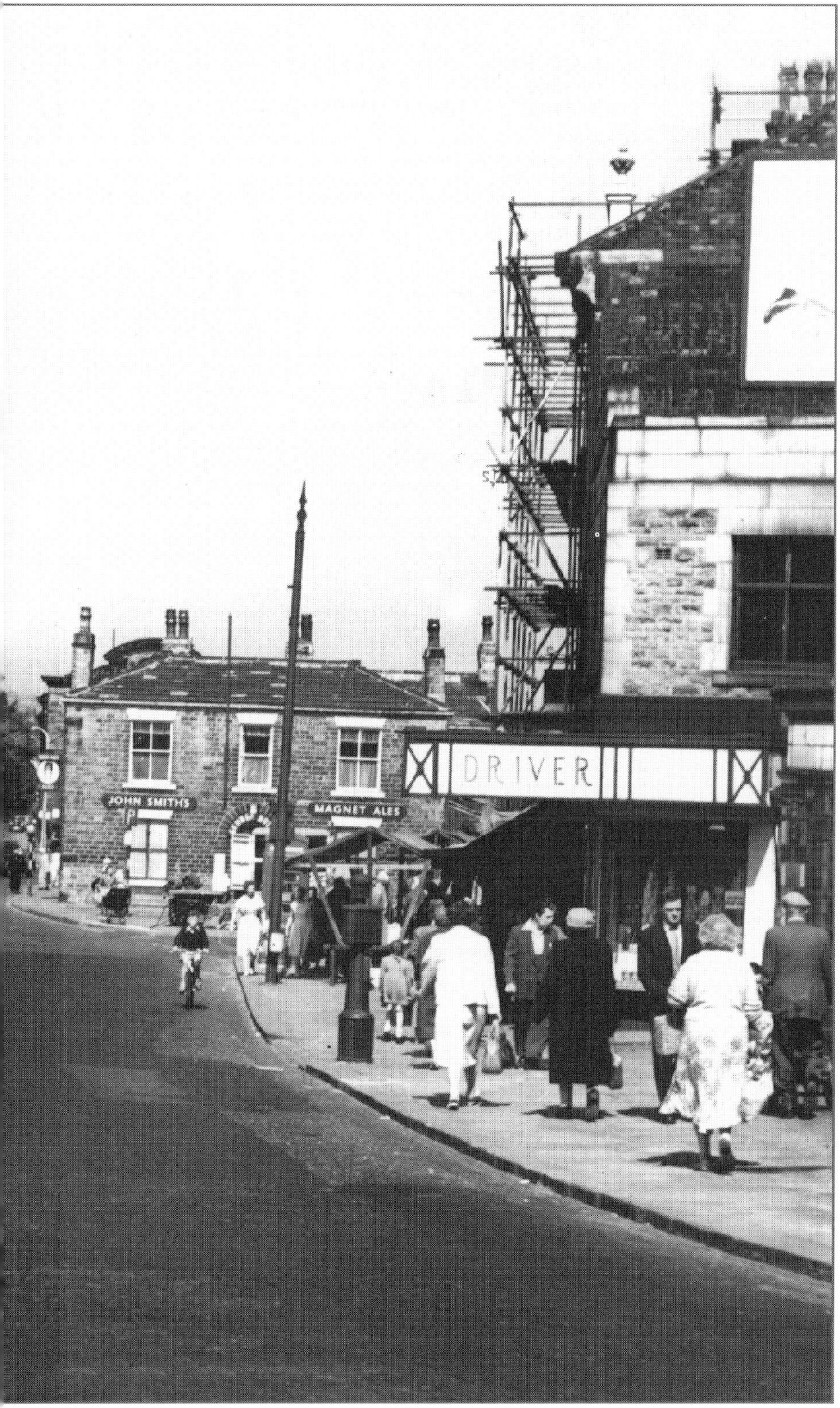

Heckmondwike Market Place and Westgate c1950

H199017

As the industrialisation of weaving gathered pace, the town was eventually reached by the railway in July 1848. Within forty years a bigger station had to be built. The last train to run from the town was in October 1963, which was even before the Beeching cuts. The market opened in 1868, and the Co-op was here from 1872, complete with its own Fire Brigade.

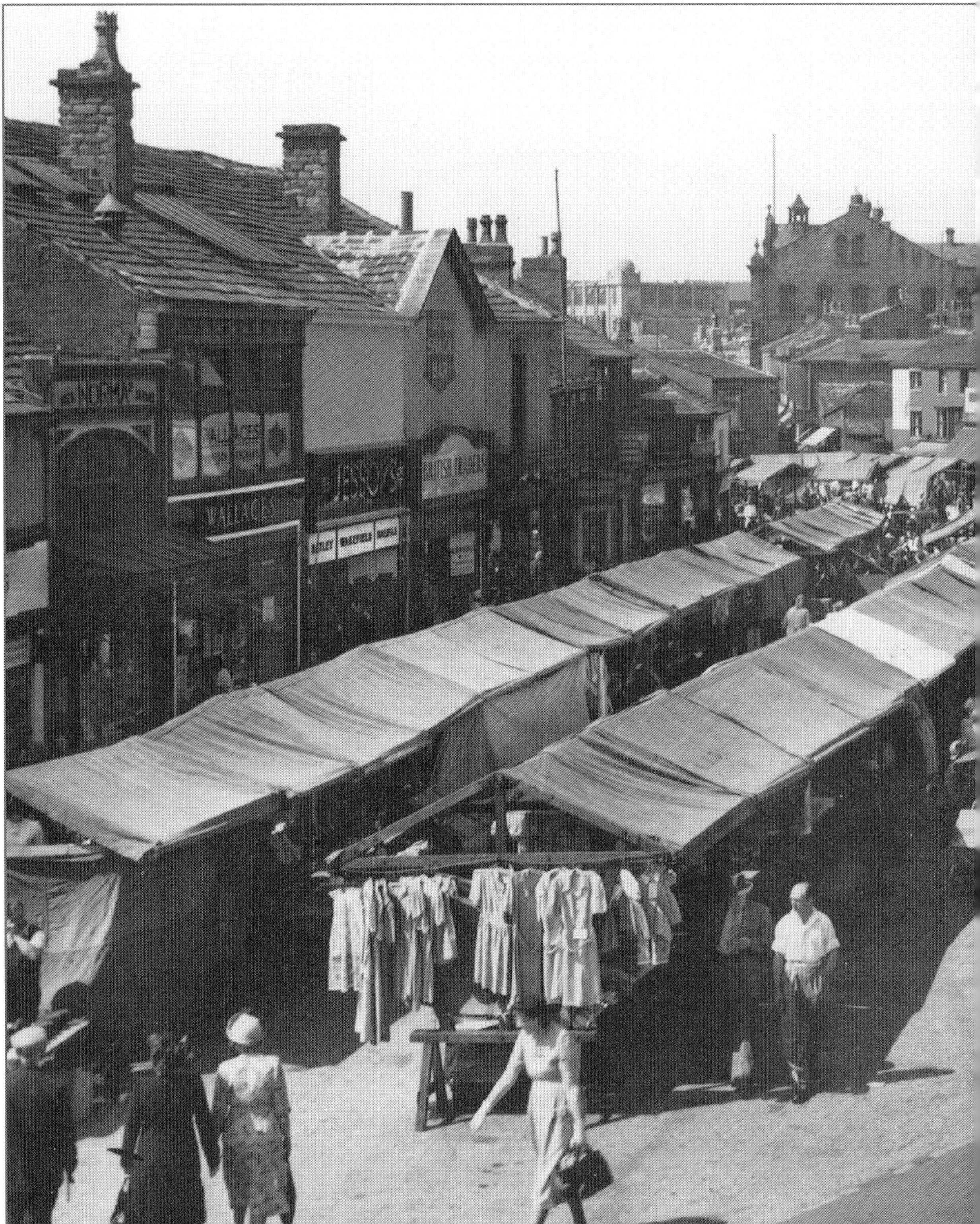
WALLACES
WALLACES
BRITISH TRADERS
BATLEY
WAKEFIELD
HALIFAX

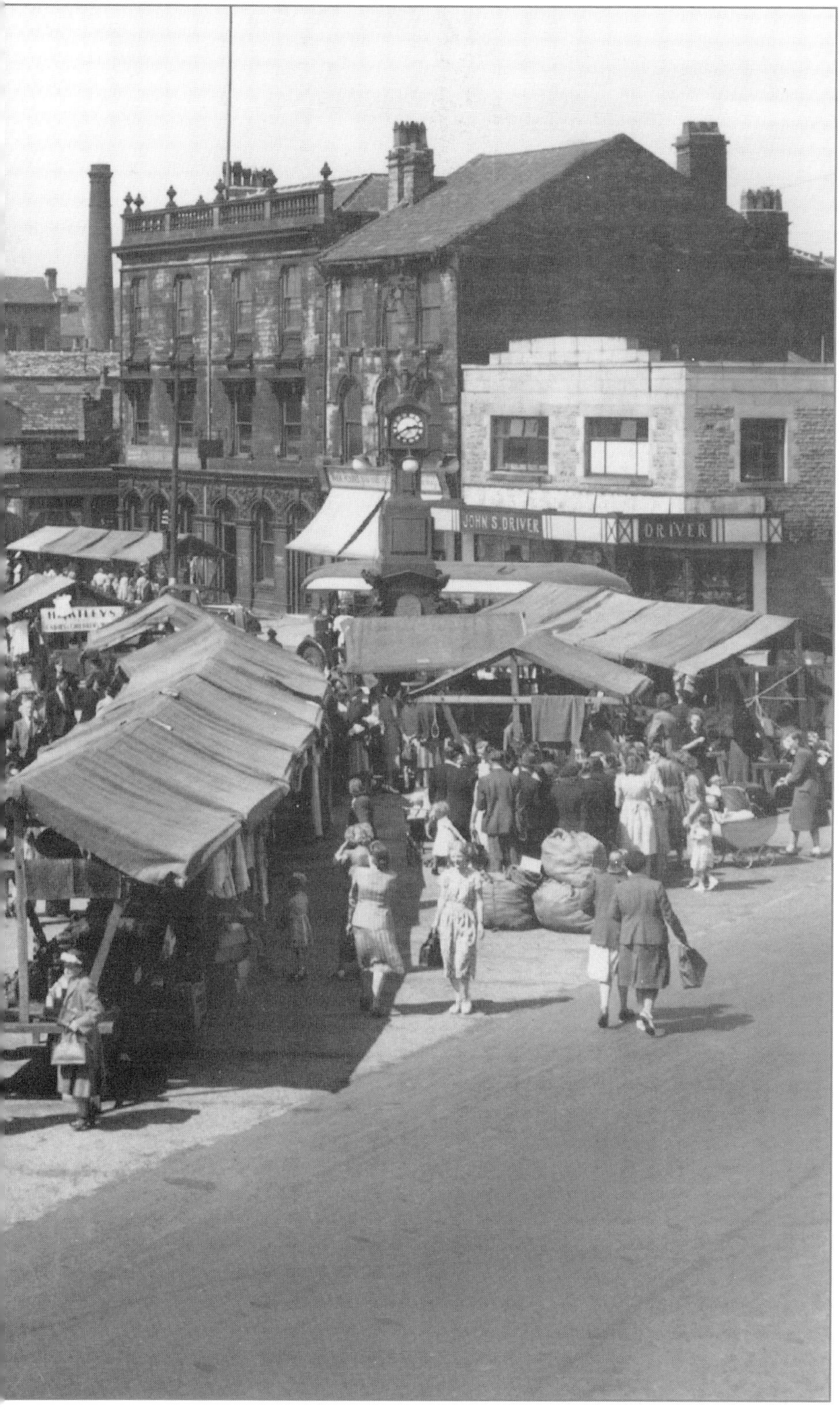

Heckmondwike The Market Square c1950 H199009

Long the centre of the town's social and political life, the Market Square contained many inns, including the George and Dragon, the Woodman, the Red Lion and the Brown Cow. Another popular place in the winter months was George Scott's blacksmiths shop. The forge lit up the whole street at night-time.

▼ **Heckmondwike, The Town c1960** H199012
This main road through the town used to be the Wakefield to Halifax road, originally built by the Romans. Business in the town was not only concentrated on blanket making. Much trade came for the dyeing facilities, especially for one major landowning family, the Beevors. King George and Queen Mary visited the town in May 1918 to thank all the townspeople for their sterling war effort.

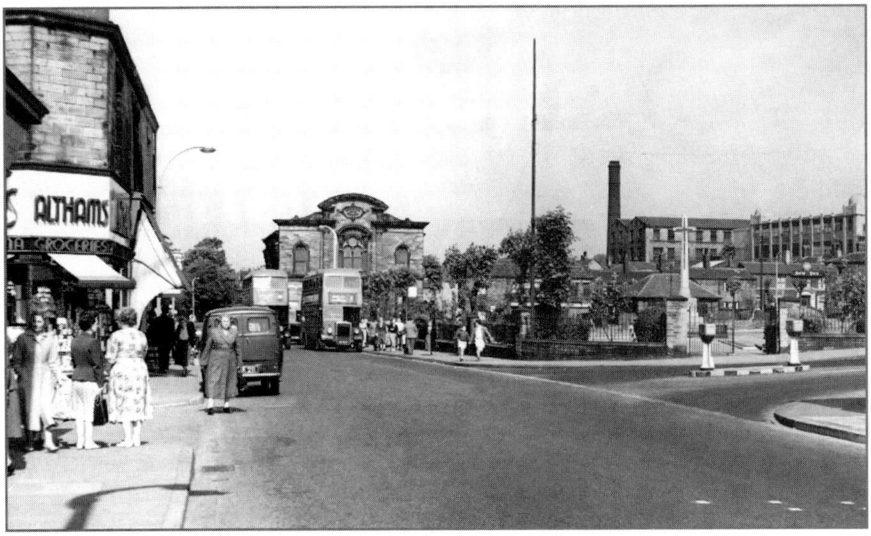

▼ **Hemsworth, Market Street 1950** H204020
The discovery of the Barnsley Main coal seam totally transformed the town from relying on agriculture to mining the new gold, coal. The sinking of the Fitzwilliam and the South Kirkby pits in the 1870s led to a huge rise in the population; the town was rebuilt with hundreds of back-to-back terraced houses. Two railways vied for the Hemsworth coal trade - the Wakefield to Doncaster in the 1860s, and the Barnsley and Hull Railway from 1880.

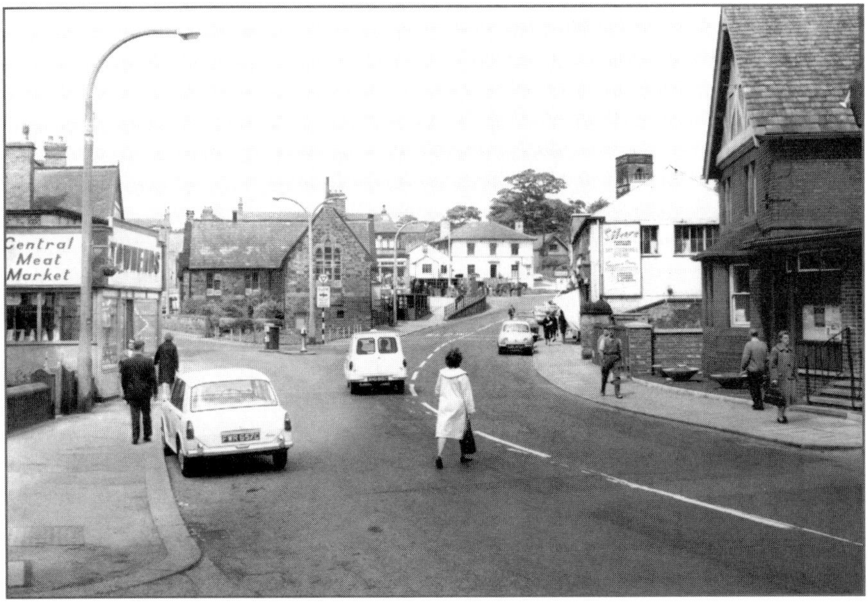

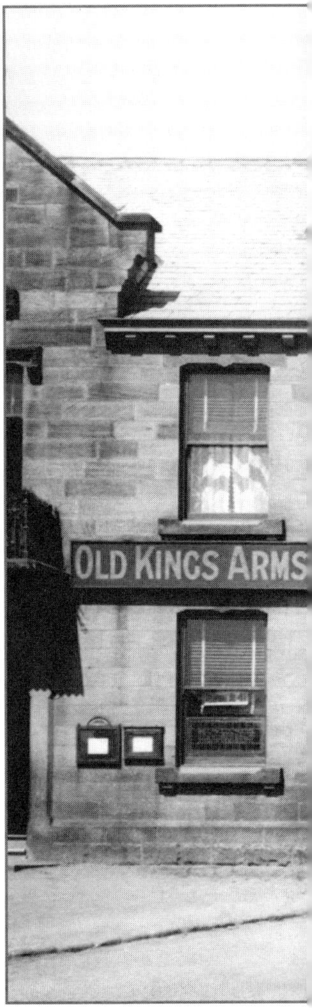

▲ **Horsforth, Town Street 1901** 47133
This is the old heart of the village. The old King's Arms opened in 1749, and opposite is the Black Bull, dating back to 1758. Also on Town Street was the Salvation Army, tithe cottages for the local clergy, and, grouped around the old Arcade, the post office, bank, bakers, florists and cobblers. At the top end could be found the Mechanics' Institute and the police station. The scene today is little changed.

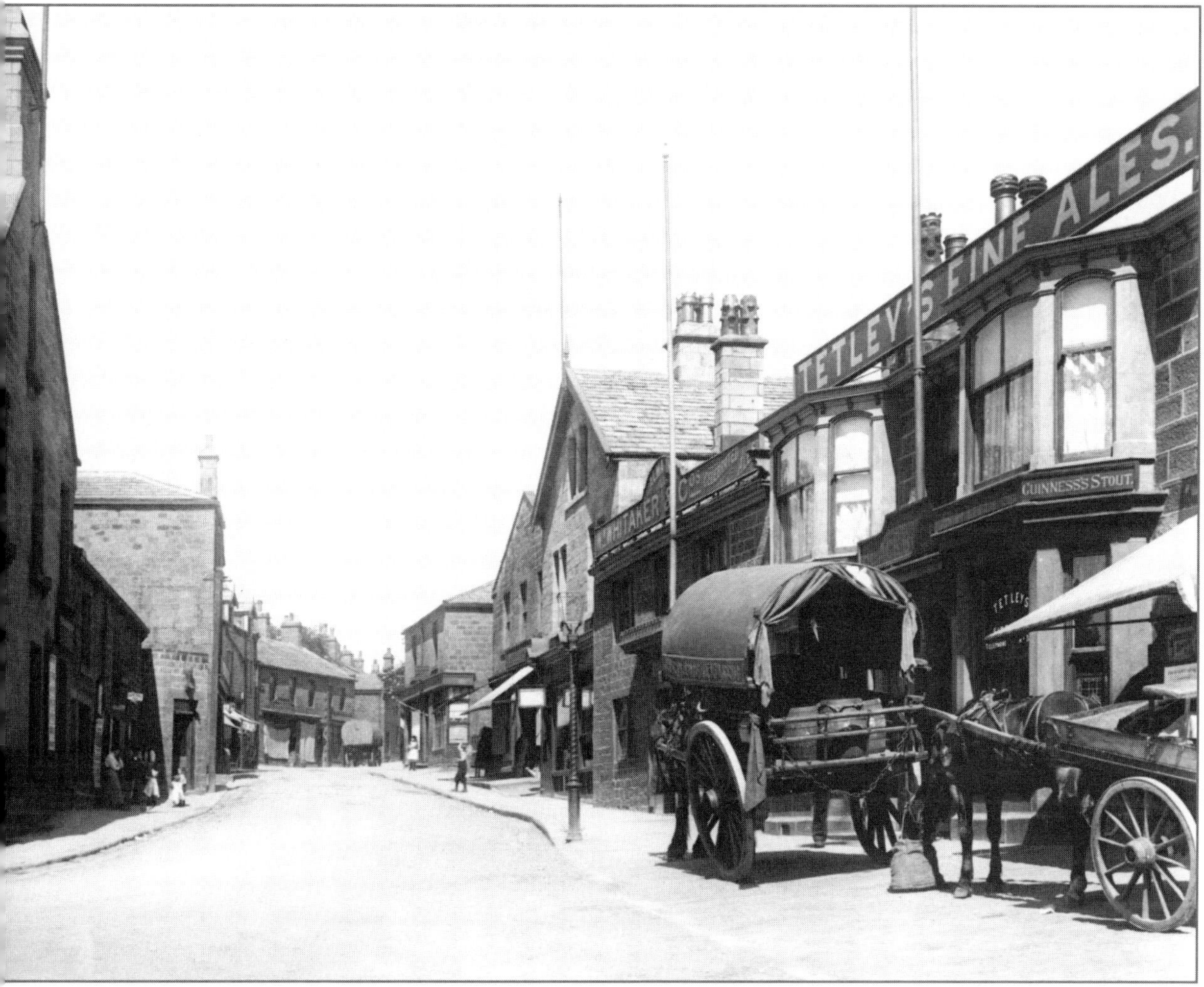

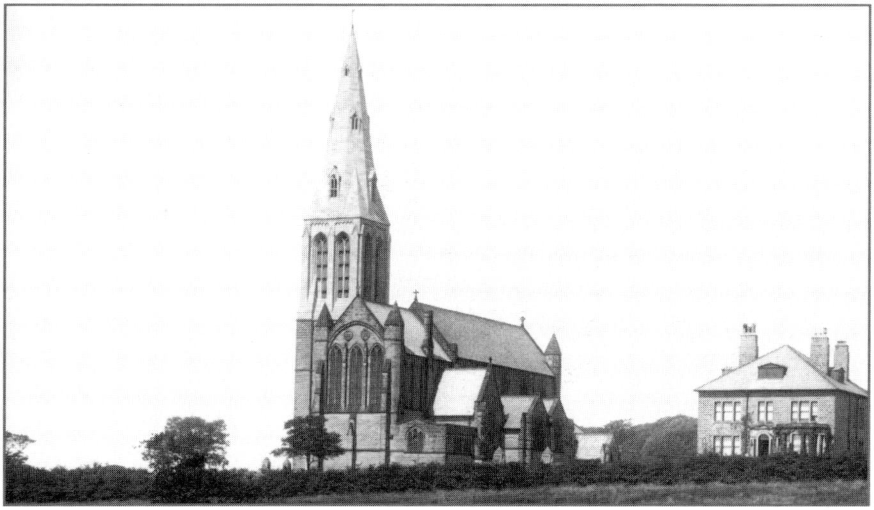

◀ **Horsforth, The Church 1902** 48566

St Margaret's Church occupies a commanding position, which gives some panoramic views over farmland and around the town. This 1883 church replaced the old Bell Chapel at the end of Town Street on the Green, which was becoming too small for the congregation. St Margaret's, built on land given to the town by the local Stanhope family, is constructed in the Early English style and contains twenty interior arches. The spire was added in 1901.

▼ **Horsforth, The Mechanics' Institute 1901** 47134

This seat of self-improvement was opened to the town's working people in 1882. It contained a reading room and a well-stocked library of over 3,000 books. Later the police station was added on the left; it was demolished to accommodate the new Horsforth library.

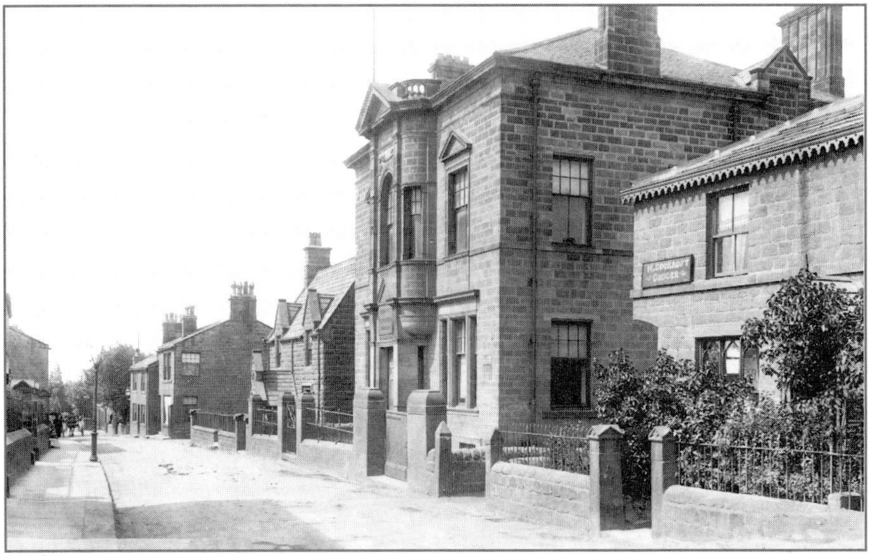

▼ **Huddersfield, The Station c1960** H151008

The station was built at a cost of £20,000, and its classic grandeur still dominates St George Square. The foundation stone, laid in 1845, weighed an incredible six tons. The first train on the new Huddersfield to Heaton Lodge line ran on 2 August 1847. Competing lines used the same station, and each sold tickets from the end offices. Staff even wore caps bearing HJS (Huddersfield Joint Station) right up to 1922. The three-mile Standedge Tunnel under the Pennines was first used in 1849 to link the town with Manchester.

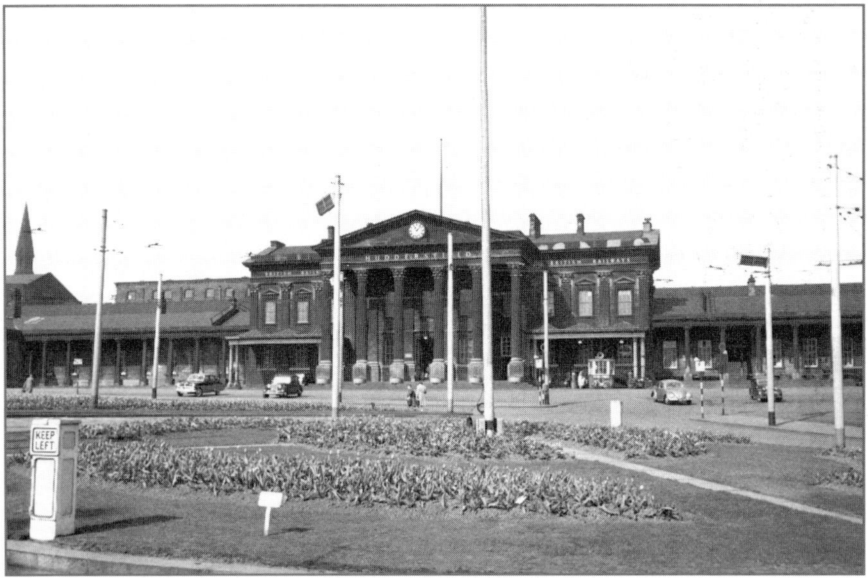

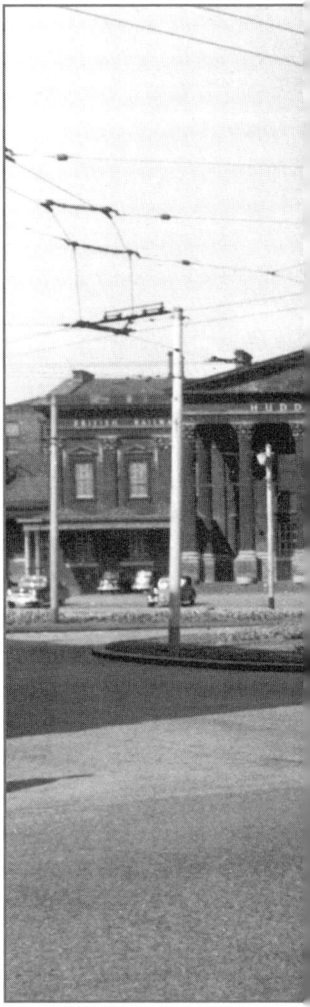

▲ **Huddersfield, The George Hotel, St George Square c1955** H151006

This was the first commercial building completed in the square to accommodate the rail travellers. It was built in 1850 by Joseph Kaye, who was well-known in the town as a merchant, a brewer and the owner of four mills at Folly Hall. He also built the station - a great achievement for a man who could barely write his own name. The George Hotel replaced the earlier George Inn, which was re-erected in St Peter's Street in 1852.

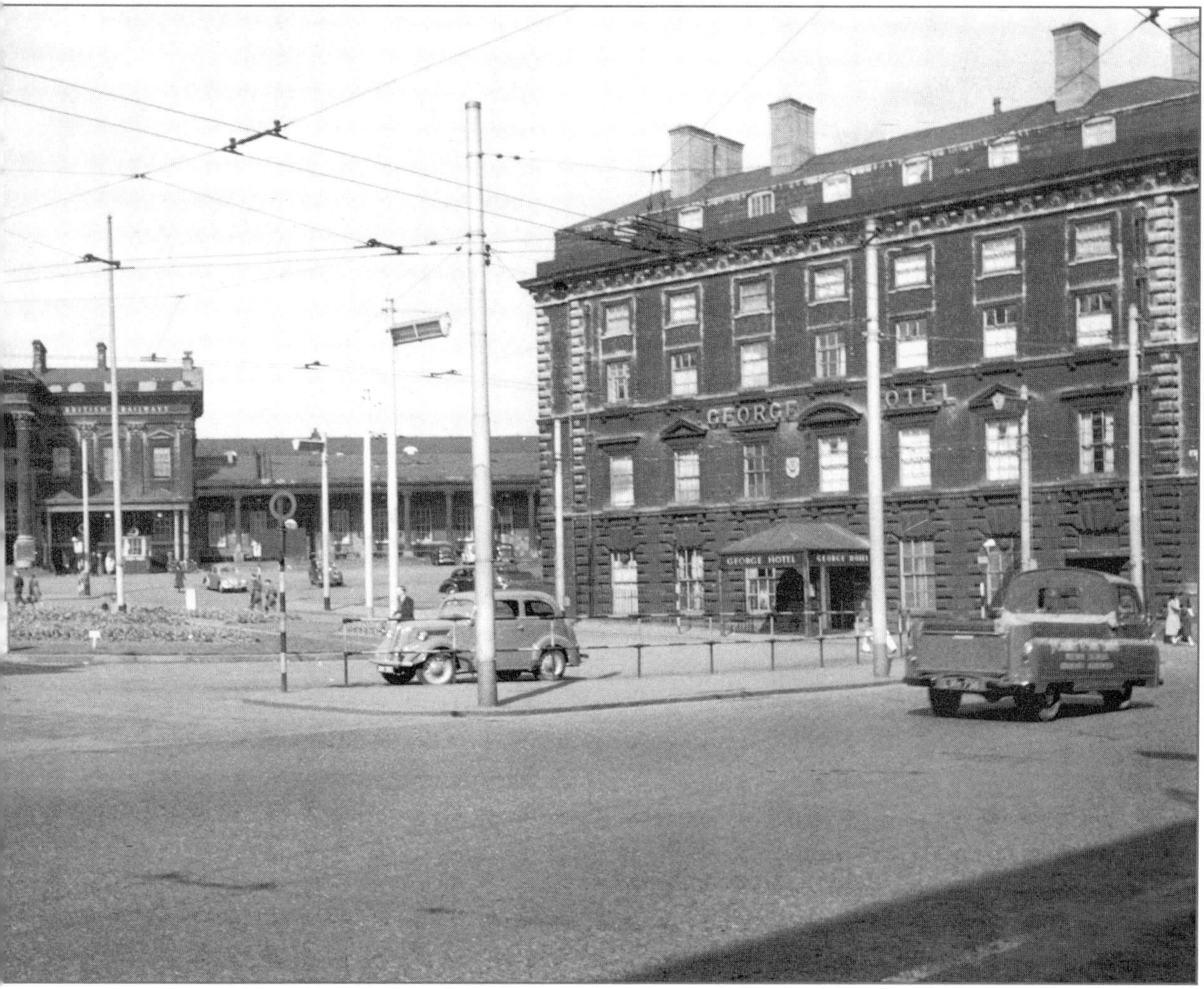

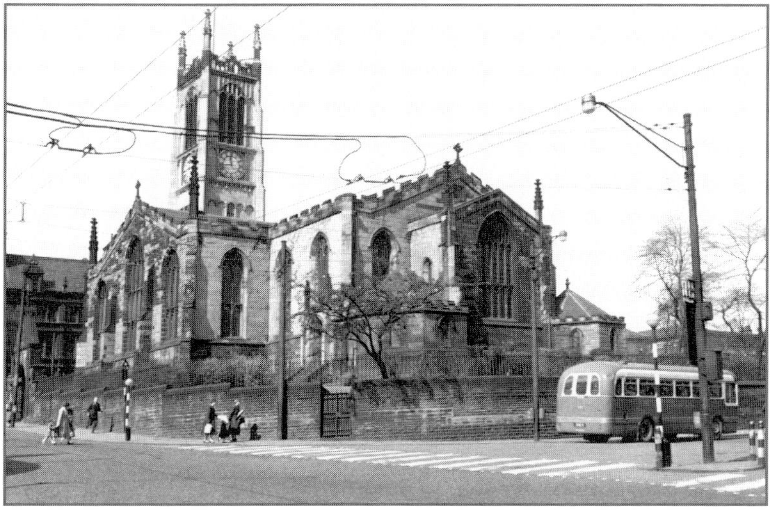

◄ **Huddersfield, The Parish Church c1960** H151015

The Battle of Waterloo partly financed this church. Under the terms of the Million Act of 1818, Austria had to pay £1 million in compensation. This money was earmarked to construct new churches in centres of growing populations. (A secondary motive was to combat the growing non-conformity movement). This church cost £10,000; it used much stone from the previous church (1509) on the site, which was demolished on 28 April 1834. The first service in the new Parish Church was held on 27 October 1836. The architect, J P Pritchett, also designed the station and Huddersfield College.

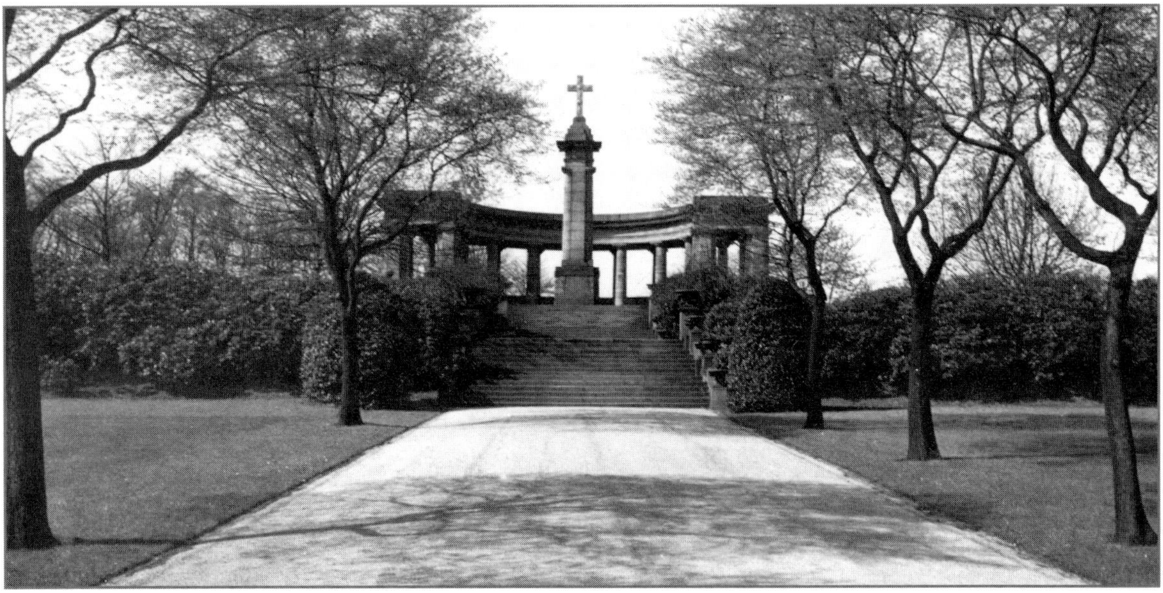

Huddersfield, Greenhead Park 1957 H151036

West Yorkshire is blessed with many fine Victorian parks. This one was acquired by the council in 1884 for £30,000 from Sir John Ramsden, who personally contributed £5,000. The land was previously part of the Greenhead Hall estate. The new park boasted two lakes, one of which is now a rose garden. The Hall was demolished in 1909 to make way for the new Greenhead High School for Girls. The memorial in the picture commemorates the many war casualties from the town.

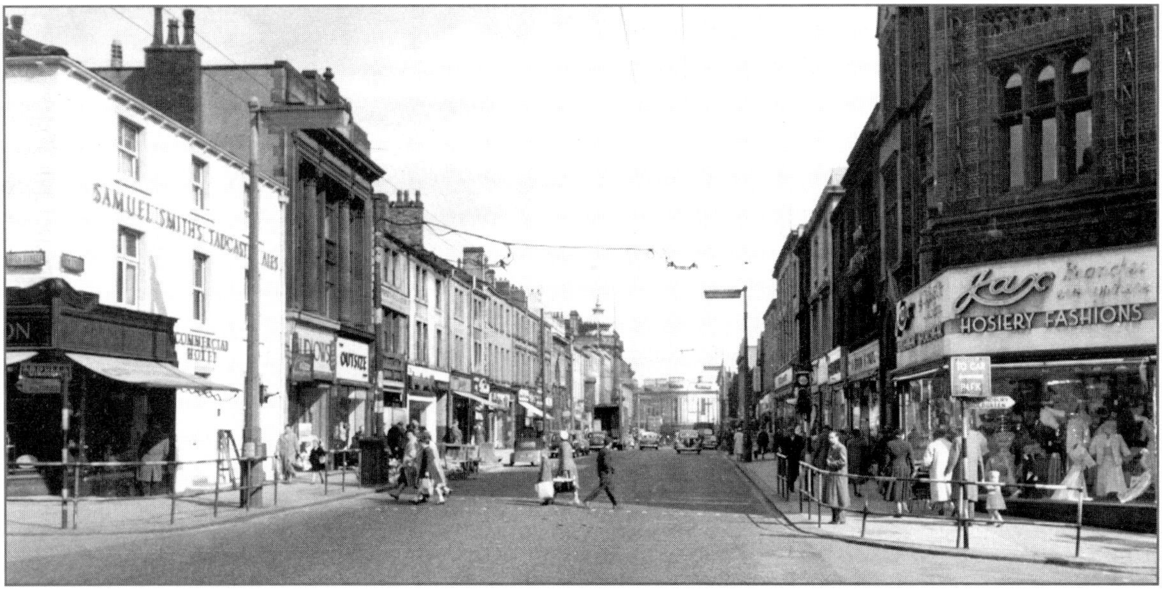

Huddersfield, New Street 1957 H151010

Previously called South Street, this was redeveloped in the late 18th century. The 'Brick' building sited opposite the Boot and Shoe was erected in 1770 out of bricks not needed for the Cloth Hall. In the 19th century, New Street became a banking location. The Cloth Hall was demolished amid much controversy in 1930 to make way for the new supercinema, the Ritz. Parts of the Cloth Hall, the clock and bell tower, were re-erected as a shelter in Ravensknowle Park.

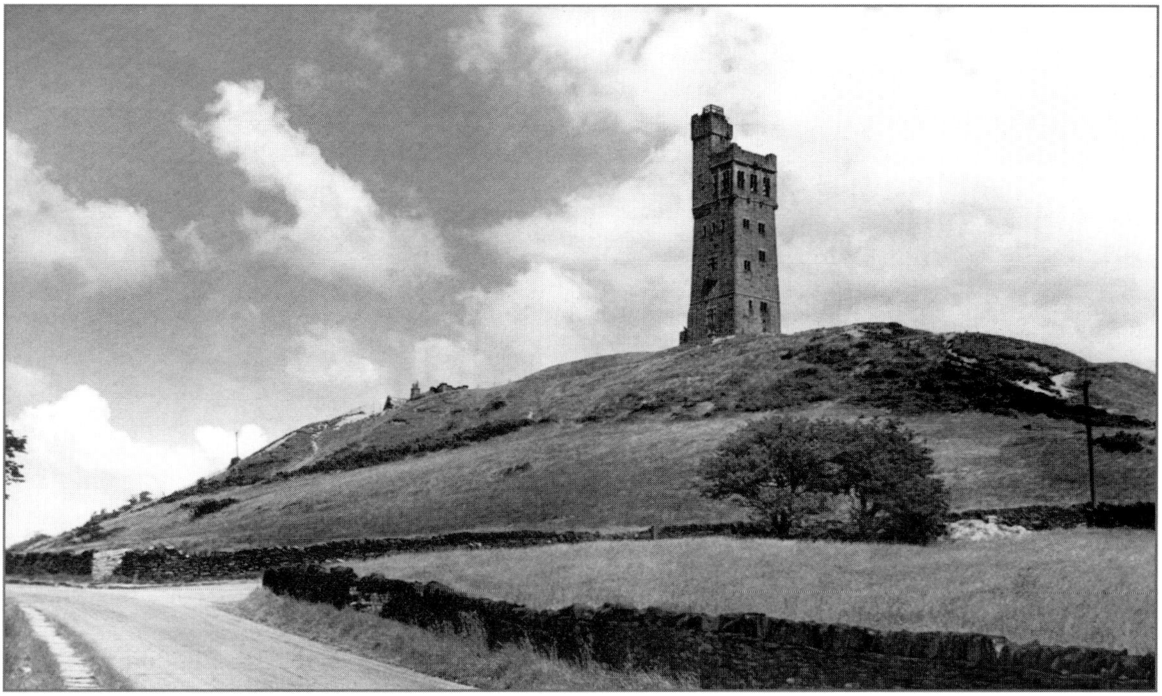

Huddersfield, Castle Hill 1957 H151031

This elevated site was settled by many early peoples, including the Brigantes, the Belgae and the Romans. The commanding view of the town led to number of schemes to erect a monument: the first was to have been the Victoria Prospect Tower in 1849. Objections kept the hill clear until 1899, when this new tower (which raised the view from 900 feet to a thousand feet above sea level) was opened on 24 June. At its base the tower is four feet thick. Stone came from the Crosland Hill quarry. During renovations in 1960 the top section was removed, and the tower now stands at a height of 996.7 feet above sea level.

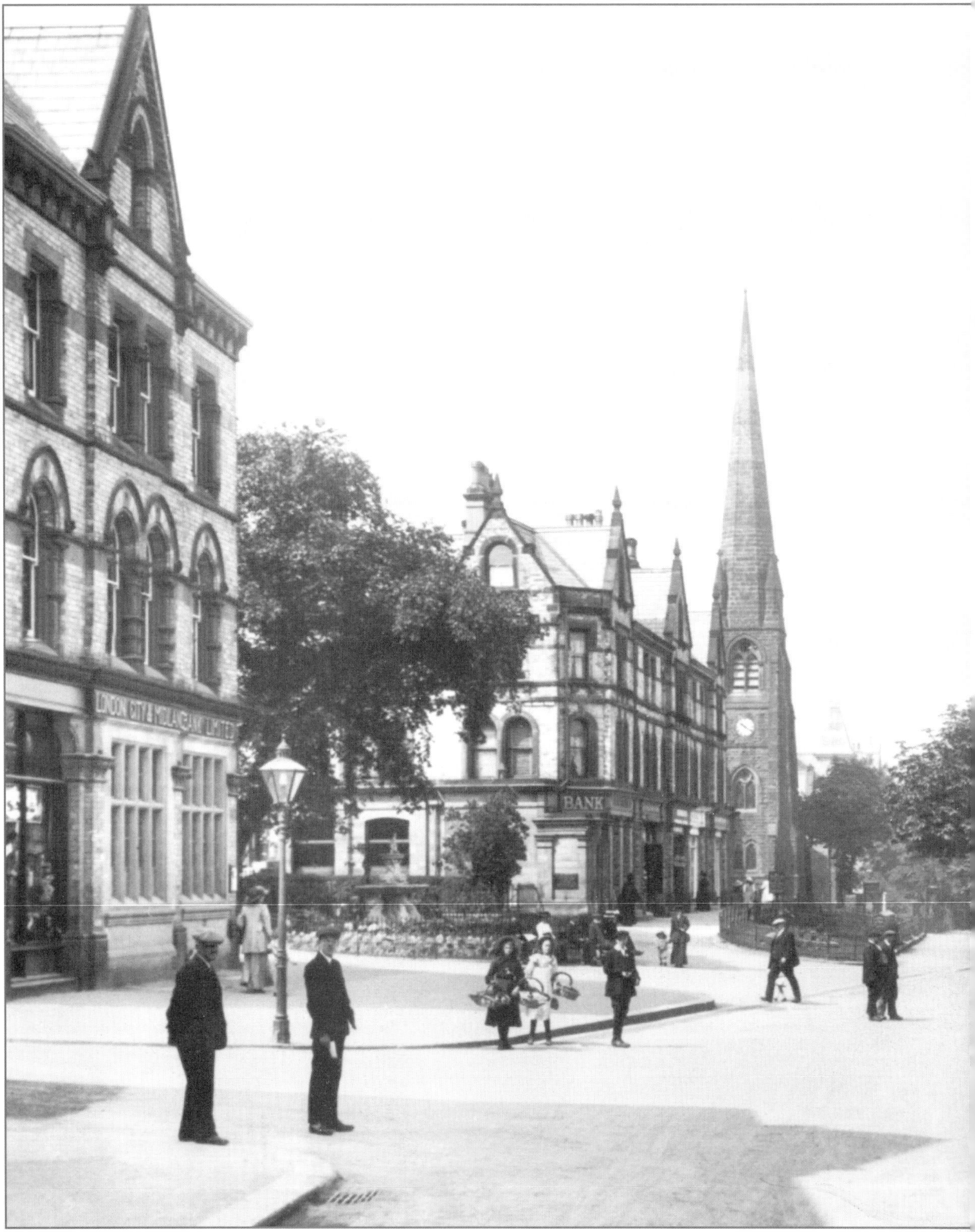
BANK

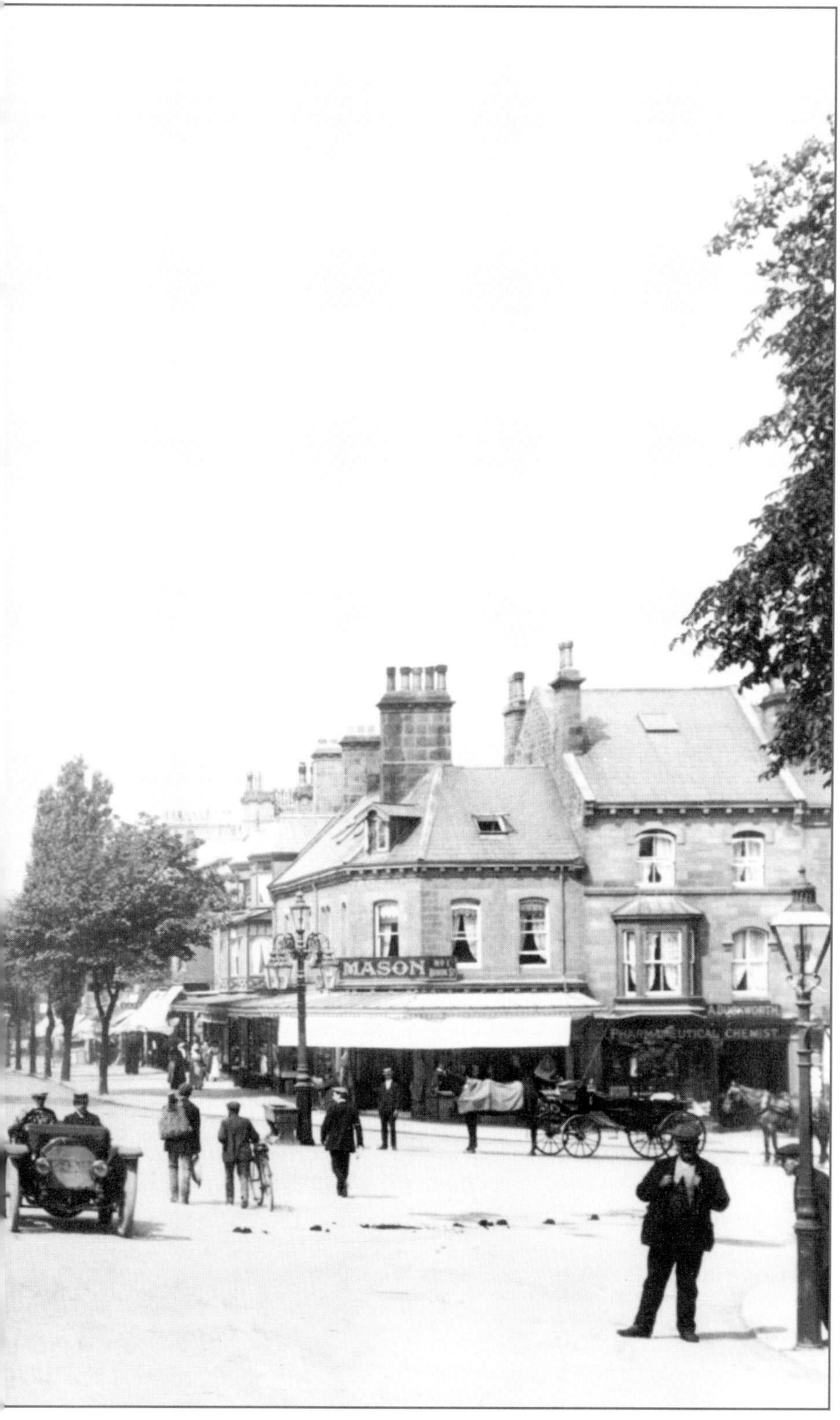

Ilkley, The Grove 1911 63556

This charming scene awaited visitors to the many hydropathic establishments, which included the Spa, the Grove, Ben Rhydding and the majestic Wells House, designed by Cuthbert Brodrick, architect of the Leeds Town Hall. Staying at Wells House in 1859 was Charles Darwin. Later, when the building was a hotel, Victor Sylvester entertained the guests. Today, the building houses Ilkley College.

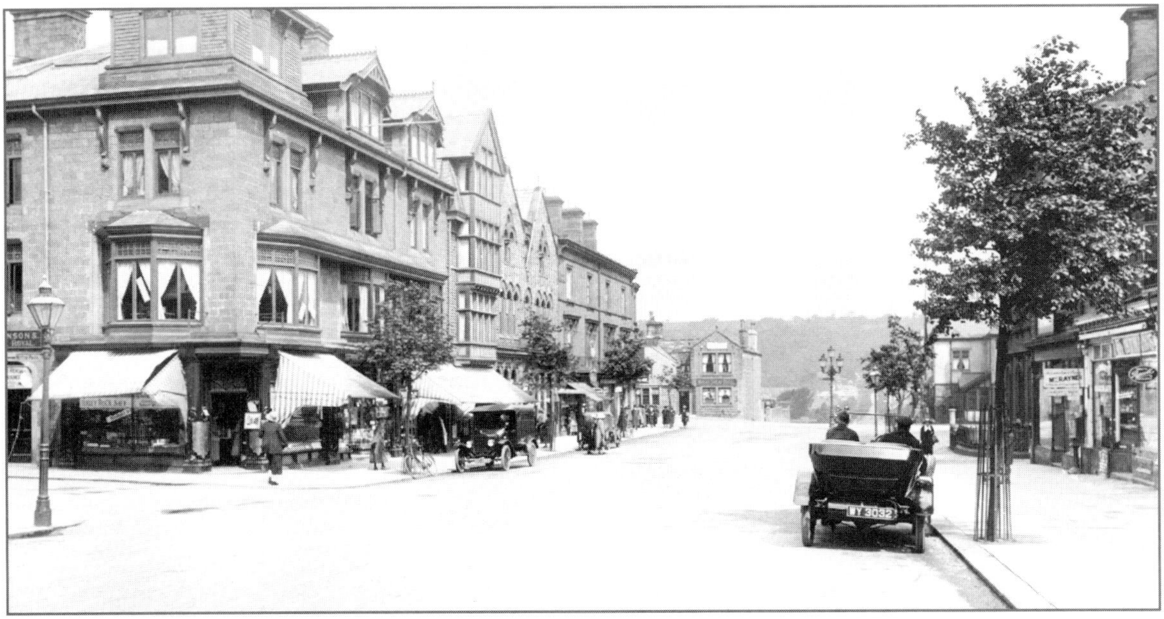

Ilkley, Brook Street 1923 74481
This view was taken from underneath the railway bridge looking down towards the Wharfe and the next village, Middleton. Fifty years earlier, before the railway increased commercial trade to the already prosperous spa town, all these premises were private houses. Ilkley's first gas lamps were installed in 1866; to economise, they were turned off four days before and four days after a full moon.

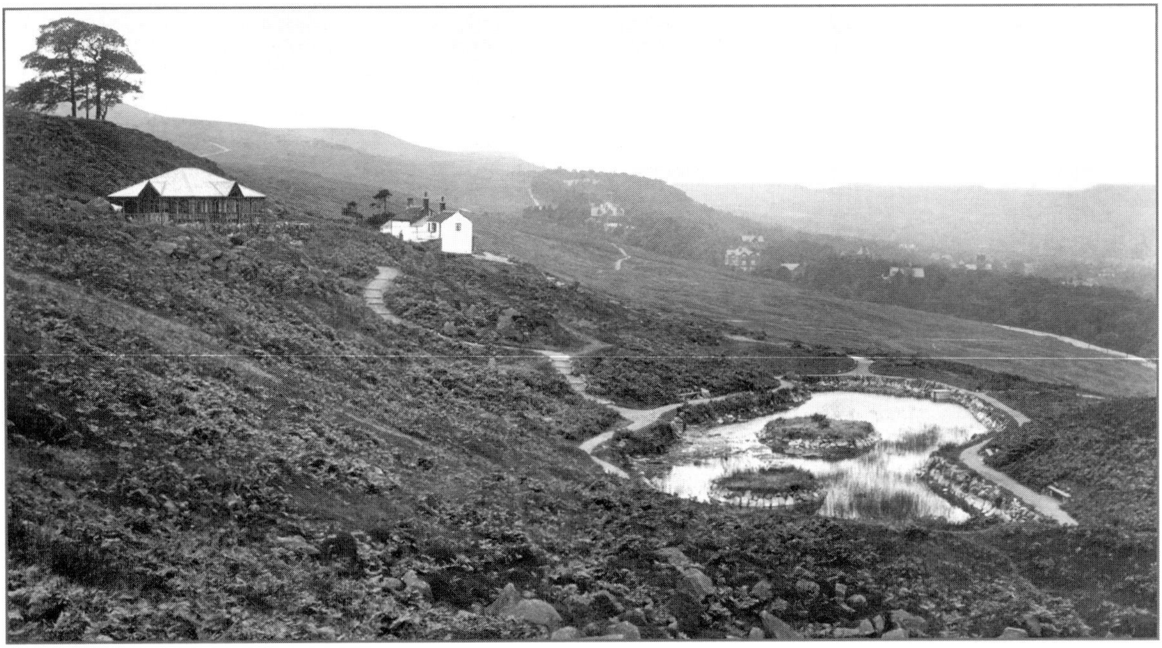

Ilkley, The White Wells 1923 74477
This cottage high up on the moors contained two stone plunge baths, one of which is still on display today. The well spring and the house date from the early 1700s. An adjoining tea house was built in the twenties; it became a favourite spot for visitors and locals, but it fell into disrepair and was demolished in the early sixties.

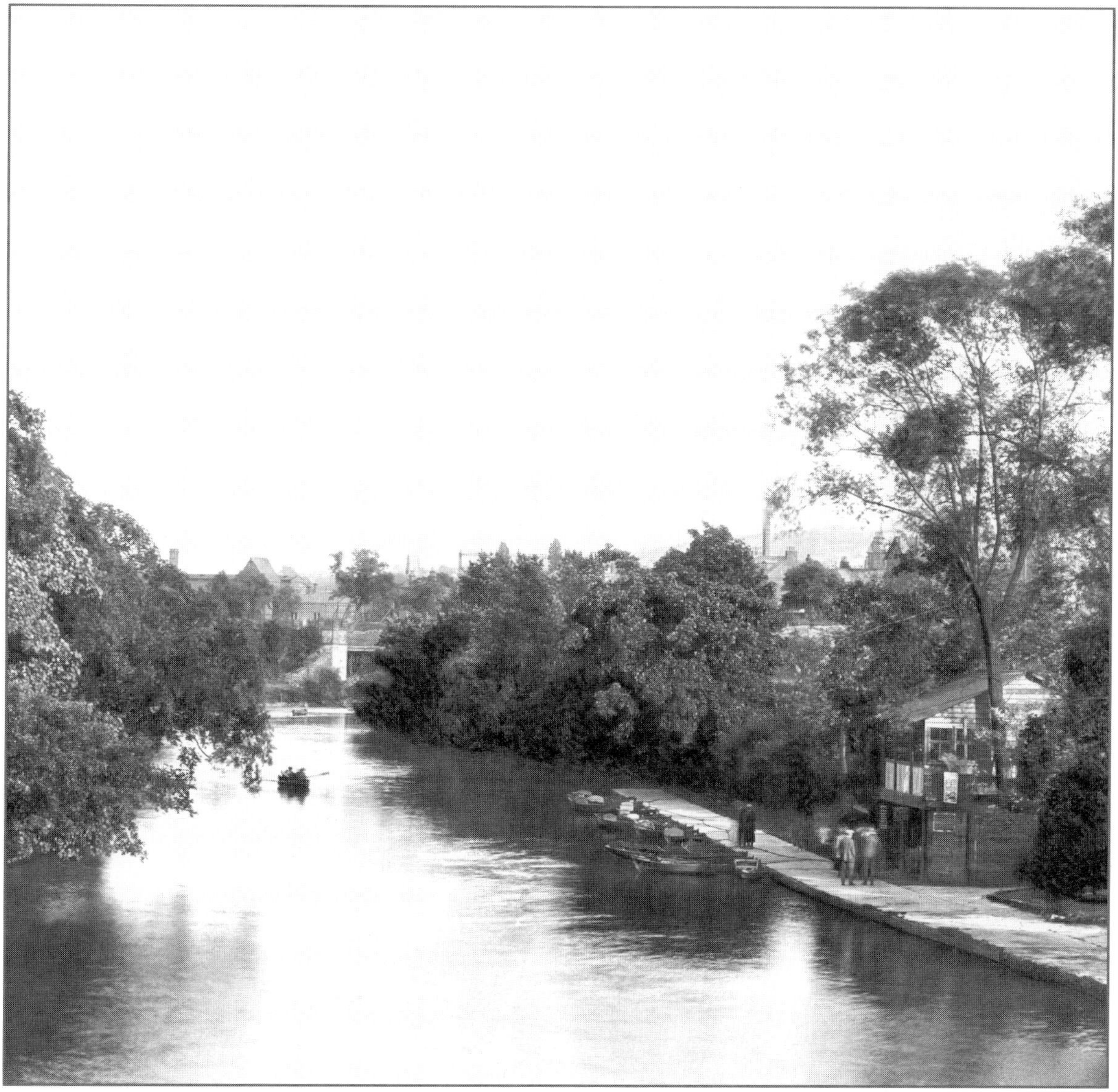

Ilkley, Boathouse and Landing Stage 1921 71271
Hiring a boat from Wray's Pleasure Gardens was always popular with visitors and locals. The new bridge (1904) can be seen in the distance; it opened up the Middleton side of the river. To the right of the bridge are the Parish Church and the Liberal Club, now the Playhouse Theatre.

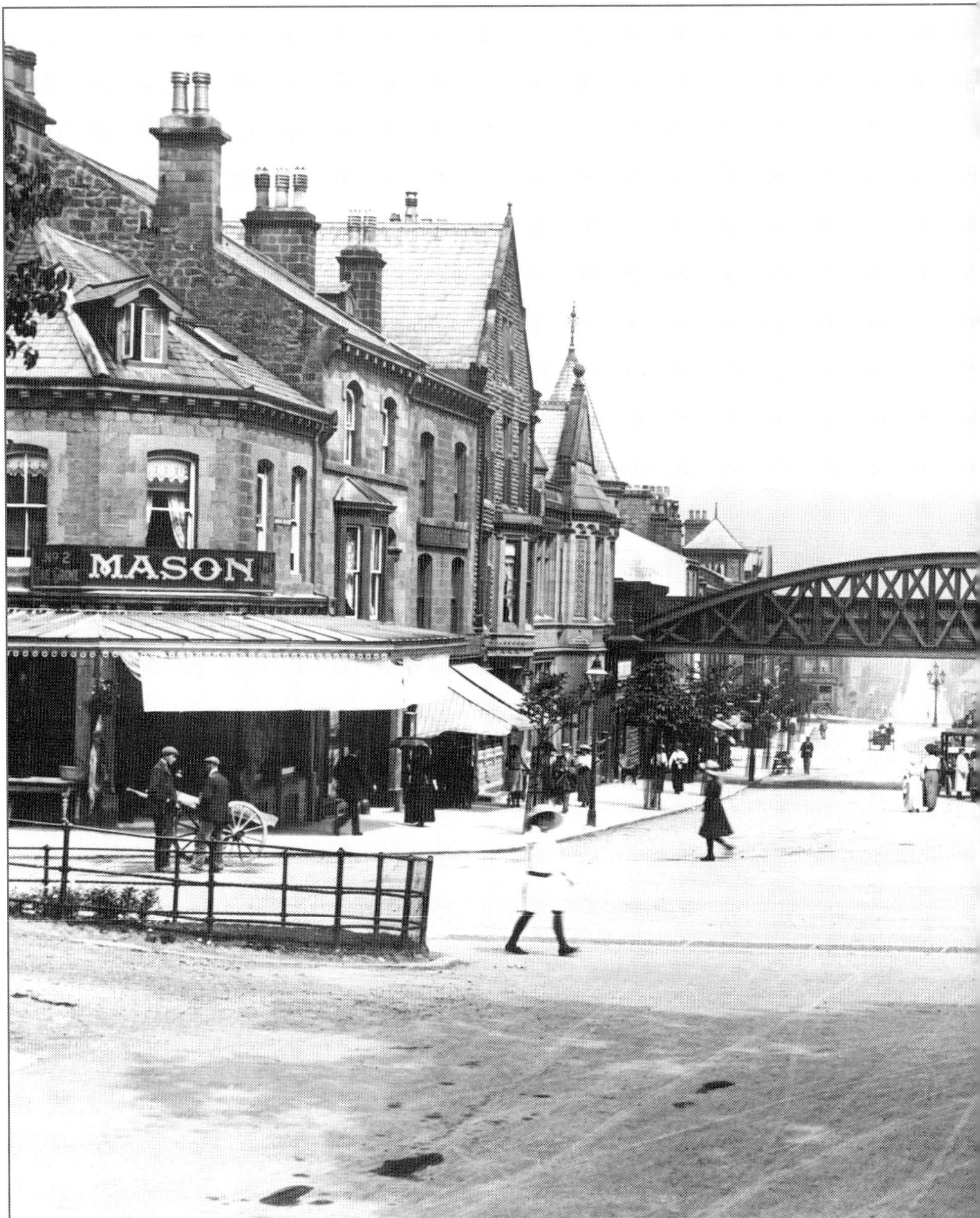
No 2
THE GROVE
MASON

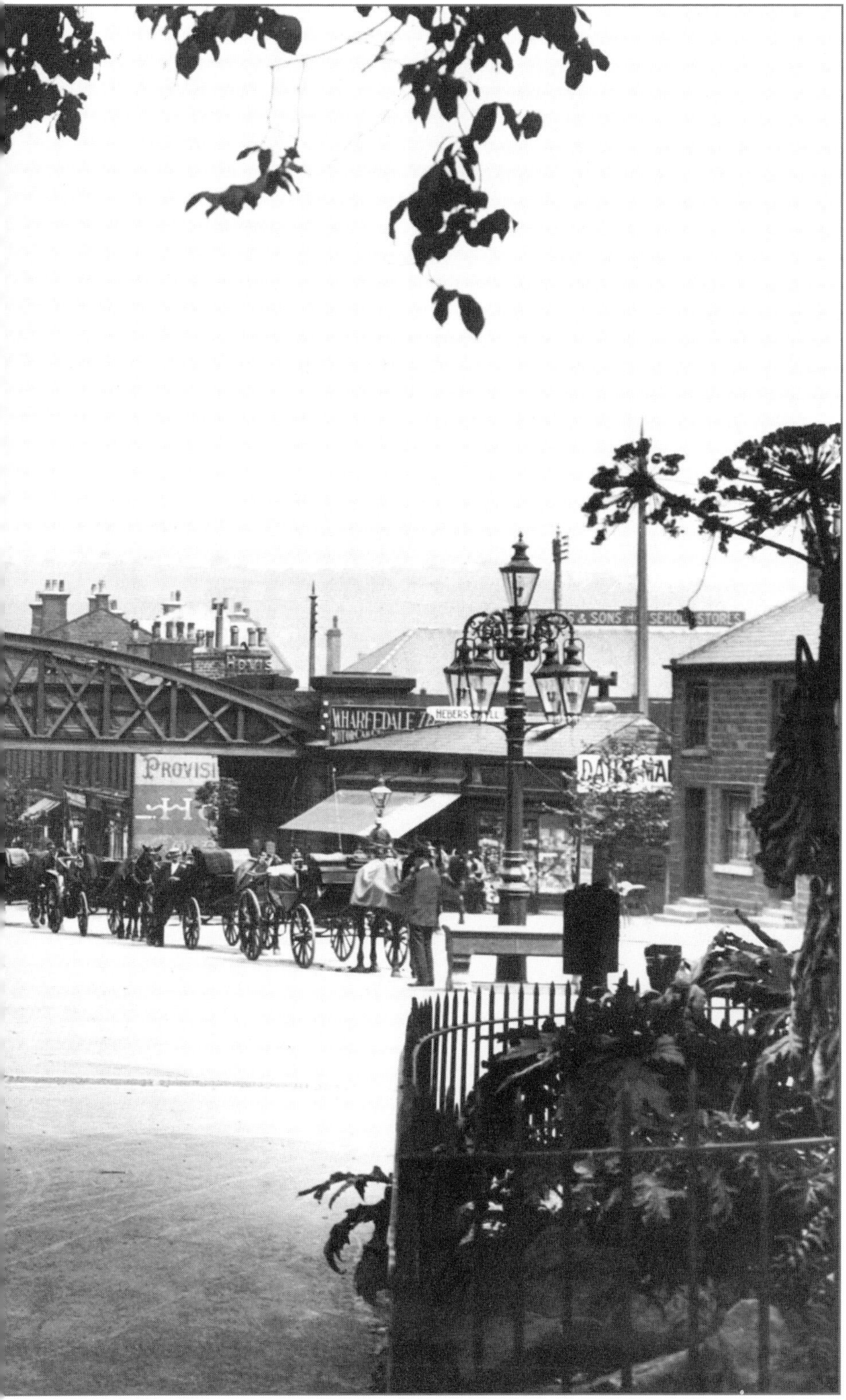

Ilkley, Brook Street 1911 63557
The first stage of the Otley to Skipton Railway reached Ilkley on 1 August 1865 - the town was decorated with bunting, and merrymaking continued day and night. The North View Hotel was remodelled as the Midland, and became a firm favourite with the new visitors. However, when the line was extended to Bolton Abbey (on 16 May 1888) the Midland was in the way, and had to be demolished. This railway bridge over Brook Street was taken down a year after the last train to Skipton left Ilkley on 20 March 1965.

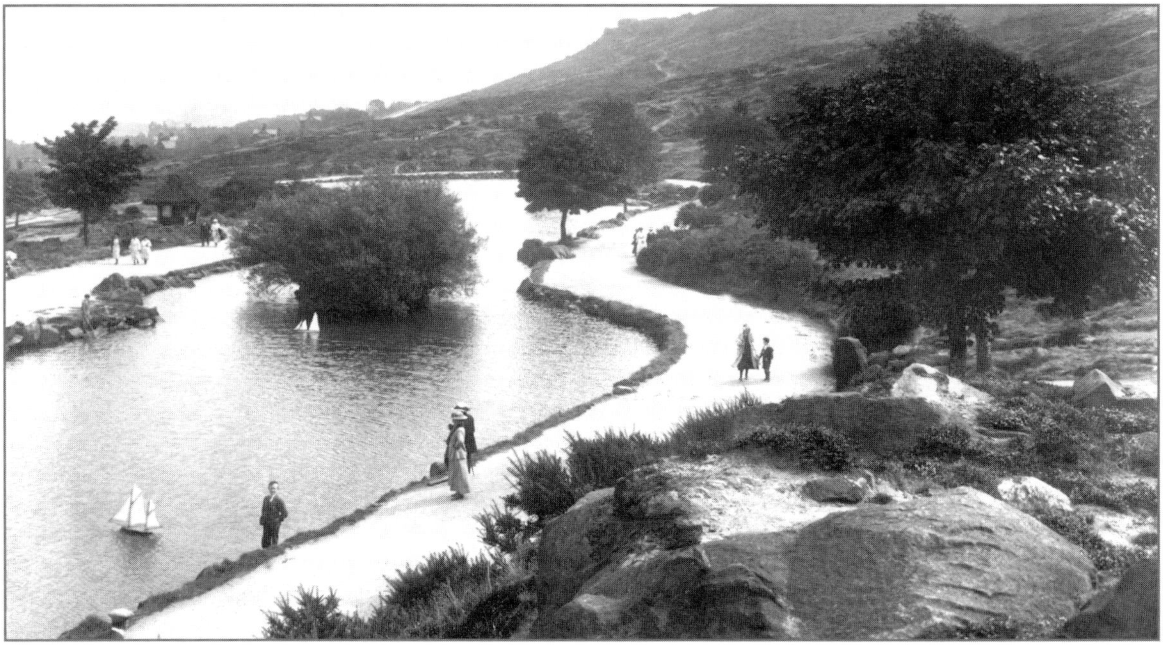

Ilkley, The Tarn 1921 71281
The attractive Craig tarn, which has a superb view over the town, was developed from a moorland pond and bog and was completed in 1874. There used to be a fountain on the central island. During the winter the tarn was always a paradise for skaters.

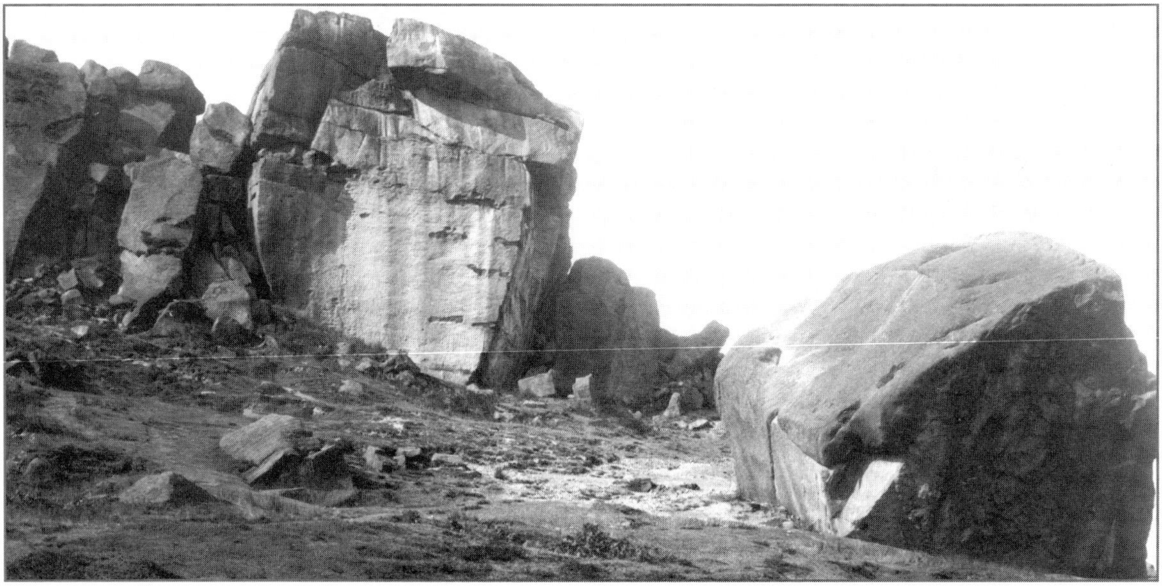

Ilkley, The Cow and Calf Rocks 1886 18564
The whole area on the western side of Ilkley is the wild Rombalds Moor, which stretches right over to Shipley Glen and the Aire Valley. The Victorians came to Ilkley in their carriages, and later by train, to enjoy fresh air and the invigorating spa water. But sunshine can quickly disappear. On one July day in 1900, the moors received over a tenth of their annual rainfall in just over an hour. Nearly 5 inches fell; water cascaded down the ghylls dragging huge boulders in its wake, causing over £100,000 worth of damage to Ilkley.

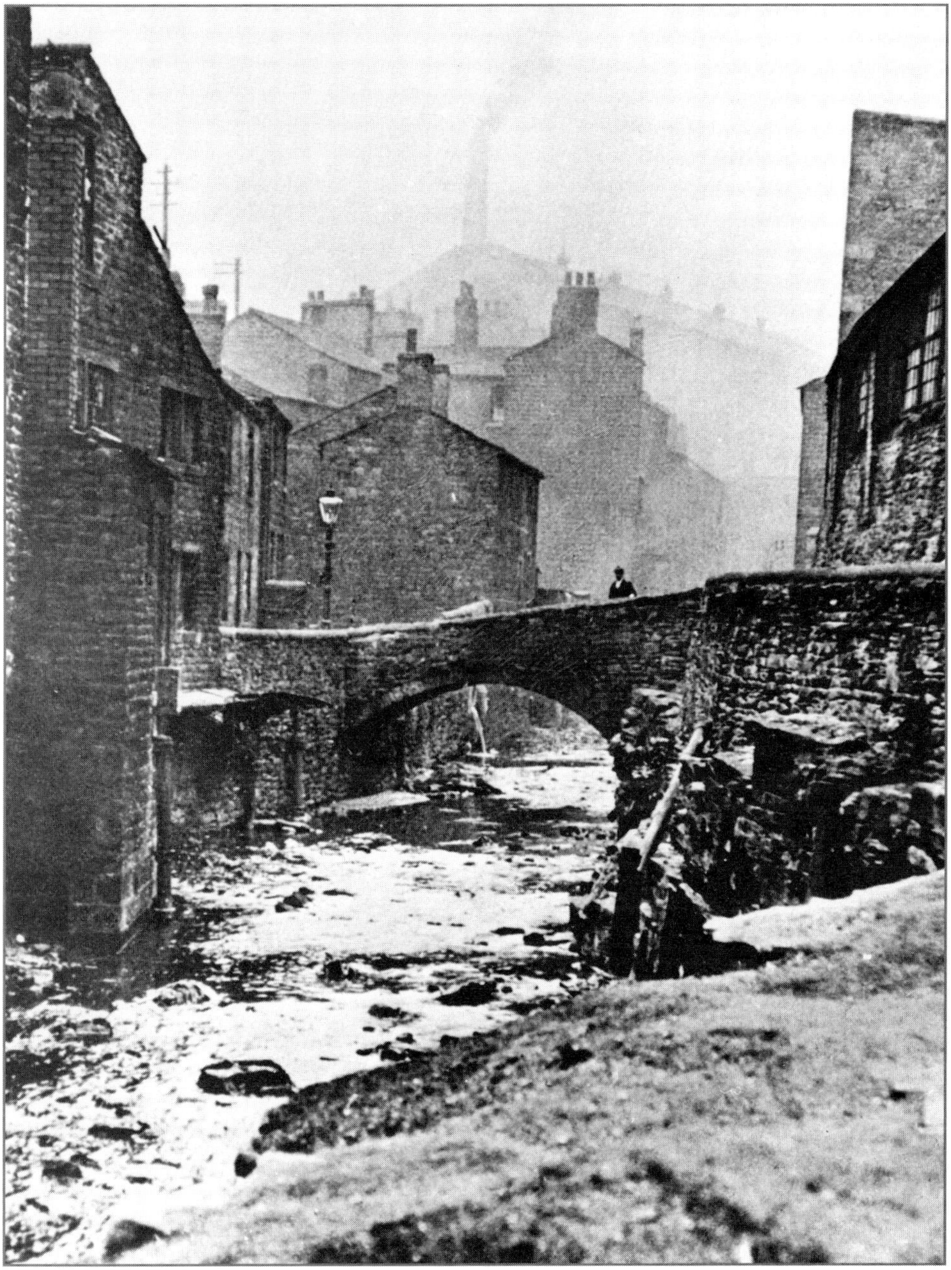

Keighley, Quebec Street c1890 K60502

This was once part of a quiet residential area, with orchards and gardens. But as the population increased massively, over five times in four decades, the streets surrounding this area became infamous for fights and drunken brawls. The bed level of the North Beck was raised five feet by the accumulation of rubbish. The bridge was eventually demolished in June 1934, and the Beck was covered over during the Westgate clearance scheme.The phenomenal growth of the cotton trade in the town led to inevitable pollution of the rivers. Gone from the North Beck were the perch and the grayling; in their place came rats and rubbish. As the population grew throughout the century, more and more cottages were built even closer together, giving this smoky tint to every street.

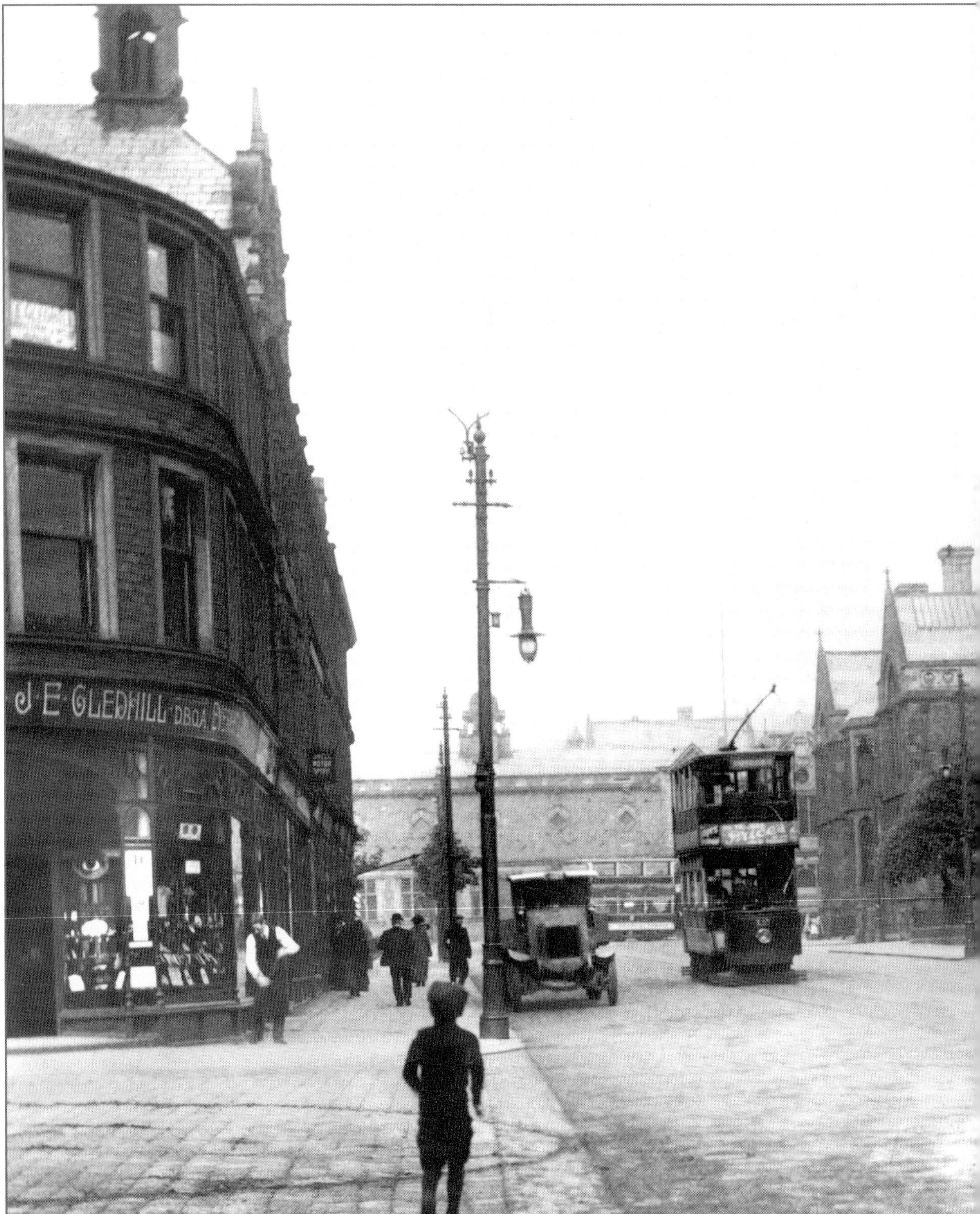
J·E·GLEDHILL

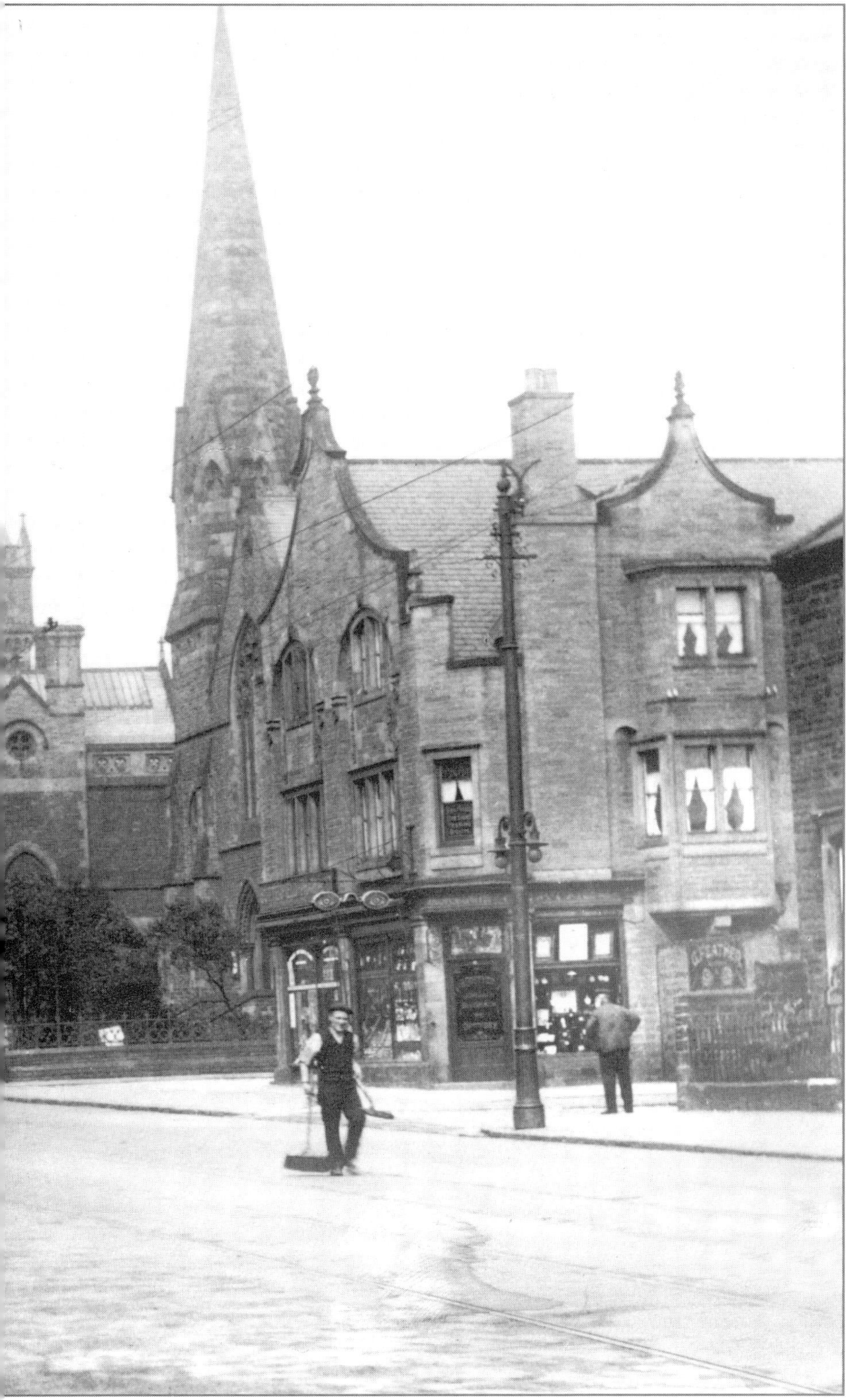

Keighley, Cavendish Street c1910 K60503
This is the town's main shopping street. Lower down, a canopy over the pavement keeps the Pennine precipitation off the shoppers. At the top of the street was the new market (dating from 1833), which took the 500-year-old trade from Church Green. It is 9.20 in the morning, and we are looking up the street from Lawkholme Crescent towards the Carnegie Public Library of 1904. The optician's shop on the left, next to the famous Cycling Club building, was replaced in 1923 by a building society. The United Methodist Church had the highest spire in town. The weathercock, at 125 feet, was a landmark for nearly seven decades until it was swept away for the Keighley College in 1953. Gordon Bottomley, poet and playwright, was born in 1874 in the Dutch-style house on the right.

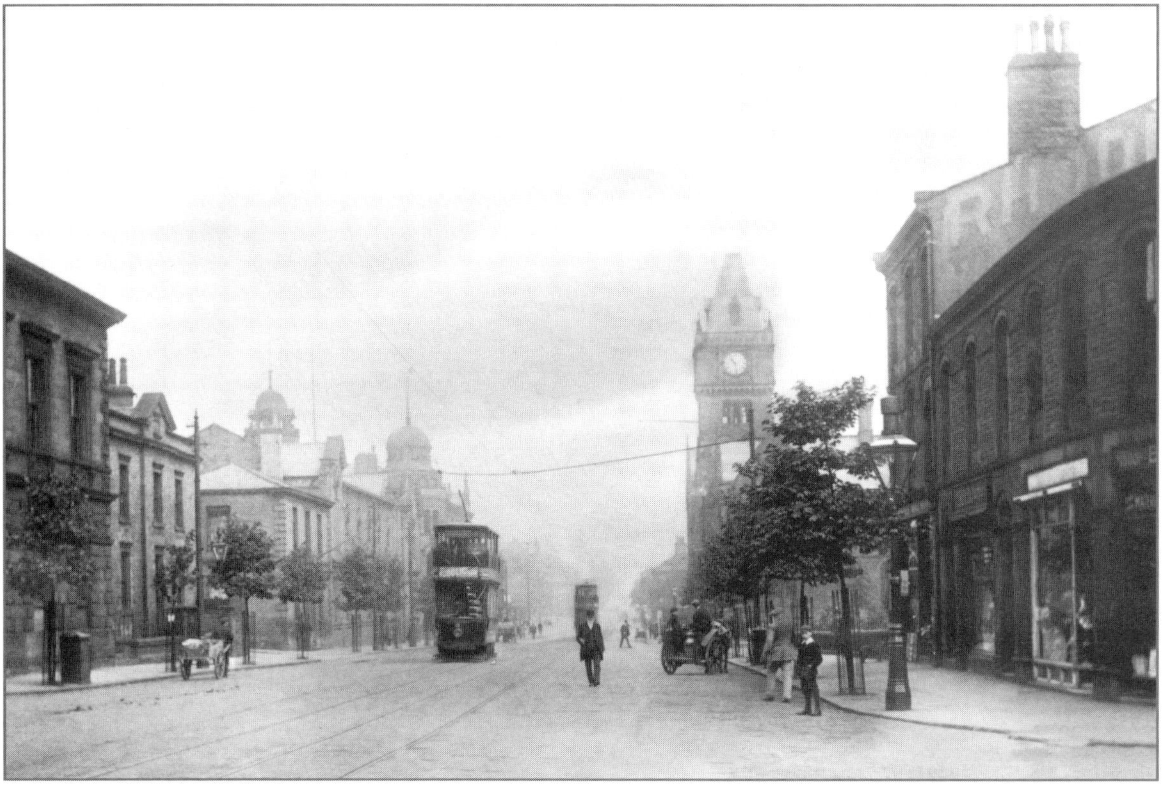

Keighley, North Street c1910 K60505
New buildings along North Street included the Court House (1831) and the Mechanics' Institute (1834). The Post Office of 1839 was superseded by a new one in Bow Street (1891). The air of Victorian prosperity is clear to see. Rails for horse trams were laid in 1889, and the system was electrified in 1904. On the left are the police station (1887), the Temperance Institute (1896) and, just out of shot, the Public Library, the first in the country to be financed by the American steel millionaire, Andrew Carnegie. The Mechanics' Institute, opened in 1870, gained its clock in 1892. The building was gutted by fire in 1962, and part of the remaining section was incorporated in the new college.

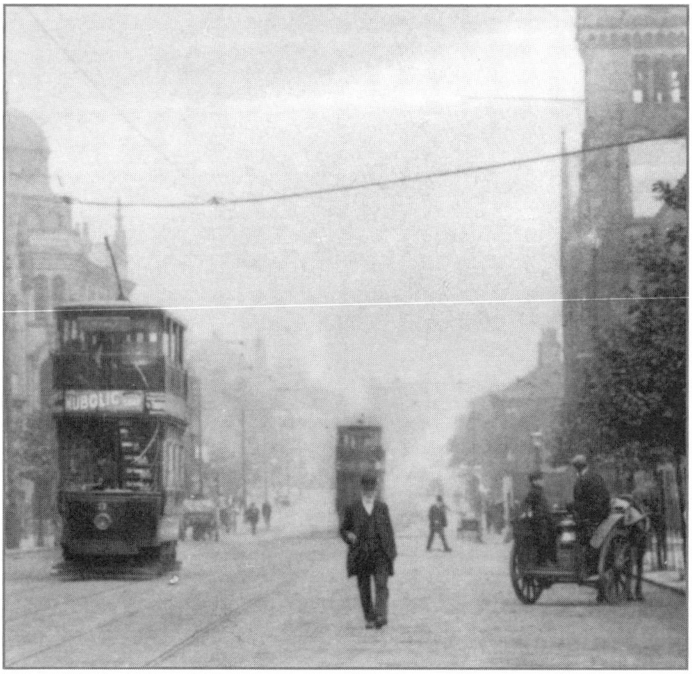

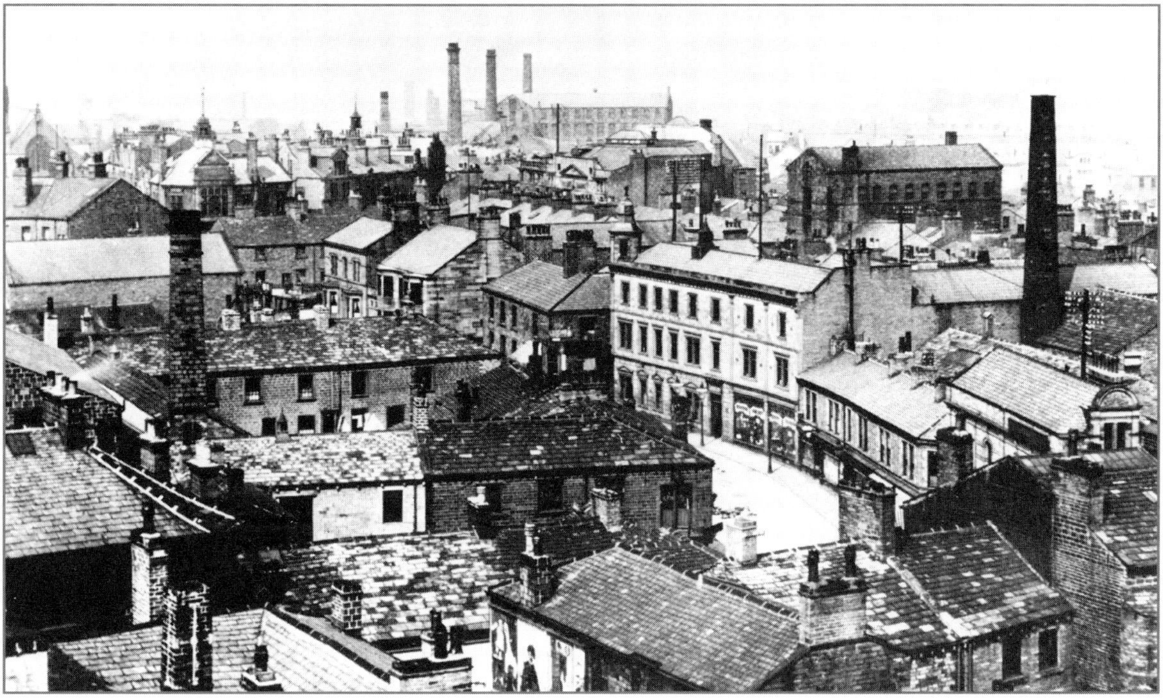

Keighley
View from the Parish Church c1900 K60501
The industrial and commercial parts of the town co-existed in a very confined space. The mill chimneys were an ever-present reminder of the source of the family's wagepacket. This view of the town is from St Andrew's Church (rebuilt in 1848 in the Perpendicular style). People came from miles around for the Sunday service, and afterwards took lunch in one of the many inns surrounding the church. Broth with dumplings cost one penny a bowl. We are looking across Cook Lane towards Townfield Gate. All of this was cleared for the new shopping centre and bus station. From the left are the Methodist Church, the School Board Offices (1893), the Hippodrome Theatre (1880-1961) and the Gas Offices (1902). Major factories in this picture include the Honduras and the Airedale Works.

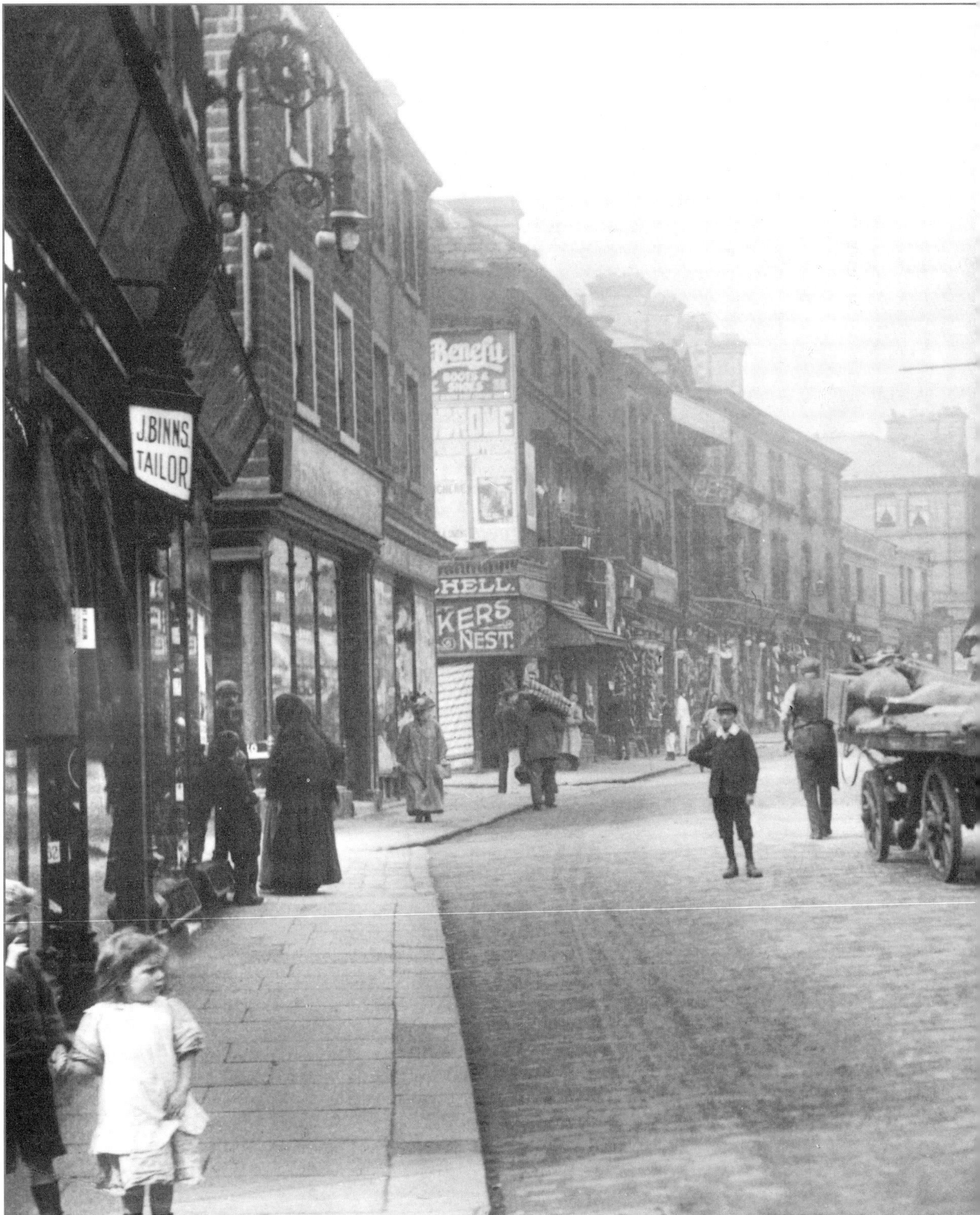
J.BINNS
TAILOR
HELL.
KERS
NEST.

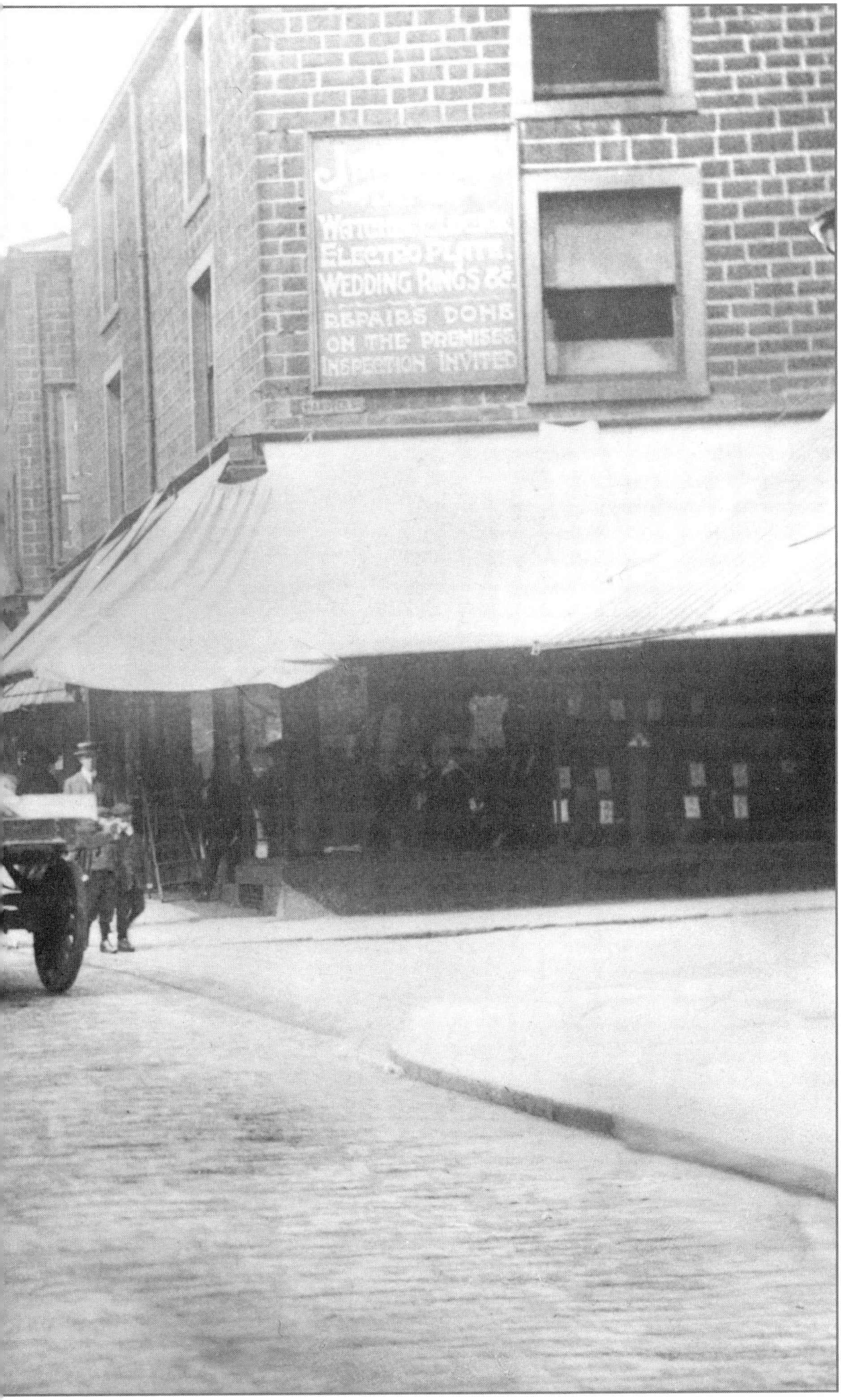

Keighley, Low Street c1910 K60506
New shopping arcades were established along Low Street and North Street at the turn of the century, as the town's population continued to enjoy the fruits of the cotton boom years. Still, though, the centre for shopping remained on Cavendish Street. Low Street was regarded as rather dreary.

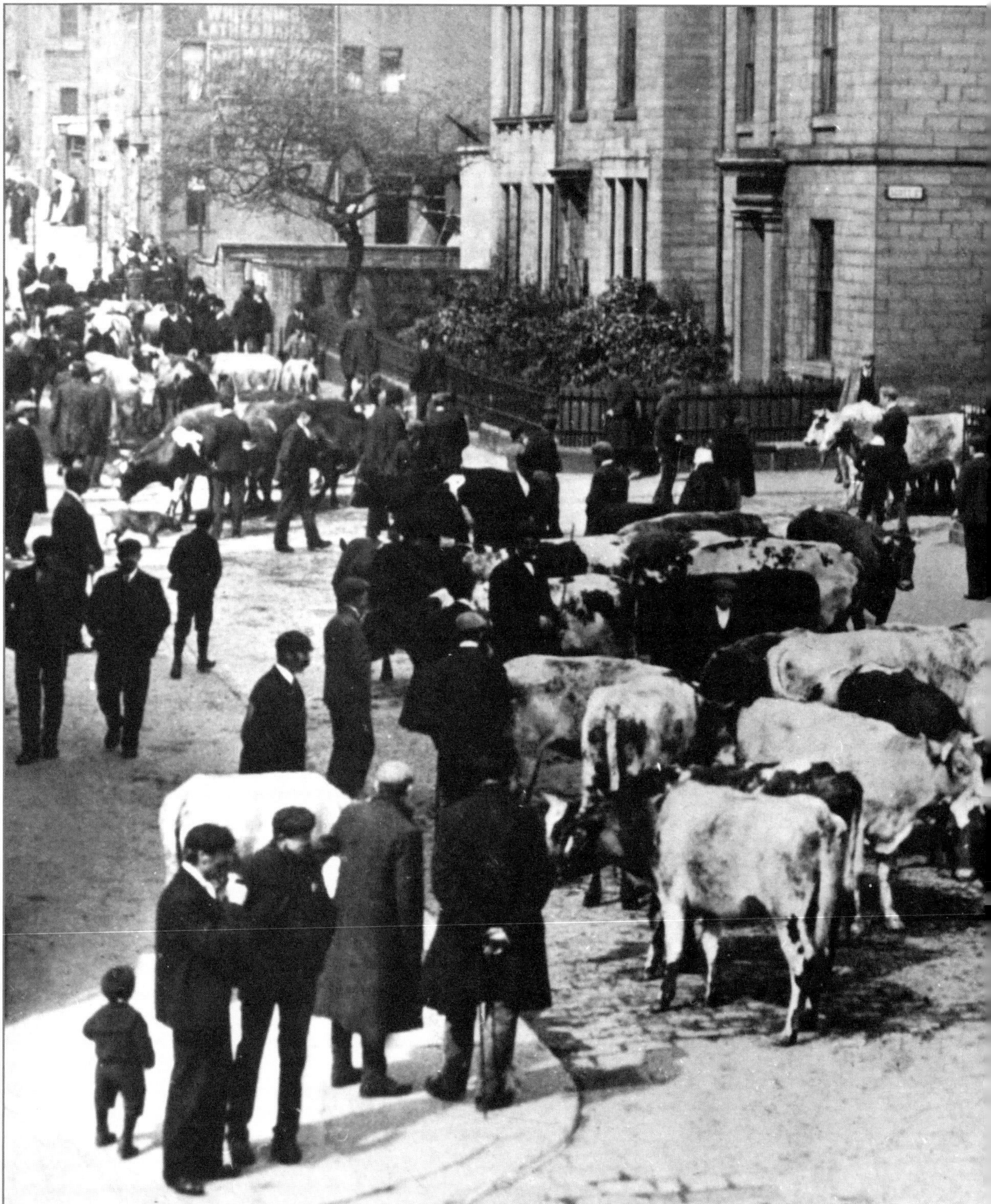

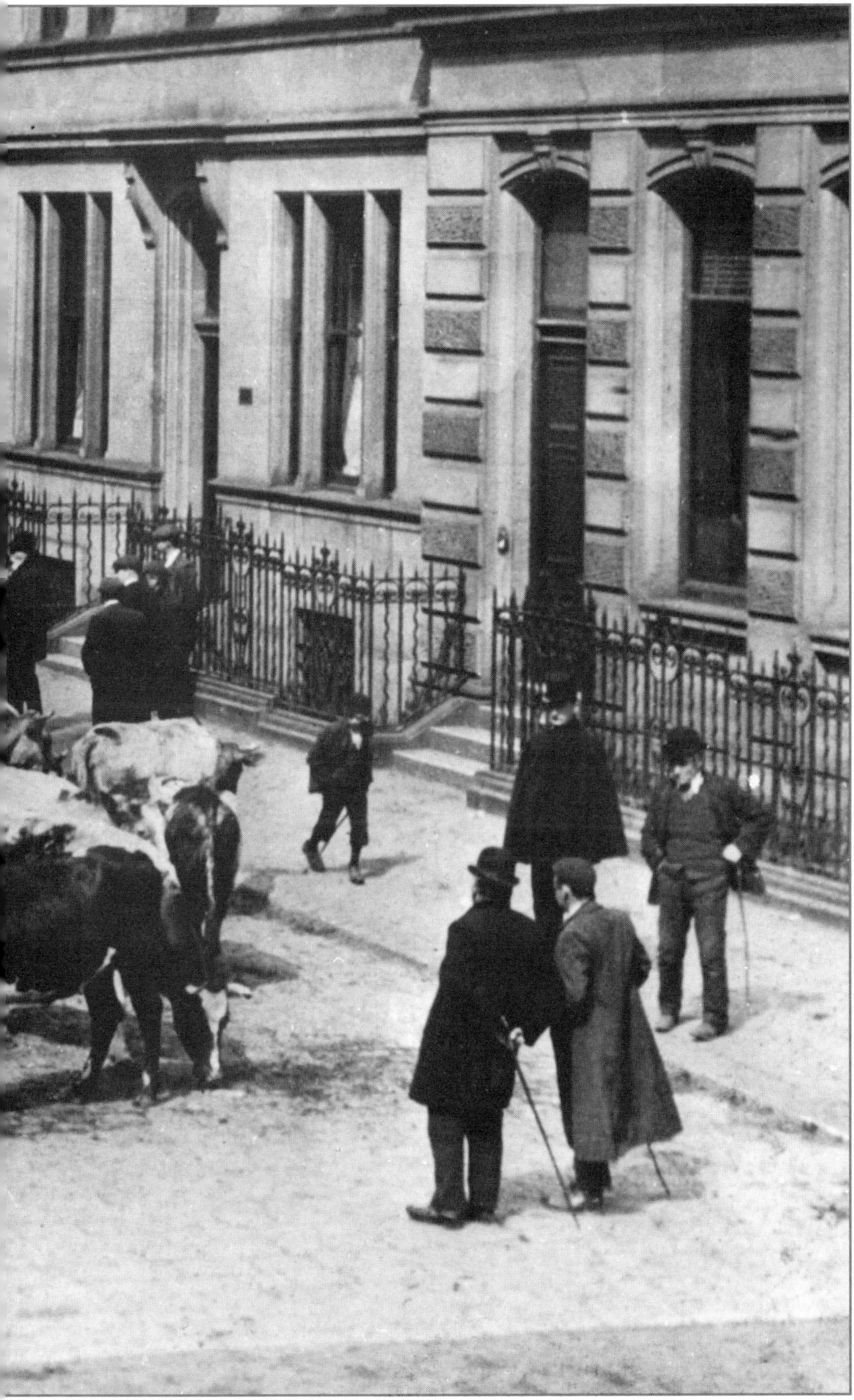

Keighley, The Cattle Market c1910 K60504
Today we would be horrified to find beasts strolling around the town centre passing offices and private houses. Back in 1910, the locals knew that the cattle fair brought prosperity and variety to an industrial landscape. Dealers came from miles around, and welcomed the chance to converse in the nearby inns. The Beast Fairs were held twice a year, in May and November, here in Russell Street. At the close of business the fire brigade would be called to hose the streets.

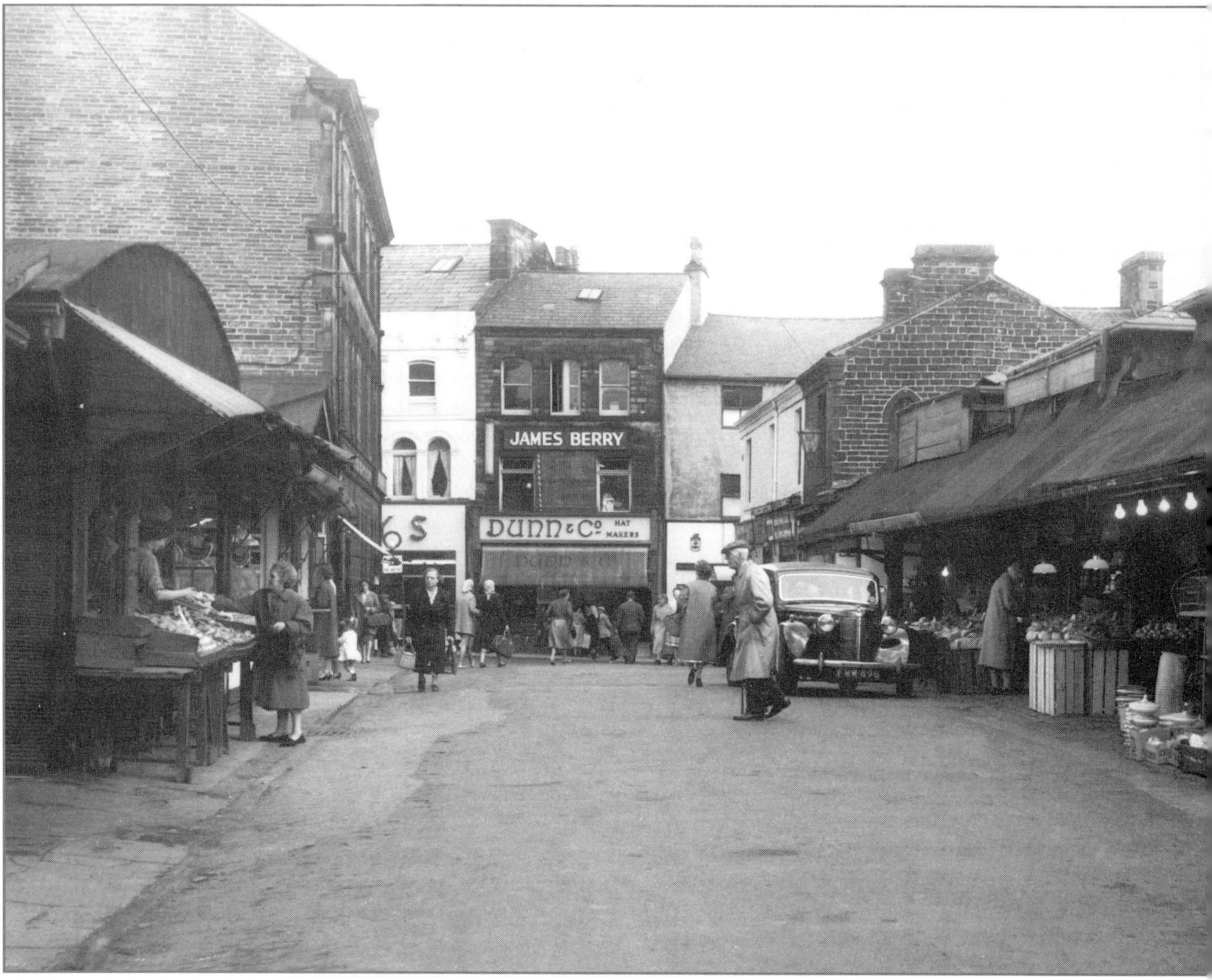

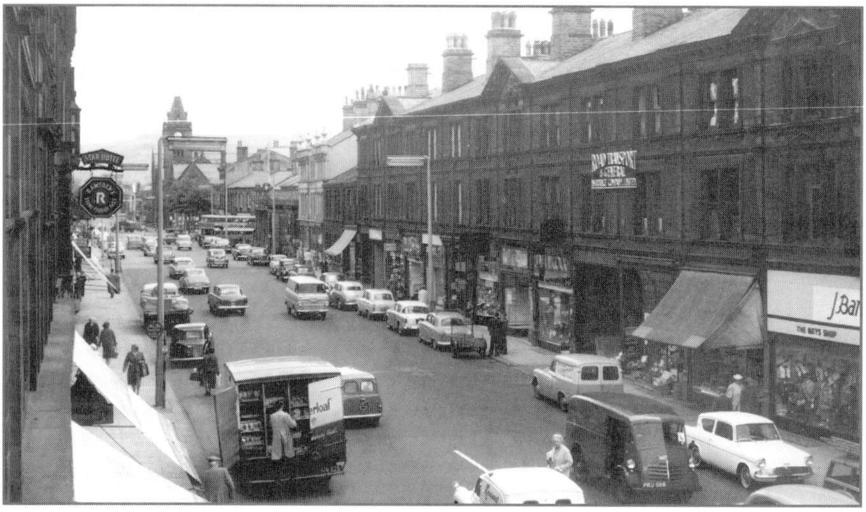

◄**Keighley, North Street c1965** K60025
The car started to become king by the mid 60s. The Picture House on North Street was still doing excellent business, in spite of competition from the nearby and more modern Ritz cinema (1938). Despite the cars, though, the delivery men could still find a parking space to service the numerous, and sadly missed, local shops.

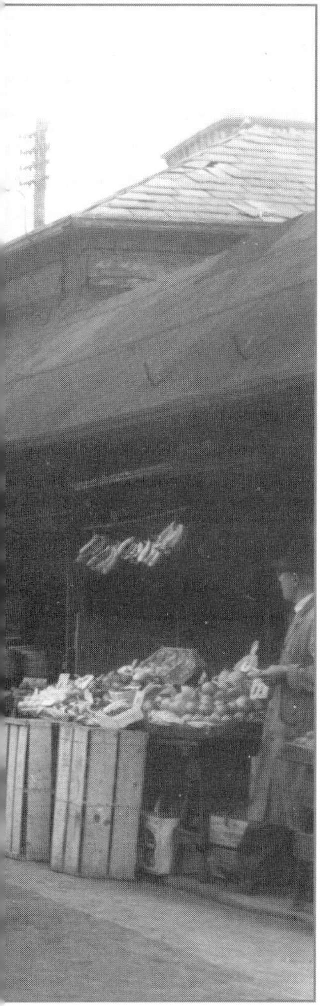

Keighley
Market Day c1955 K60031

From 1833 to 1971 this old market near the Parish Church served the town well with fresh produce from across Yorkshire. But when Keighley saw the developments in neighbouring towns, it demanded a more modern version as well. The old market was swept away in 1971 and the new hall was incorporated into the modern shopping precinct. It was not always hard work here; the market workers frequently enjoyed barrel-rolling and basket-stacking contests.

Kippax
High Street c1960 K72044

Situated just to the east of Leeds, the village of Kippax was the scene of much coal mining since 1410. The estate surrounding the old Kippax Hall contained many unusual black deer. The house, built in yellow stone, was 600 feet in length, but it was demolished owing to mining subsidence in 1965. The one-time owner, Sir John Slingsby, is said to have discovered the sulphur springs in Harrogate.

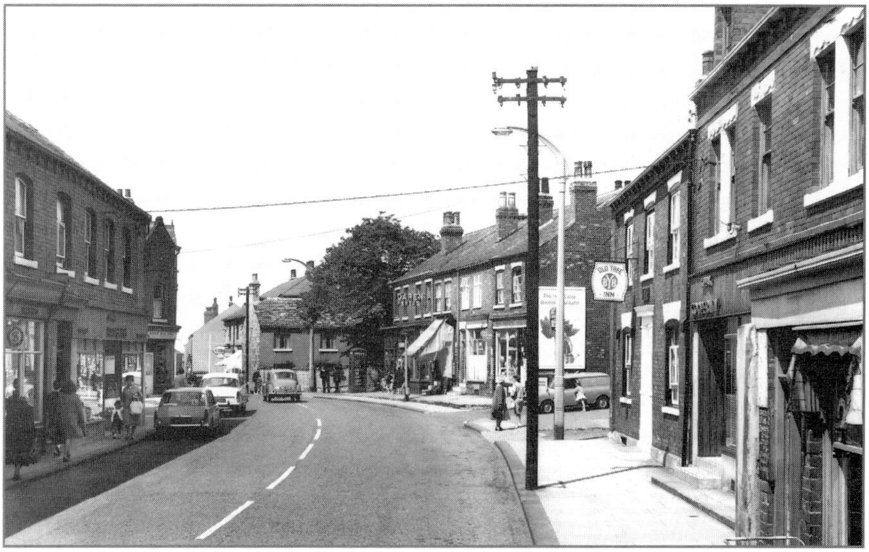

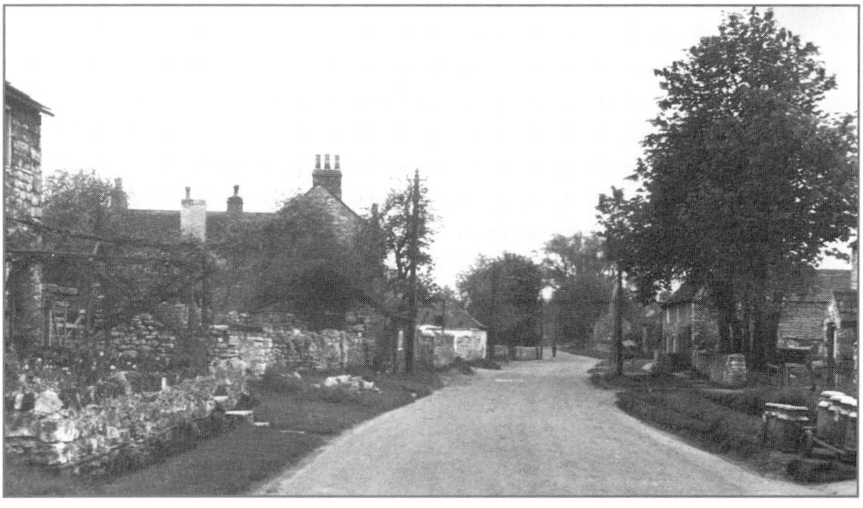

Kippax, Ledston Village c1955 K72019

The rural charm of this delightful village was preserved owing to its proximity to nearby Ledston Hall. A manor house of 1556, it was built on the site of an old monastery. After the house was inherited by Lady Elizabeth Hastings in 1701, a royal gardener redesigned the grounds. With Temple Newsam, it remains a rare example of an Elizabethan/Jacobean house. Evidence of Iron Age activity was unearthed just off the Main Street of the village.

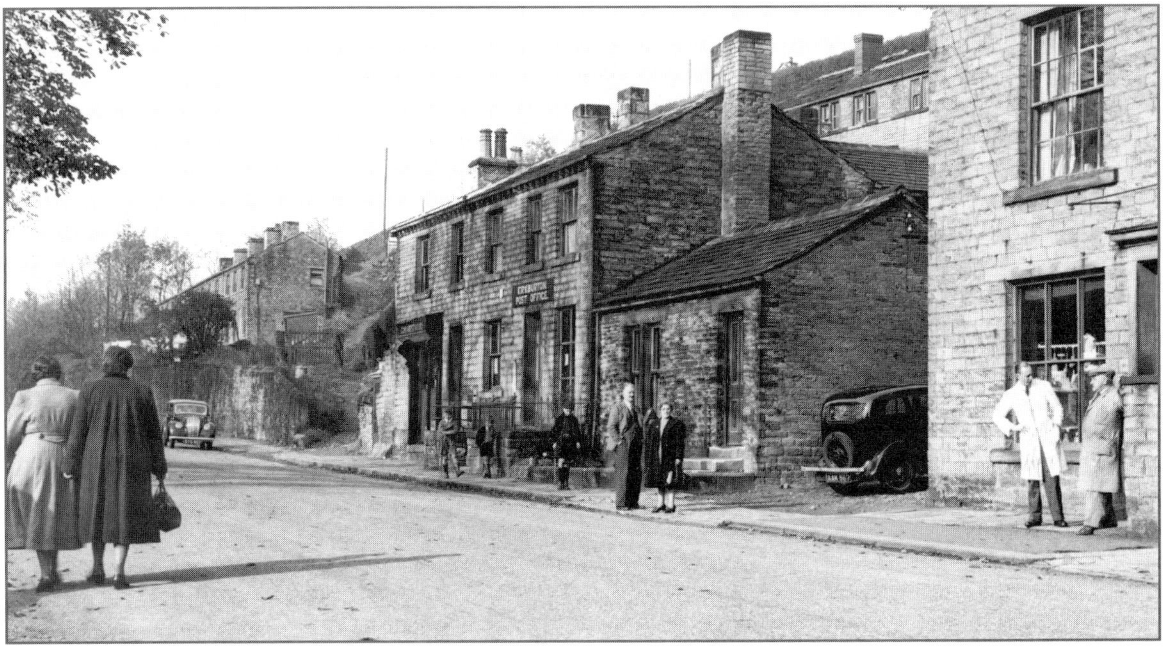

Kirkburton, North Road c1955 K75020
Just five miles south of Huddersfield on the road to Wakefield, Kirkburton in the 19th century was just as polluted by smoke as its near neighbours. The town was full of woollen mills and corset factories and was surrounded by numerous collieries. Later, the town became a centre for 'fancy' goods such as cords, velveteens and fine woollens.

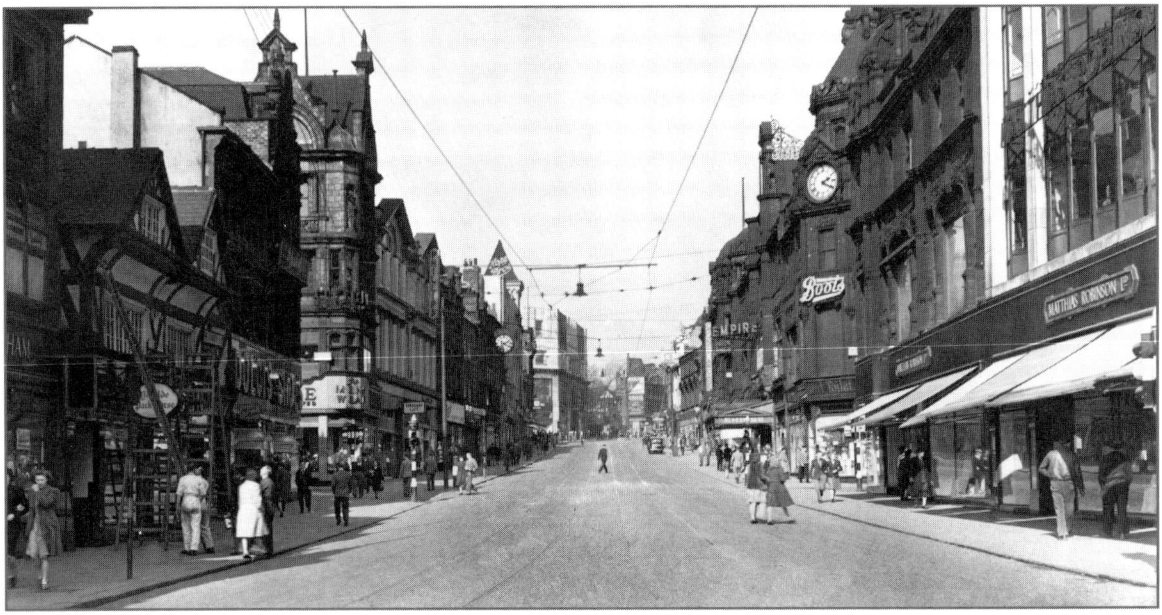

Leeds, Briggate 1955 L28012
The heart of the city for 800 years, Briggate leads directly off the Leeds Bridge. A major redevelopment in 1870 brought many new shops and arcades to the thoroughfare. The last bow-windowed shop here, William Green's, was demolished in 1922, and the last surviving medieval building on Briggate, Wallis's Hosier and Glover's, was taken down and replaced by Timpson's shoe shop in the year of this photograph.

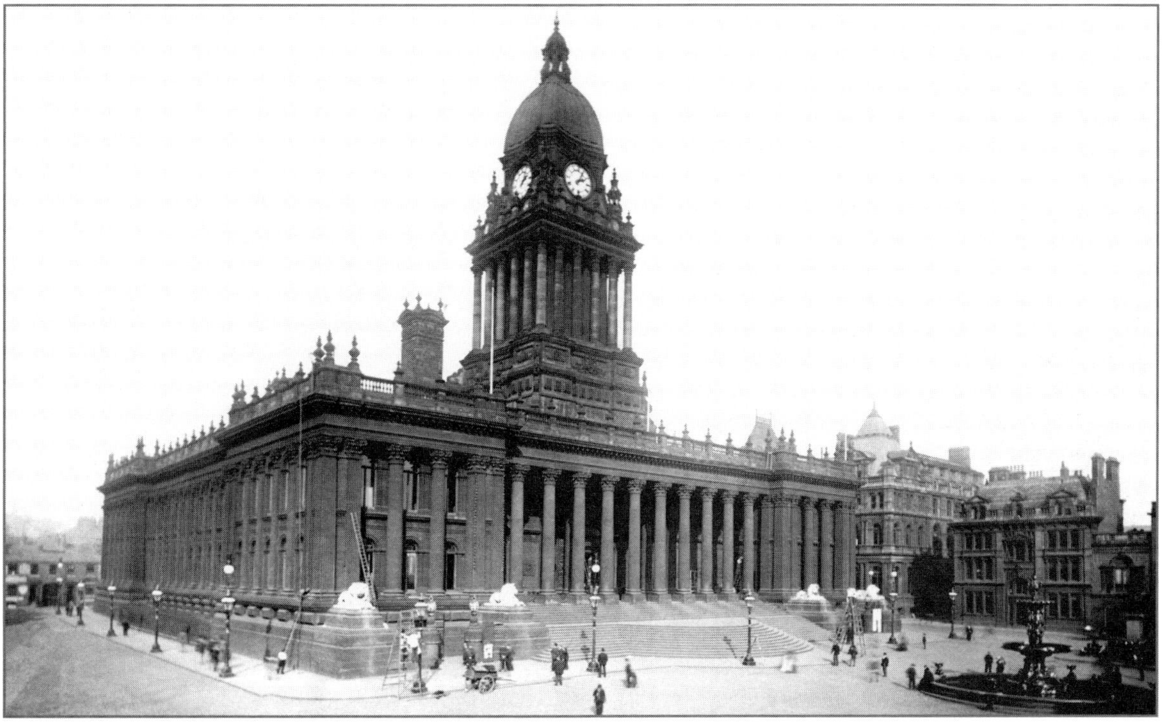

Leeds
The Town Hall 1894 34765

The architect of the Town Hall, Cuthbert Brodrick, also left many other Leeds legacies, including the Corn Exchange (1860), the Mechanics' Institute (1860), the Oriental Baths (1866)and shops on Cookridge Street (1864), together with a private house in Headingley at 17 Alma Road (1859). Further afield, he was also the architect of the imposing Grand Hotel in Scarborough (1862). After a spell in France, he retired to Jersey where he died in 1905. At the time of the opening of the Leeds Town Hall in 1858, an arch commemorating Queen Victoria's visit was erected in north Leeds. It was renovated in 1984 and still stands, but it is well-hidden in woodland at Beckett's Park in Headingley. The Calverley office building behind the fountain was demolished for the widening of the Headrow in 1933.

▼ **Leeds, Yorkshire College 1894** 34767

This was originally Yorkshire College of Science; it opened in 1877, and the first student was a miner. The college was renamed the Victoria University in 1887, when the science specialism was extended to embrace languages and history. It became the Leeds University on 25 April 1904. This original site now nestles behind the 1951 Portland stone Parkinson building.

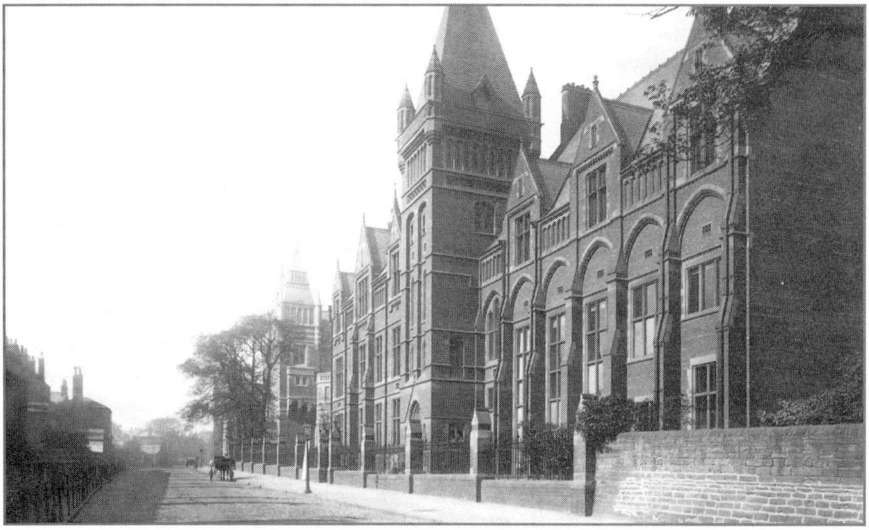

▼ **Leeds, Kirkstall Abbey 1890** 28286

Kirkstall Abbey was founded by Cistercian monks from Fountains Abbey and was financed by the landowner Sir Henry Lacy. Construction took twenty-three years; the Abbey survived until its dissolution in 1539. The gatehouse was then converted to a domestic house, and it is now the city's folk museum. After three centuries of dereliction, the Abbey was purchased from the Cardigan estate by Colonel North in 1888. He had made his fortune from nitrates by discovering that the droppings of tropical birds contained that substance; he had the droppings collected and shipped to Europe as a fertiliser. North presented the Abbey to the city, and after much restoration it was opened to the public.

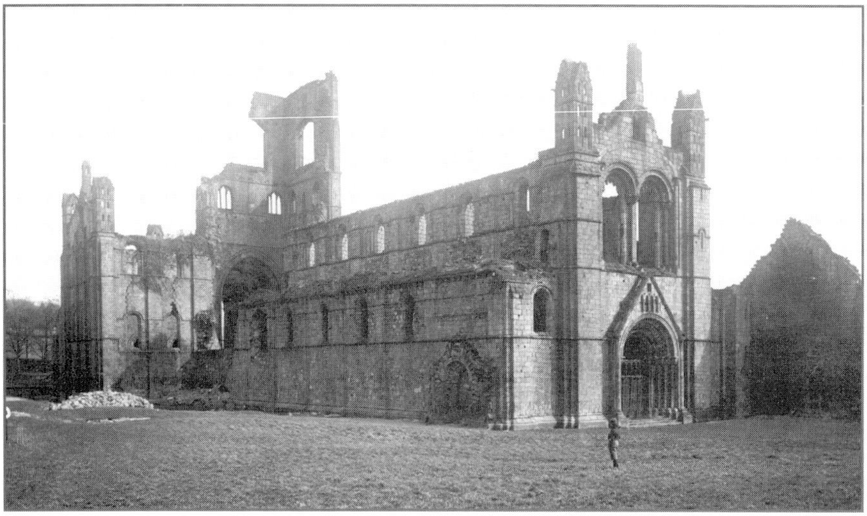

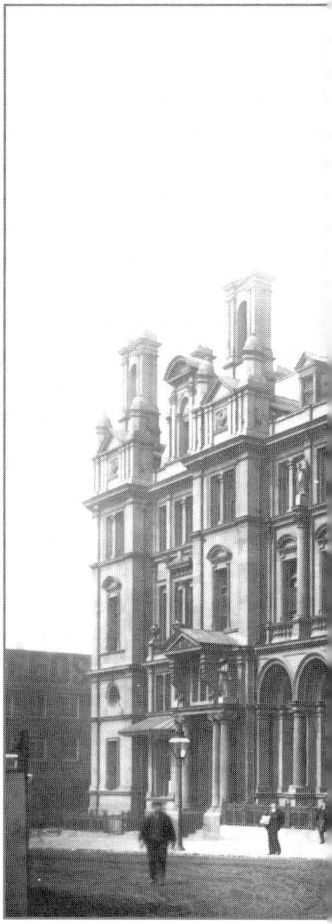

▲ **Leeds, The Post Office 1897** 39088

The Coloured Cloth Hall once stood on this site. Here, traders were allowed just one hour's trading per day. After demolition, the cupola from the roof tower was used, and can still be seen, on the nearby Metropole Hotel. The Post Office (1896) overlooks City Square, around which are now grouped the railway station, the Queen's Hotel and the former News Theatre. A statue of Sir Robert Peel once stood opposite the Post Office, but it was moved to the Town Hall square in 1903. Then from 1937 he kept Queen Victoria company on Woodhouse Moor.

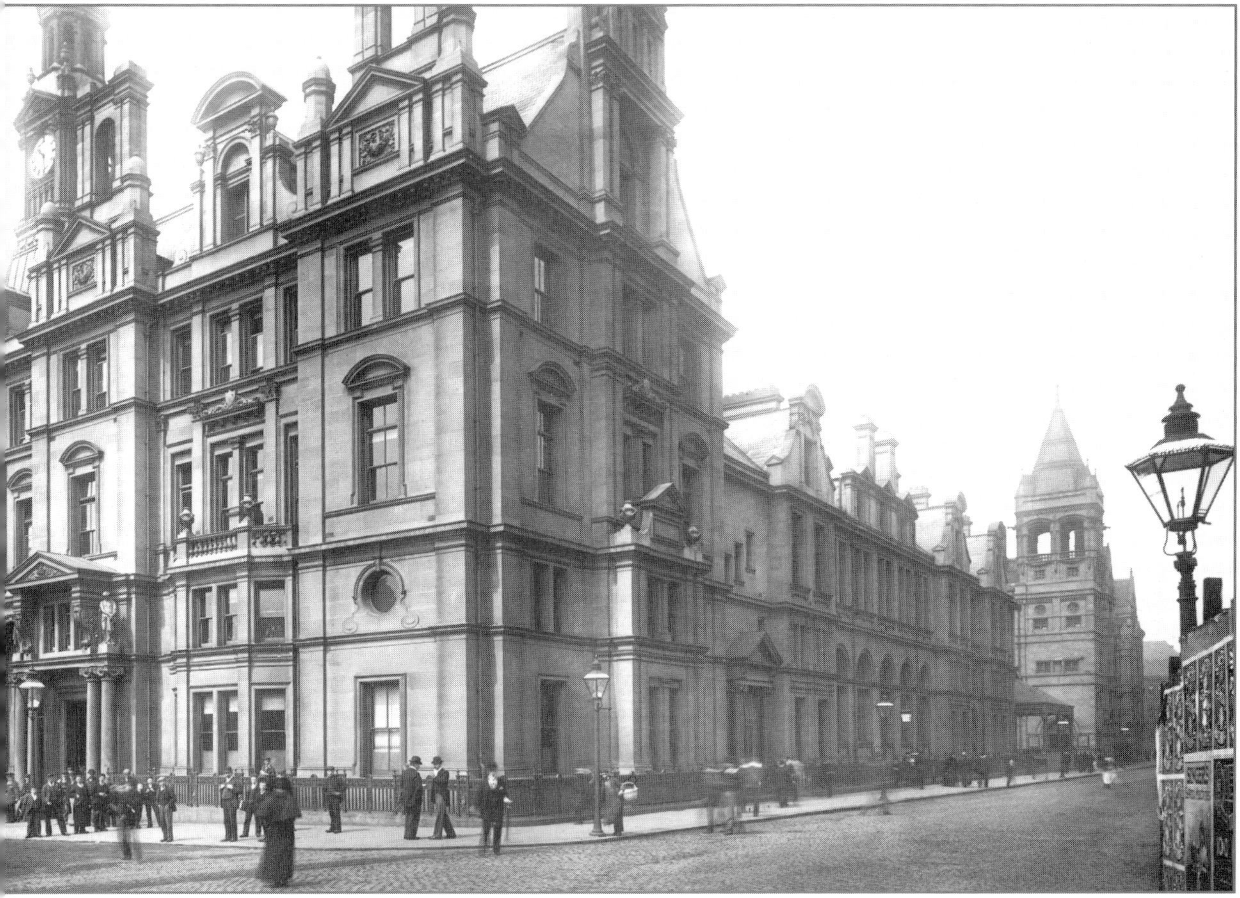

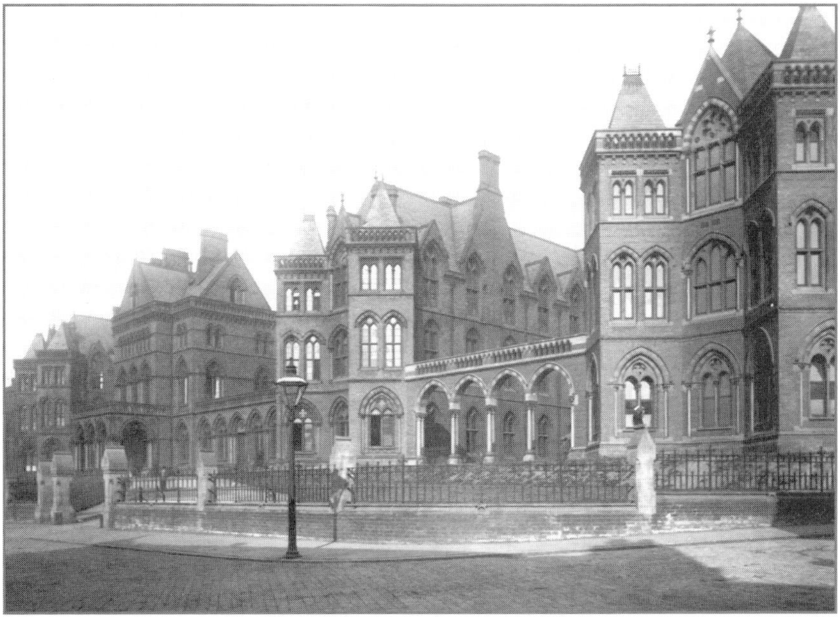

Leeds, The General Infirmary 1894 34769
Completed in 1868, the Infirmary was designed by Gilbert Scott, whose other major work at this time was the hotel at St Pancras Railway station in London. In Leeds, Scott was also responsible for the old Beckett's Bank building in Park Row (1862, now demolished). Advice on the interior design of the Infirmary came from Florence Nightingale, and it was acclaimed as being the best among European hospitals. The Winter Garden for the patients contained tropical plants and trees.

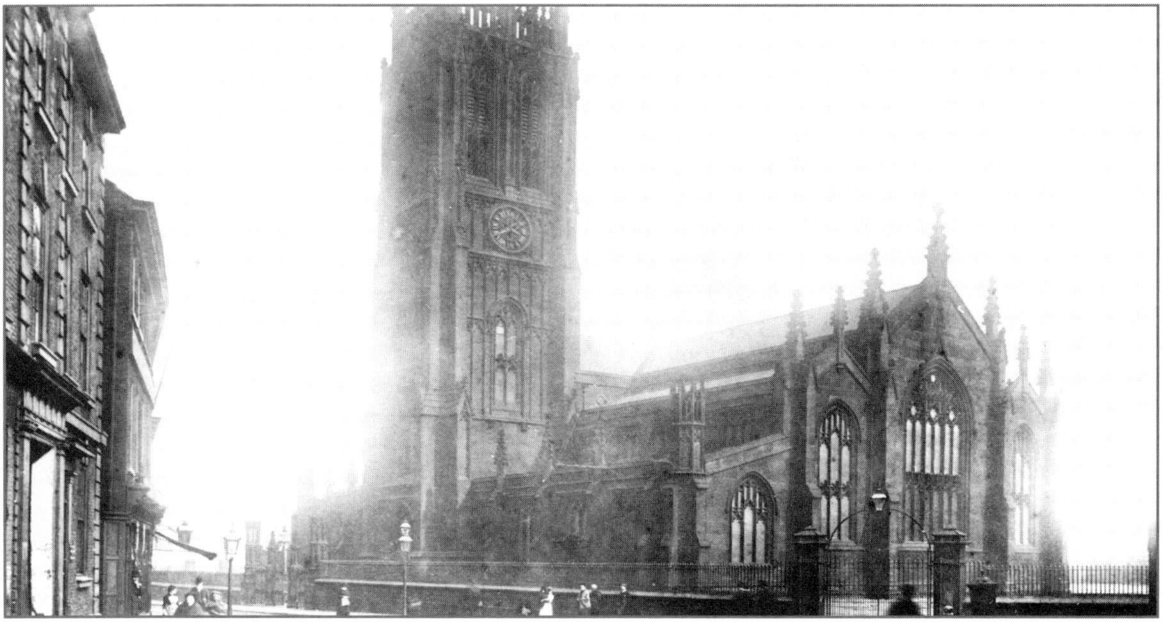

Leeds, The Parish Church 1891 28281
The new Vicar of Leeds in 1837, Dr Hook, decided to rebuild the much-altered 16th-century and rather cluttered central church. Unusually, the tower is positioned in the middle of the frontage. Completed in 1841, the Parish Church is now at the centre of much riverside regeneration. Back in Victorian times it was surrounded by a degenerate Leeds, including drinking-houses and prostitution.

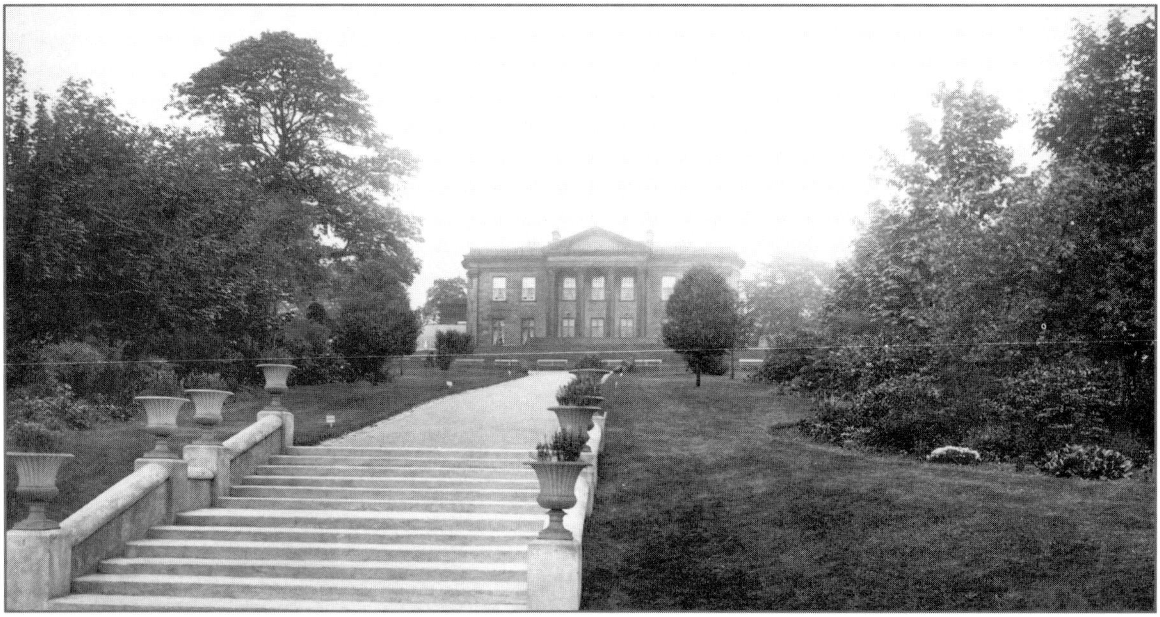

Leeds, Roundhay Park 1897 39090
Once a hunting estate for John of Gaunt, the land was purchased in 1803 by Thomas Nicholson, who created the two lakes and the parkland. Mansion House dates from 1826. The Mayor of Leeds, John Barran, the pioneer of mass clothing, bought it at auction in 1871; he then sold it at cost to the Leeds Corporation. The old Roundhay estate was then opened on 20 September 1872 as the country's first municipal park.

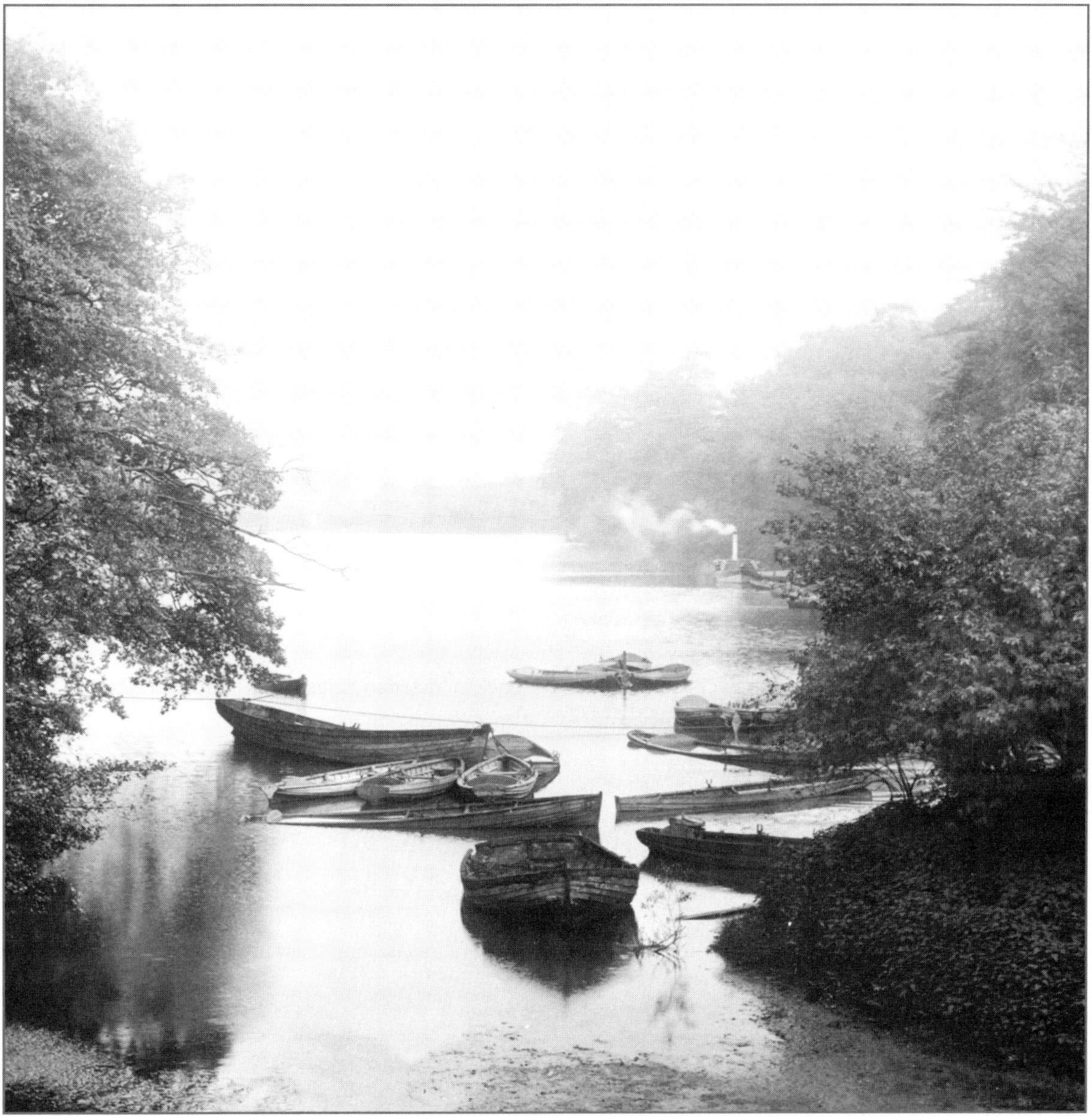

Leeds, Roundhay Lake 1897 39092

This 33-acre lake was constructed from an old quarry. The depth at its deepest point is 100 feet. The delightful steam boat is the 'Maid of Athens'. A trip round Waterloo lake was 2d for adults and 1d for children. The steam boat was launched in 1895, but she was replaced four years later when the new steam yacht 'Mary Gordon' was launched. The boathouse at the other end of the lake was constructed in 1902, and held 150 rowing boats. In the 1930s an amnesty on war weapons produced 300 firearms, which were sunk in the lake during the darkest nights. A few years ago the lake was drained for maintenance, and the police patrolled the area to stop weapons being retrieved.

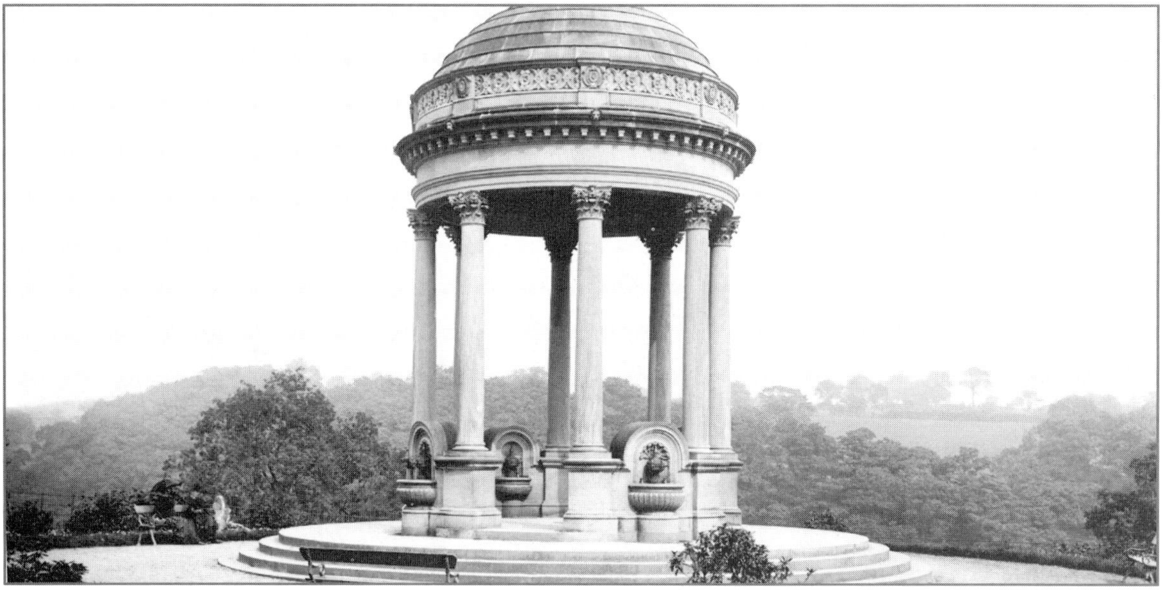

Leeds, The Fountain 1888 21003
Because Roundhay was on the outskirts of Leeds, transport to the Park was difficult; those who did venture along the old turnpike road found a beautiful site - but it lacked basic facilities. To try to alleviate at least the drinking water supply, John Barran constructed this delightful fountain at his own expense (£3,000). A tramway opened to the park in 1891, and the fountain must have quenched many a Loiner's thirst. It remains to this day, but appears to be no longer connected to the city's Eccup reservoir.

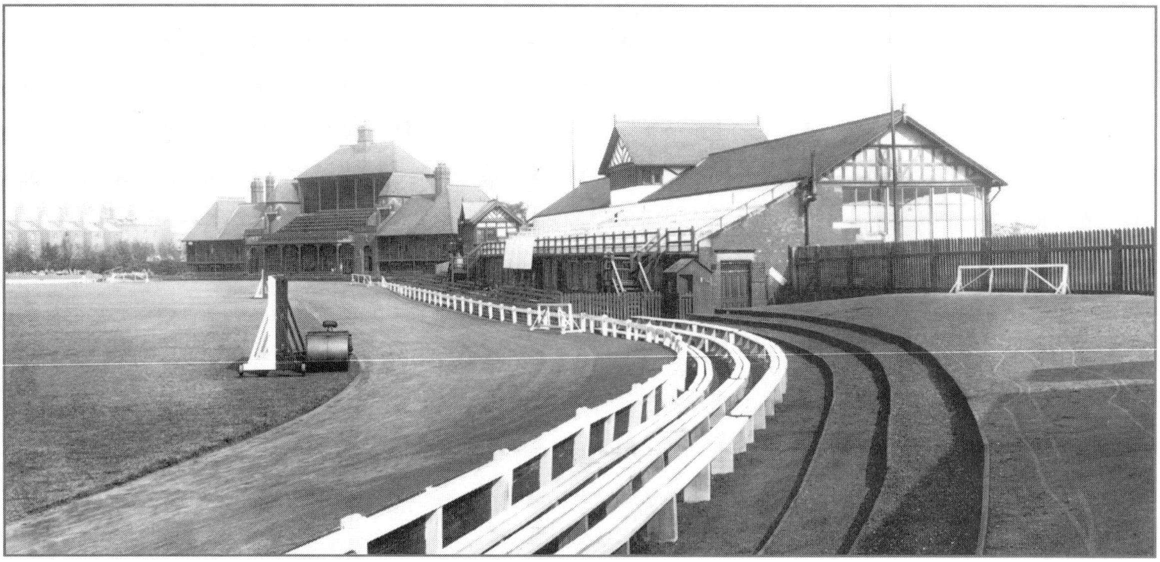

Leeds, The Cricket Ground, Headingley 1897 39099
When the Cardigan estate at Kirkstall and Headingley was sold at auction in 1889, a group of businessmen with an enthusiasm for sports purchased Lot 17A. This was to become the home of the Leeds Cricket, Football and Athletic Company. The very first cricket match played here in 1890 was between Leeds and Scarborough. Also, in the same year a North of England XI entertained the Australian team. In the first Yorkshire cricket game in June 1891 the home team lost to Derbyshire by 45 runs. Test cricket came in 1899, and rugby was first played here in 1895 by Leeds FC, one of the twenty original clubs that formed the Rugby League.

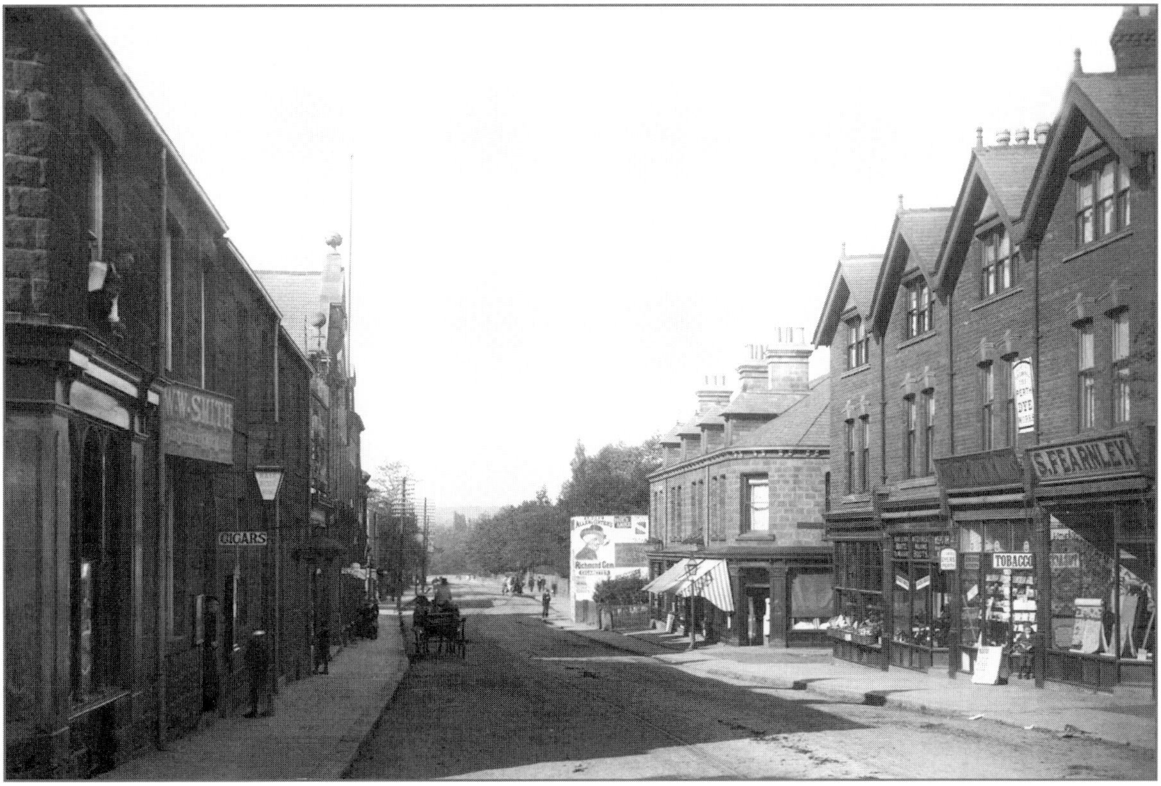

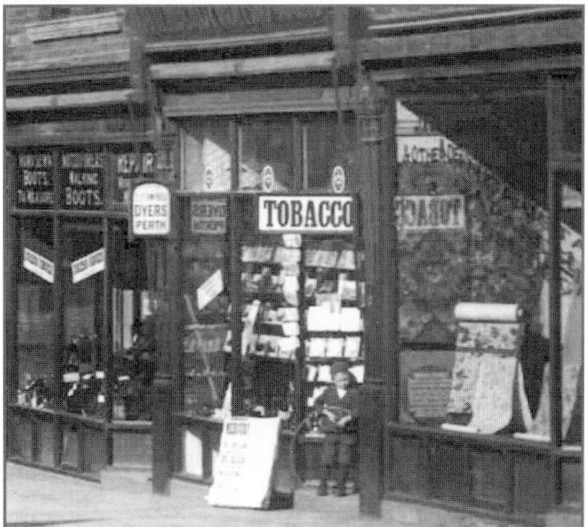

Leeds, View of Headingley 1894 34773
In the mid 19th century, many middle-class residents of central Leeds began to move out to the north of the city near to the country estates of Beckett's Park and Hollin Hall, and Headingley became a rather exclusive suburb. Here the merchants of the city built their imposing new houses, most of which remain today.

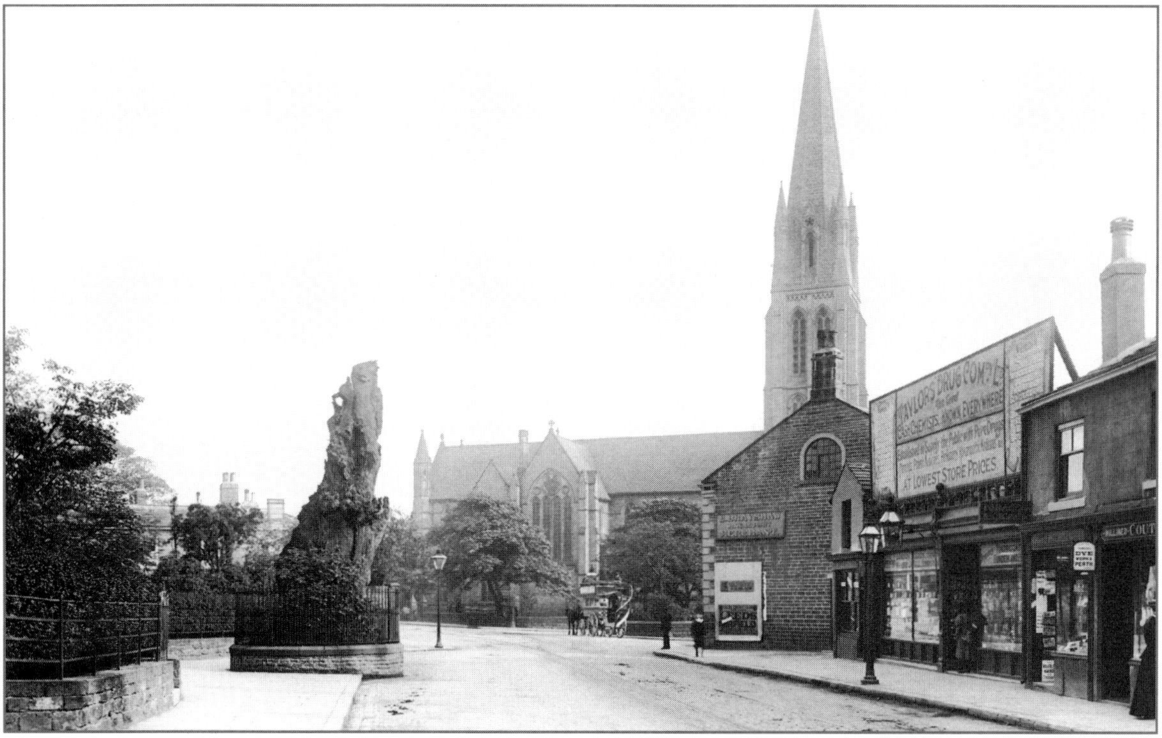

Leeds
Headingley 1897 39097
This ancient oak tree finally collapsed on 16 May 1941, just a month after the council had proposed the adding of a steel support. It is said that the tree had been used in Roman times as a signal station. The parish church of St Michael and All Saints, in the background, was rebuilt in 1864.

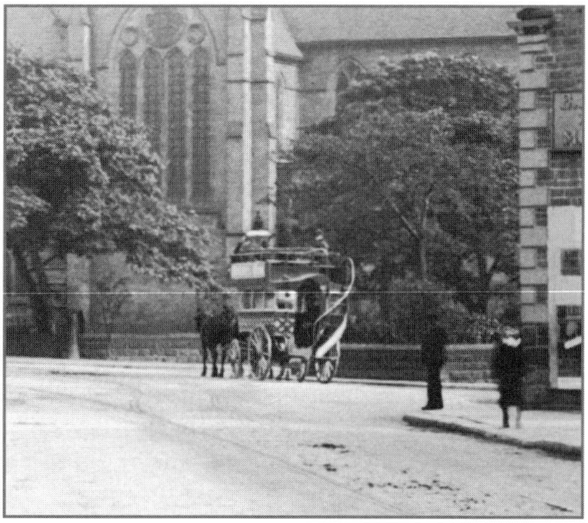

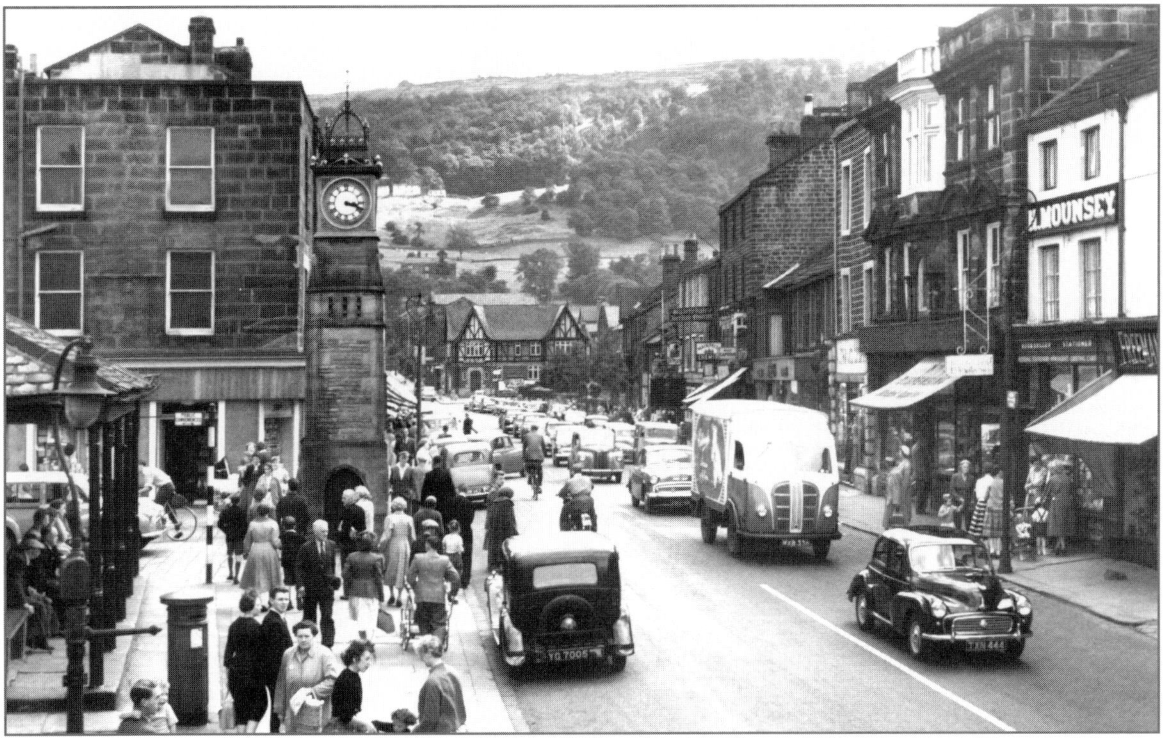

Otley
Kirkgate c1960 049040

Up to the 15th century, Otley was of more importance than either Leeds or Bradford. England's oldest agricultural show began here in 1799. The market town is bisected by the 75-mile River Wharfe. So much of the past remains in Otley, such as the Jubilee Clock erected in 1888, which contains two plaques, one for two soldiers lost in the Transvaal war, the other a gift from Belgian refugees who found sanctuary here in the First World War. The cabinetmaker Thomas Chippendale was baptised in the Parish Church on 5 June 1718. The Tudor-style building at the end was constructed in 1940, and above that on the magnificent Chevin is the White House, a former barn, later used as refreshment rooms for the Victorian perambulators.

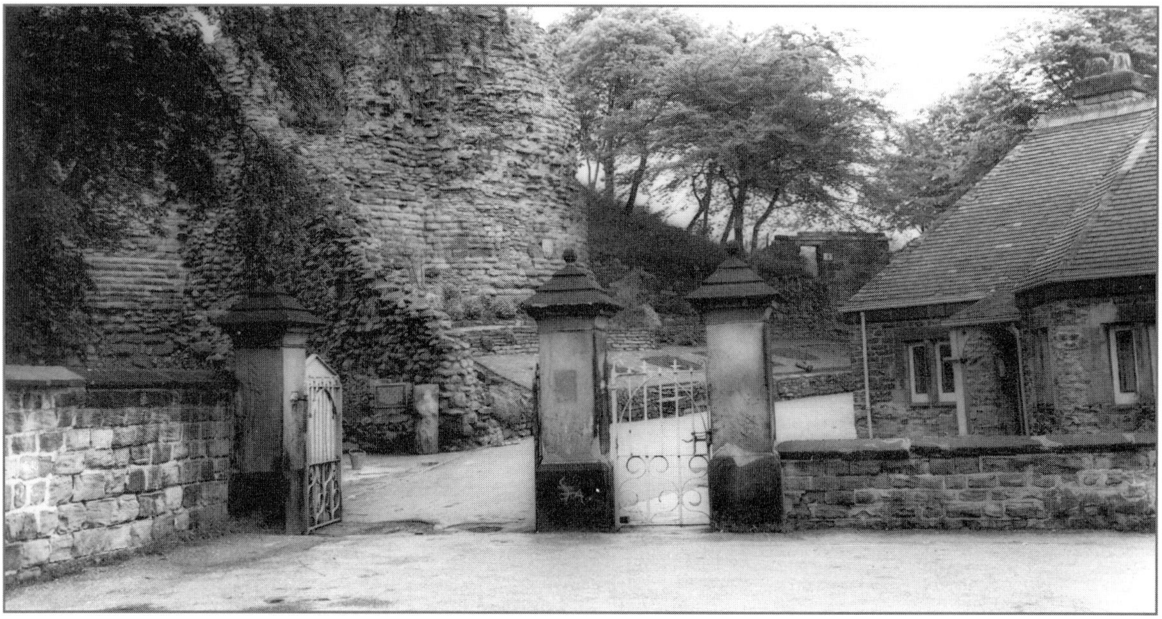

Pontefract, The Castle Entrance 1964 P155030
The 17th-century Civil War put an end to this Norman stronghold of independence. At the end of its third siege supporting King Charles (the sieges were in 1644, 1648 and 1649) the Castle was forced to surrender on 25 May 1649. Parliament ordered its demolition, and within a month the site was in ruins, thus ending a six hundred-year history. The charge for this act was noted as £1779.

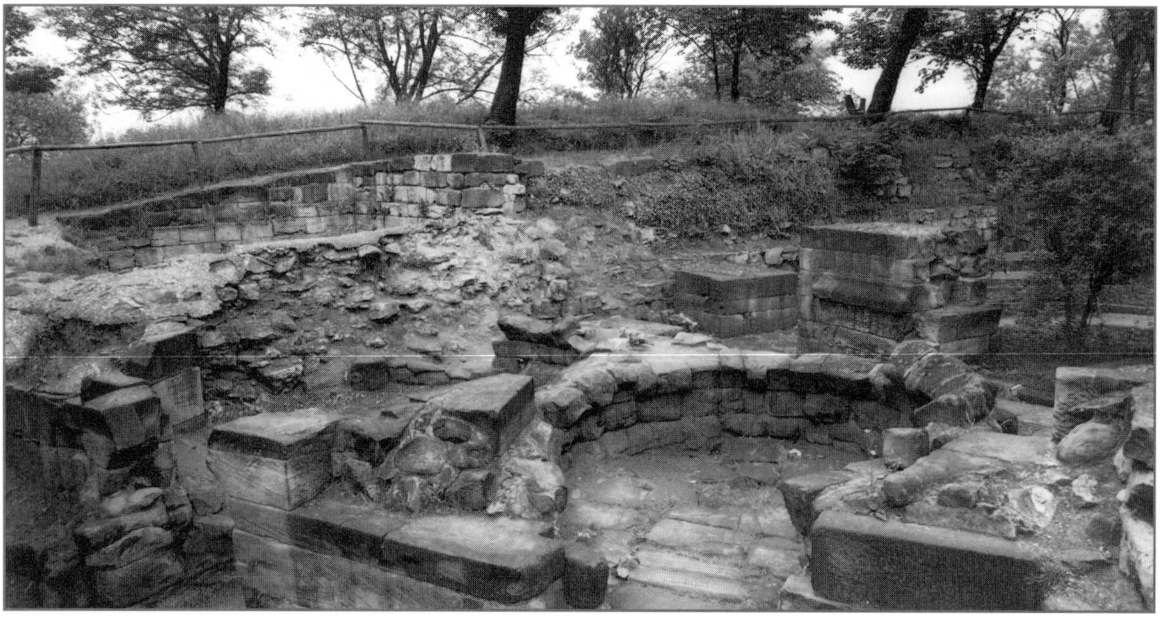

Pontefract, The Castle Kitchens 1964 P155036
After centuries of starvings, beheadings and executions, the site later became a haven of tranquillity in 19th-century Pontefract. The grounds were let in 1863 for the growing of liquorice, and a few years later the council laid out the grounds for a public amenity. Six hundred trees were planted, the ruins were made safe, and on the 400th anniversary of the town's incorporation the grounds opened to a crowd of 5000 on 28 July 1884.

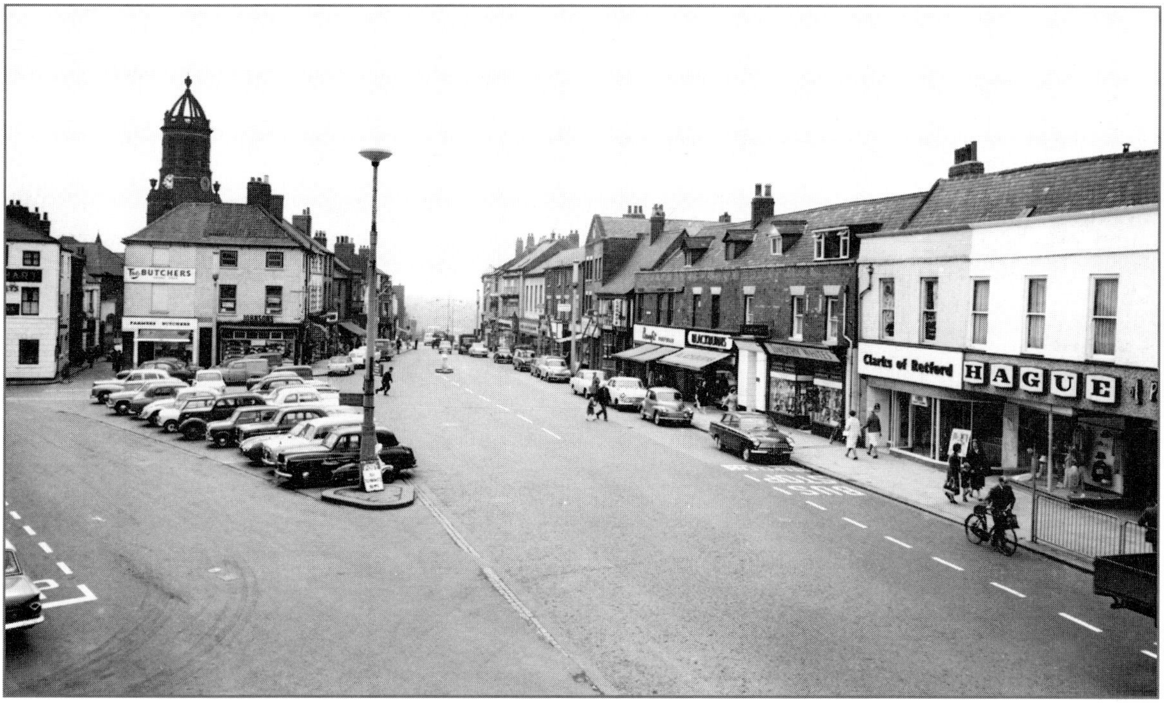

Pontefract
Beastfair c1960 P155023
This was the original site of the huge cattle market. In the 19th century the street was lined by saddlers, but these premises gradually closed when horses gave way to the horsepower of cars. The last tram ran through the town on 1 November 1925. The parish church of St Giles can be seen at top left.

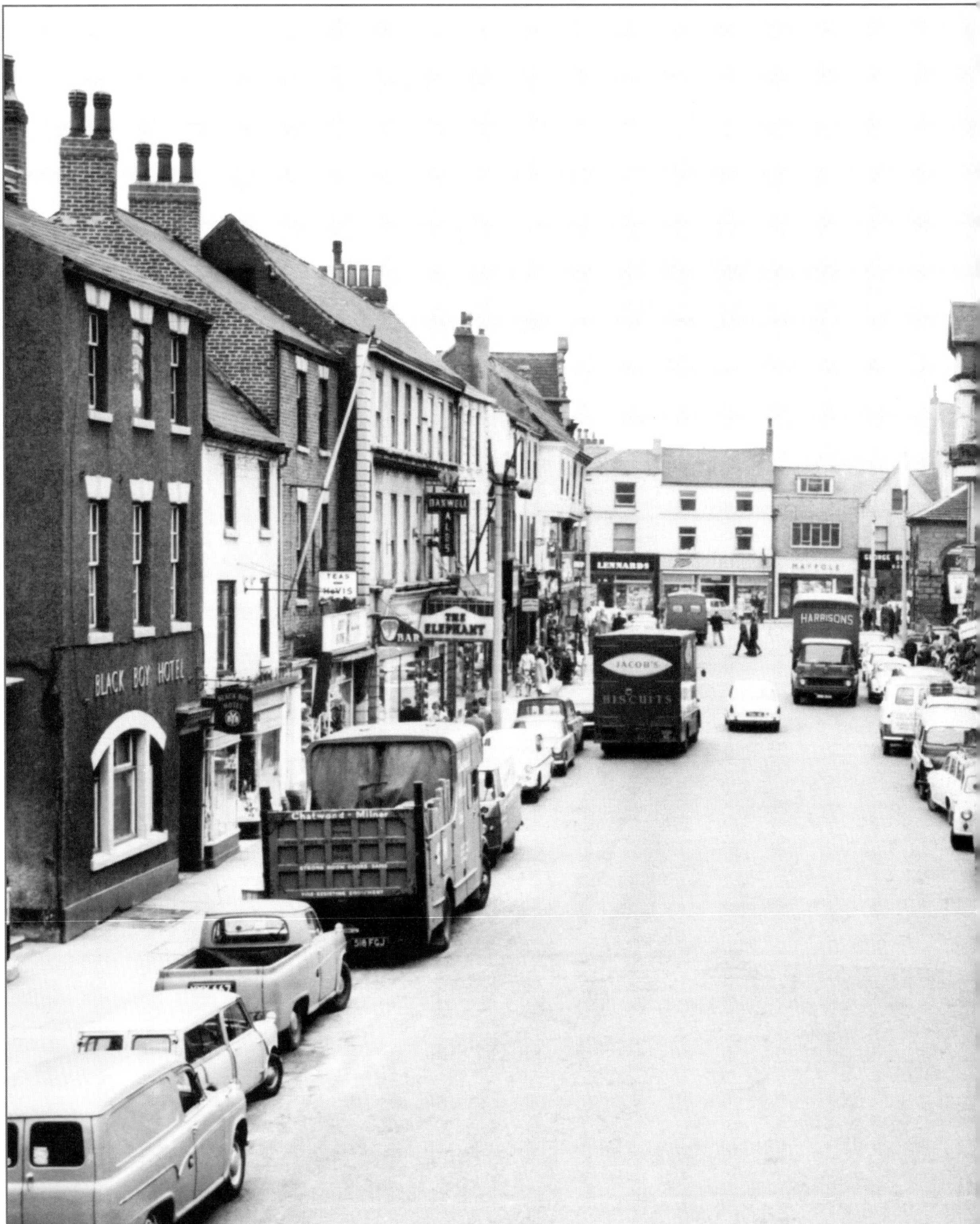
BLACK BOY HOTEL
THE ELEPHANT
LENNARDS
MAYPOLE
JACOB'S
BISCUITS
HARRISONS

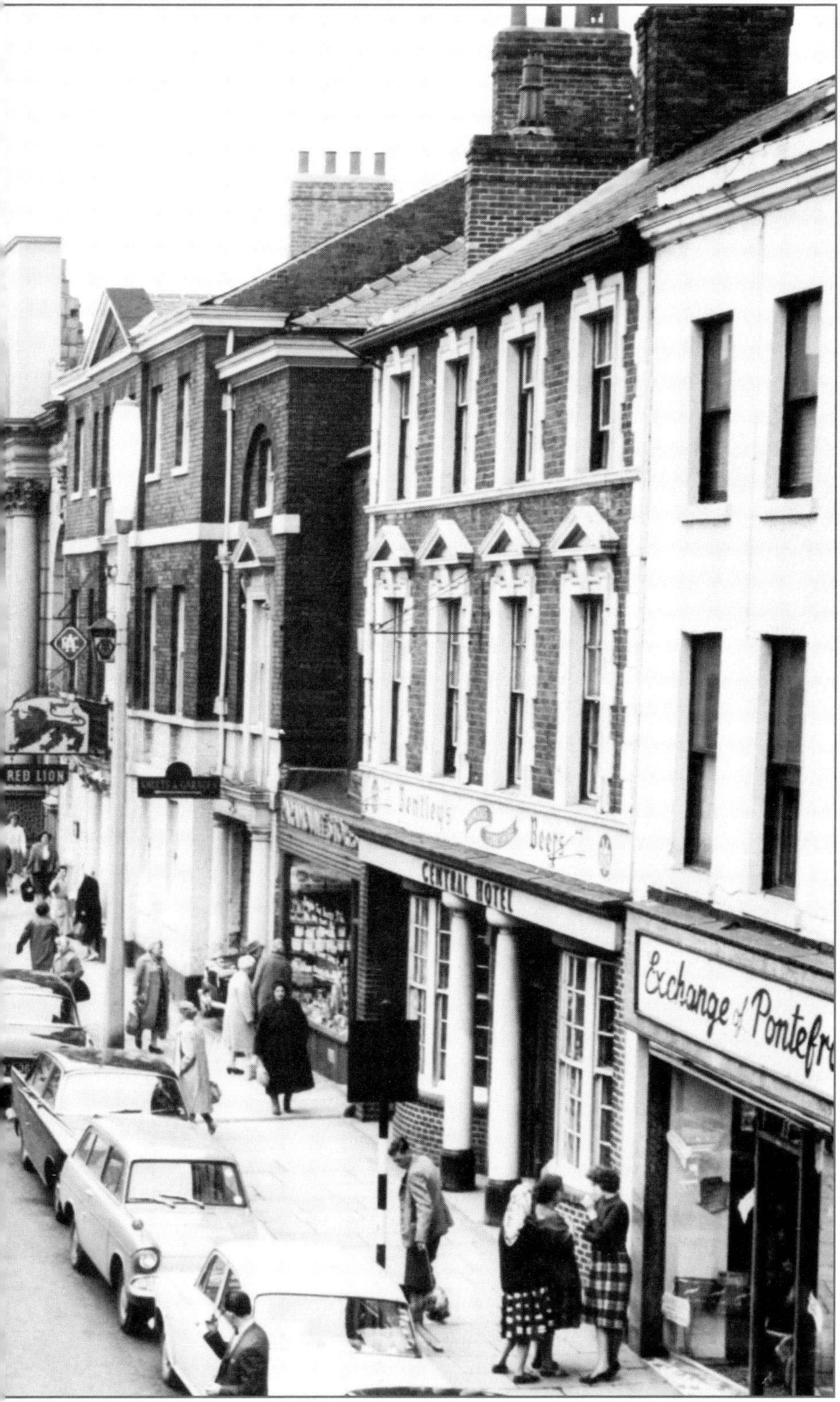

Pontefract
The Market Place
1964 P155029
Cars begin to clog the roads, even in the sixties. Pontefract was a major coaching town, and many inns were established for this trade. On the right are the pillars to the Market Hall (1859), and the Buttercross can be seen on the right at the end of Market Place.

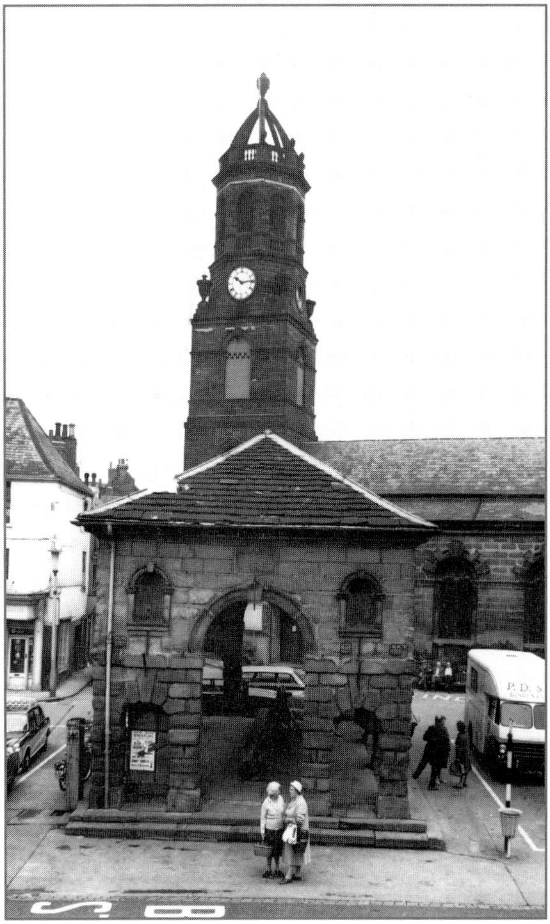

◄ **Pontefract, St Giles's Church c1960** P155024
The church was badly damaged during the last siege of the castle after being used as a lookout for the opposing side. In the foreground is the Buttercross, built on the site of the former St Oswald's Cross. The Buttercross was erected in 1734 by the wife of Solomon Dupier, a former garrison commander in Gibraltar, who later lived in the town.

▼ **Ripponden, Oldham Road 1966** R242019
Cotton spinning brought rich rewards to the town. The new mills, ten of which were established as early as 1758, used water power from the fast running River Ryburn. The valley later became renowned for its dyeing of dark blue cloth, which was used by the whole of the Royal Navy. Because of its industrial heritage, Ripponden village has been given conservation status.

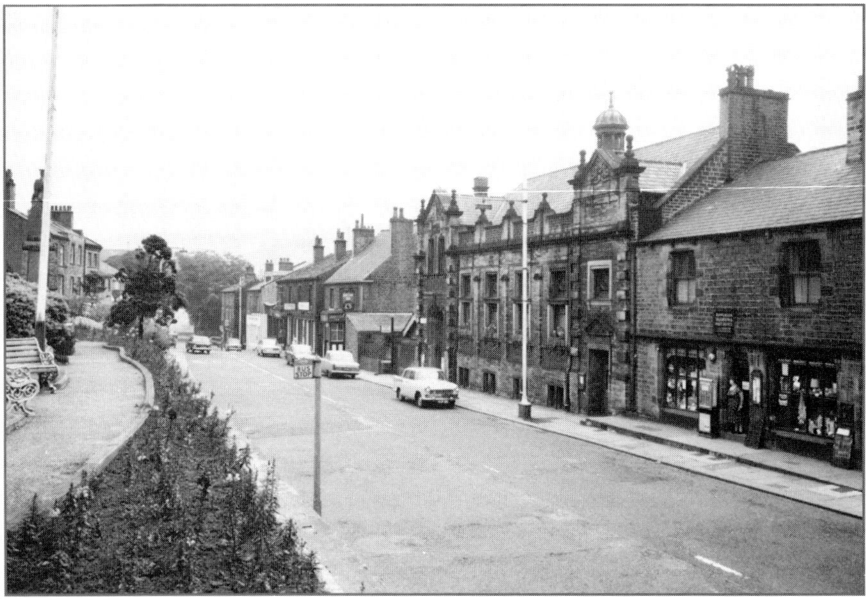

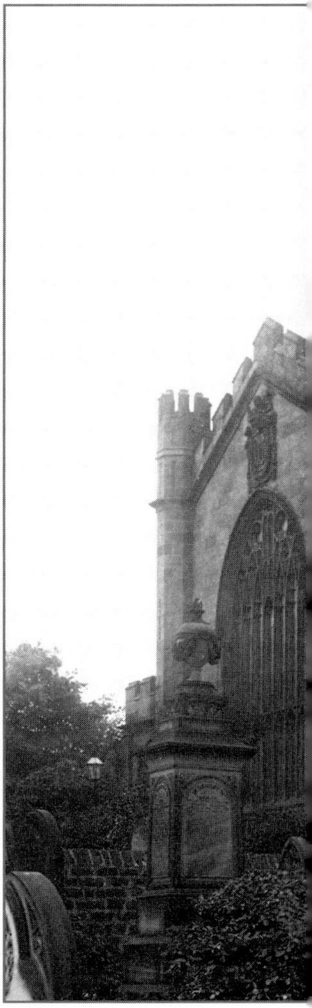

▲ **Shipley, The Parish Church of St Paul 1893** 33195
This church was a gift to the nation under the Million Act of 1818 (see Huddersfield).The church seats 1488, and cost £7687. Inside the tower can be found six bells. A replica of this church at nearby Wilsden was also consecrated on the same day, 1 November 1826.

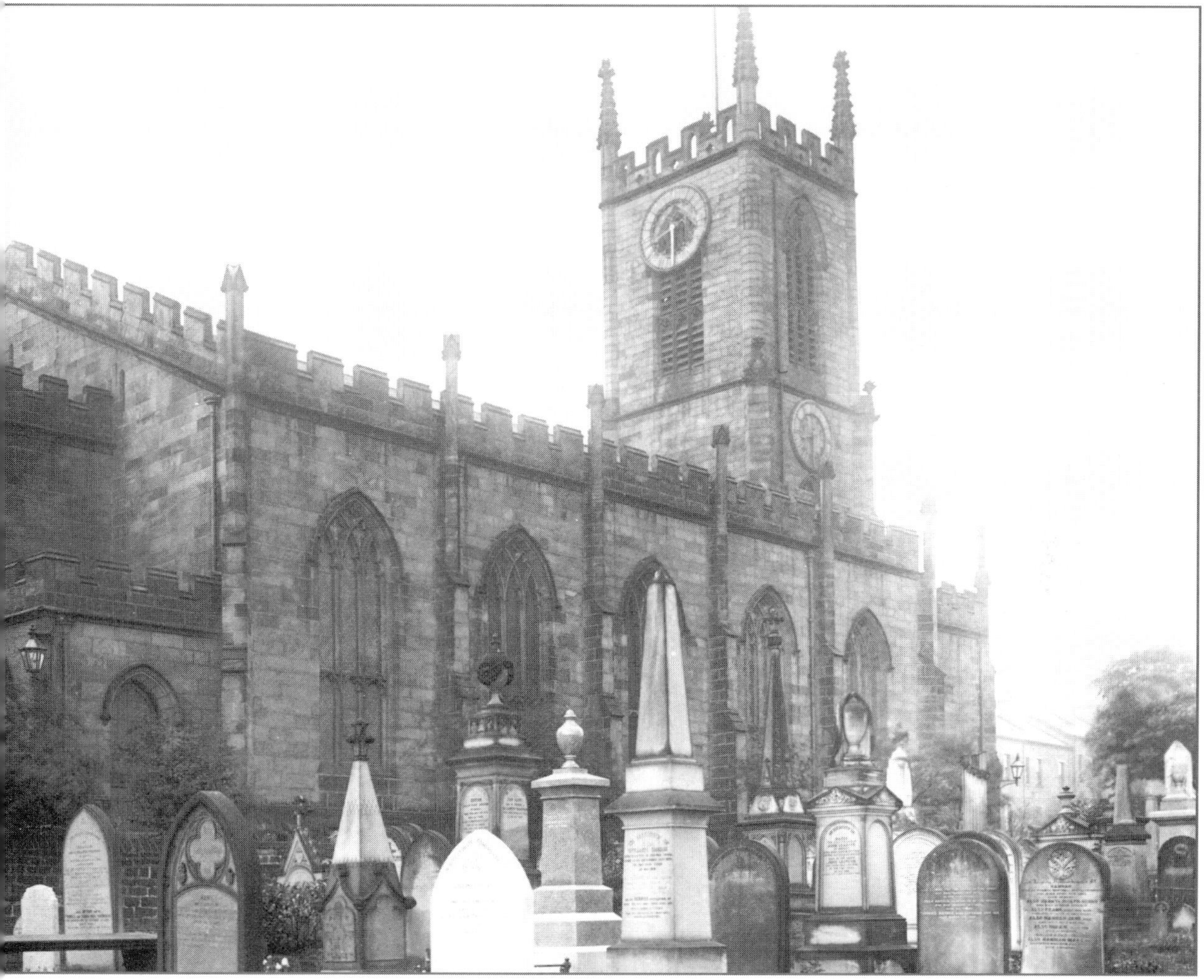

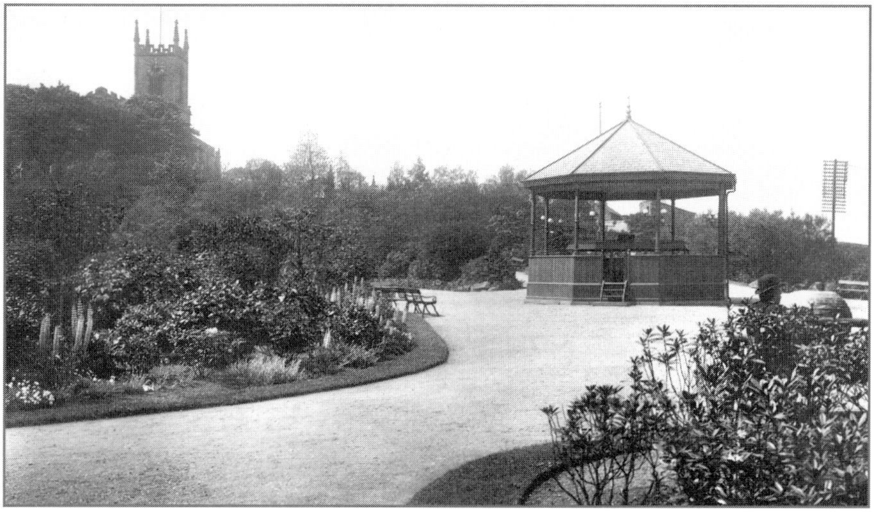

Shipley, Crowghyll Park 1903 49702

Crowghyll Park was opened to the residents on 31 May 1890 following a civic ceremony led by Mrs Titus Salt. The land was formerly a quarry, and was given to the town by church administrators in lieu of common rights. The charming bandstand was illuminated by gas light at this time. Following the demolition of Shipley Old Hall in Kirkgate, parts of the building - a wall, water chutes and a roof truss - were re-erected in this park.

▼ **Shipley, The Glen 1921** 71640

This stream, the Lode Pit Beck, flows off the moor into the Aire at Shipley. A former drovers' track took trade over the hills to Ilkley and Otley. At the top of the glen a pioneer amusement park was established from 1887 when the switchback railway from the Saltaire Exhibition was moved up the hill. This was joined by an 'aerial flight' in 1889 and a toboggan run in 1897. The whole area became a paradise for thousands of West Yorkshire mill workers. The cable tramway of 1895 still operates.

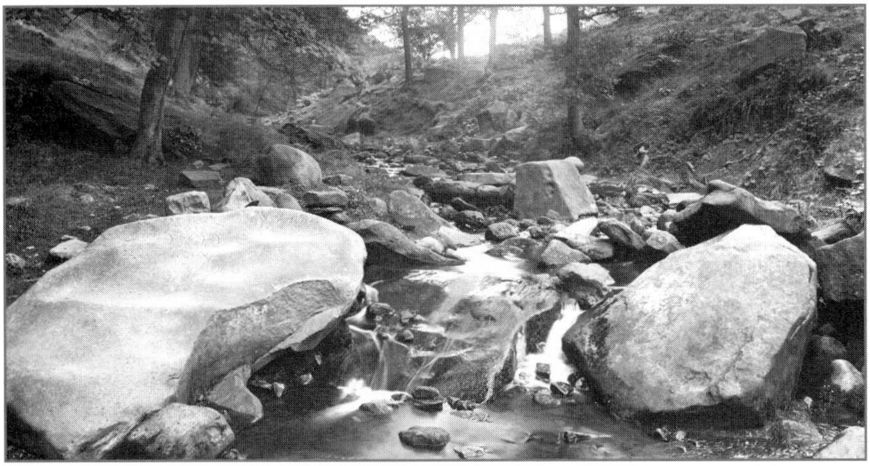

▼ **Wakefield, The Cathedral c1960** W464008

The foundation stone is dated 5 September 1789; this building replaced earlier churches on the site. St Mark's Chapel, on the right, was added in 1904, sixteen years after the Parish Church was elevated to a Cathedral. The first Bishop in 1888 was William Walshaw How, a famous composer of hymns; his best-known hymn is 'For all the saints who from their labours rest'.

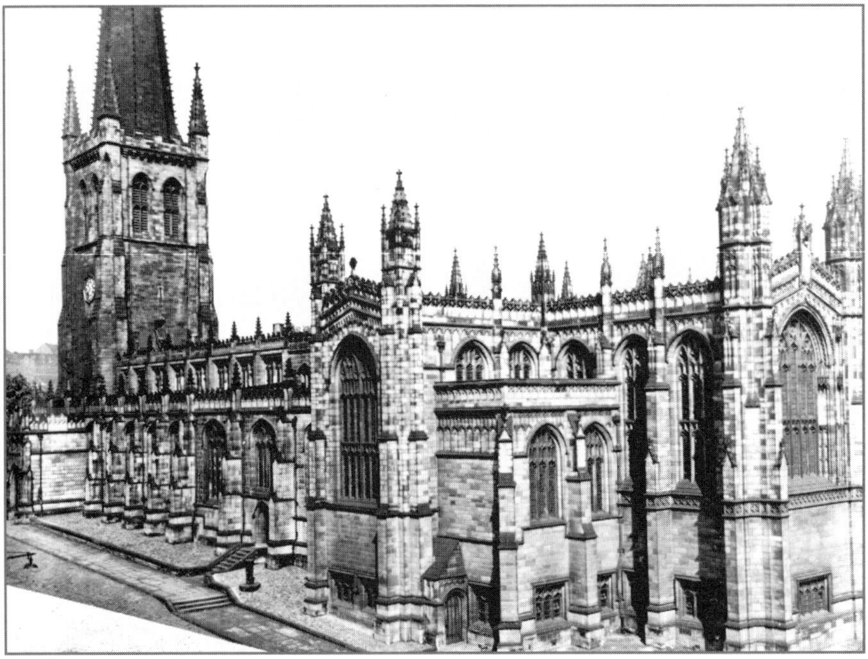

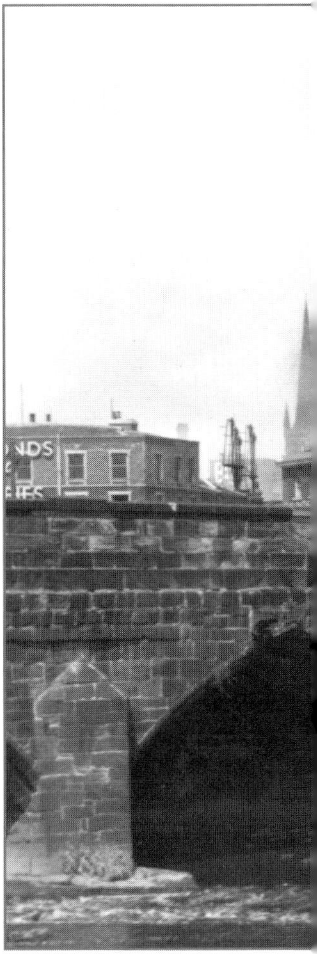

▲ **Wakefield The Chantry c1955** W464002

This 14th-century chapel was built on the bridge as a memorial to Richard, Duke of York, who was killed at Wakefield. It was hoped that travellers crossing into the town would benefit from simple prayer. The building was renovated in 1848, but within forty years smoke and pollution had again damaged the pinnacles. The old chapel front was purchased during renovation and can still be found sited by the lake at Kettlethorpe Hall.

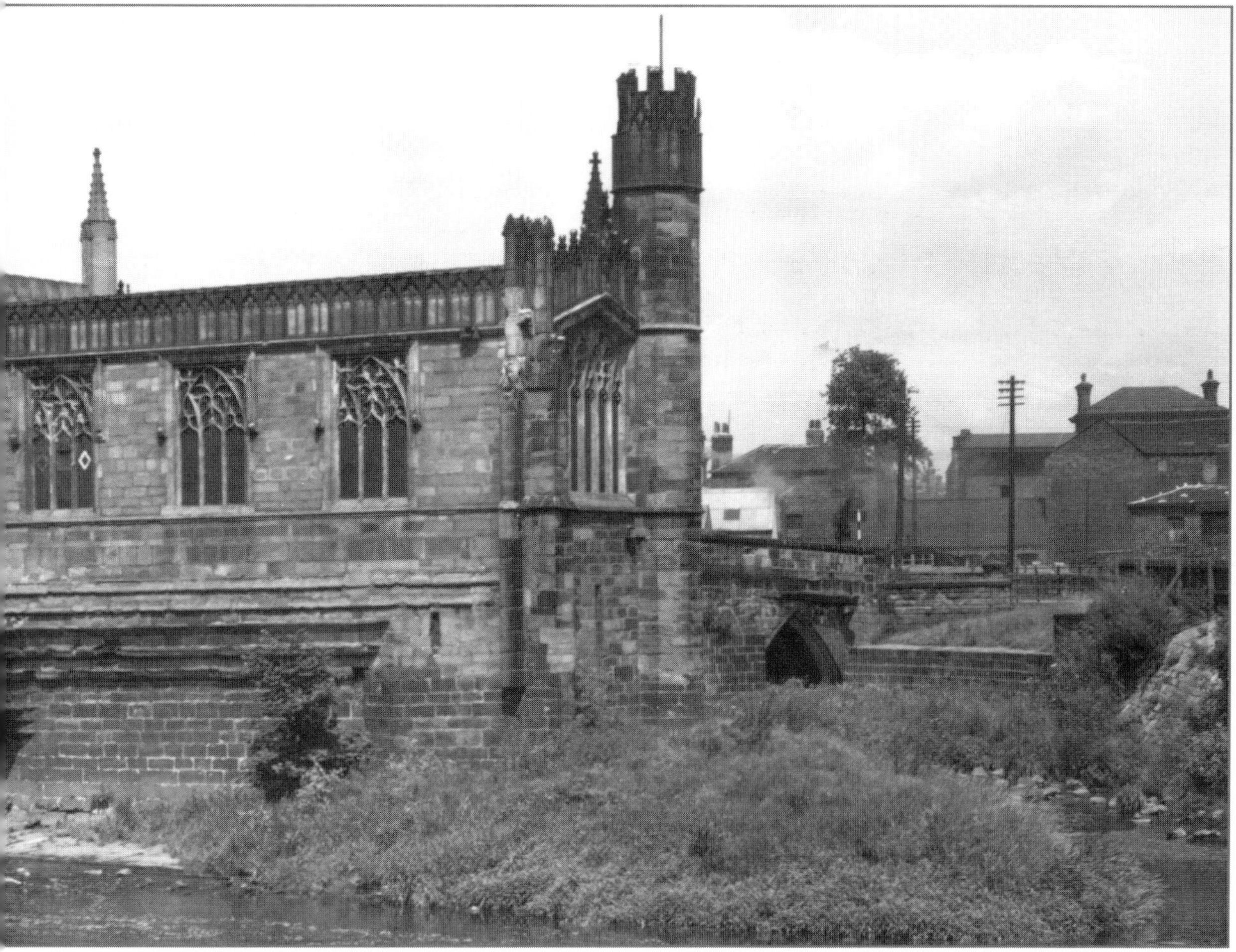

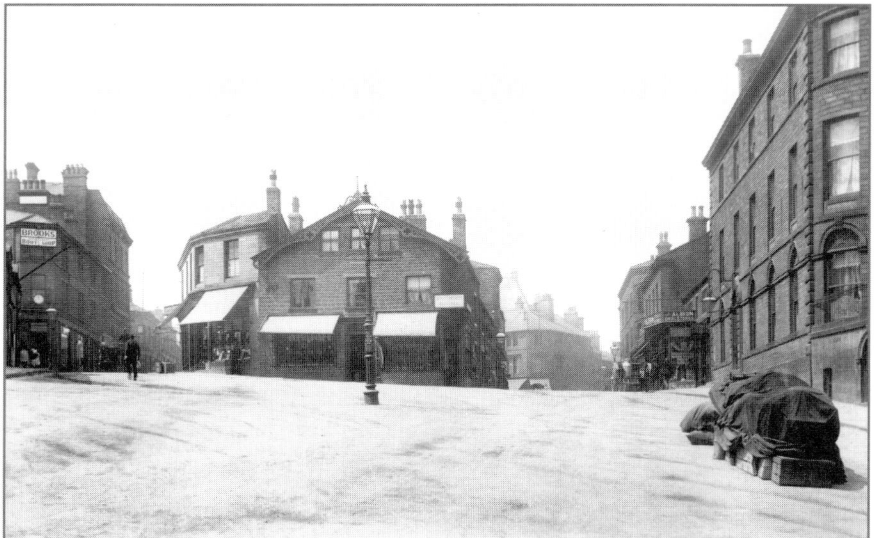

Shipley, Market Place 1903 49697

A weekly Friday market was held on this site for well over a century.

A feast and fairground also took place between here and the canal side. Work on a new Market complex began in 1956, and one feature of this is a clock tower where the hours are chimed by a mechanical man.

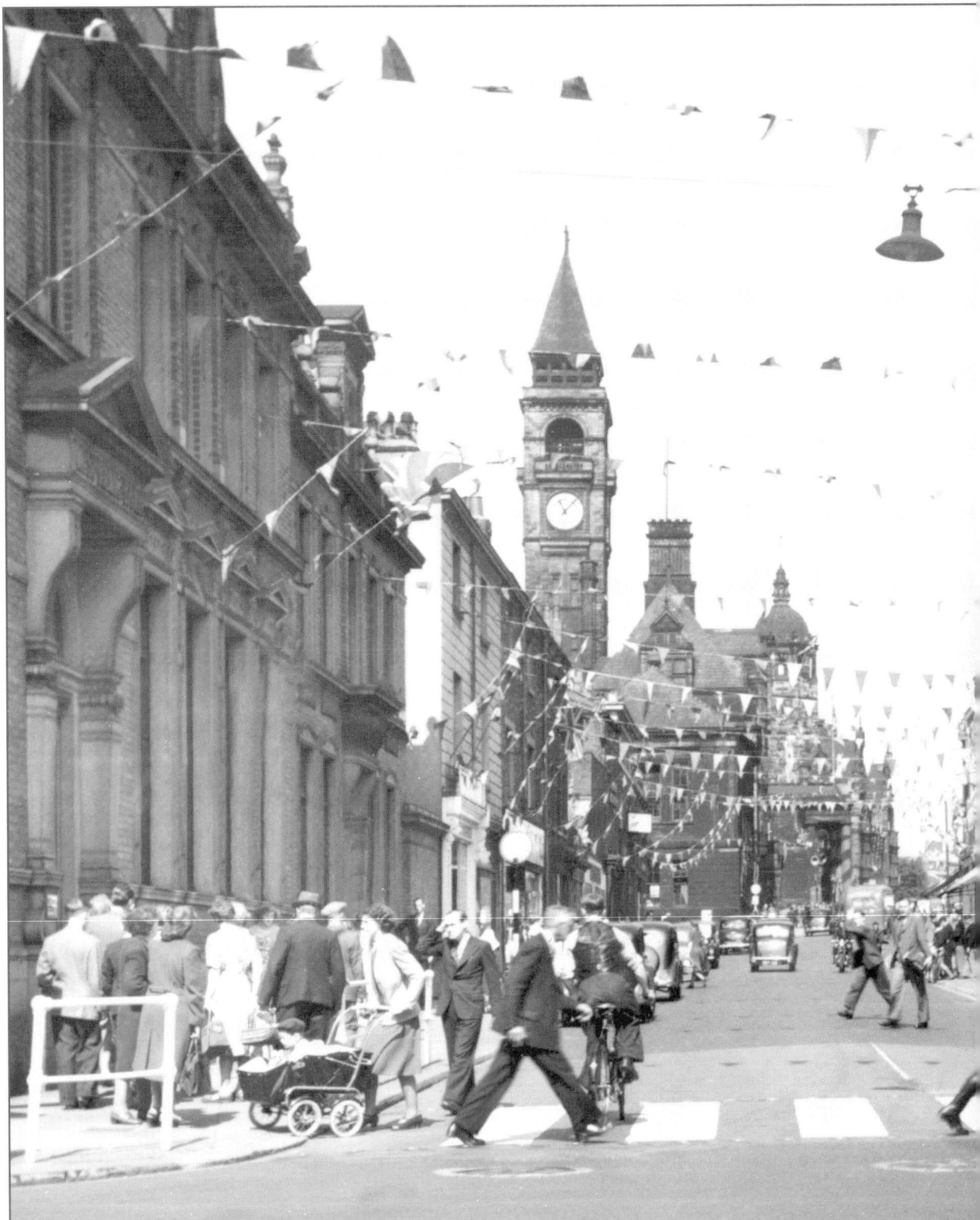

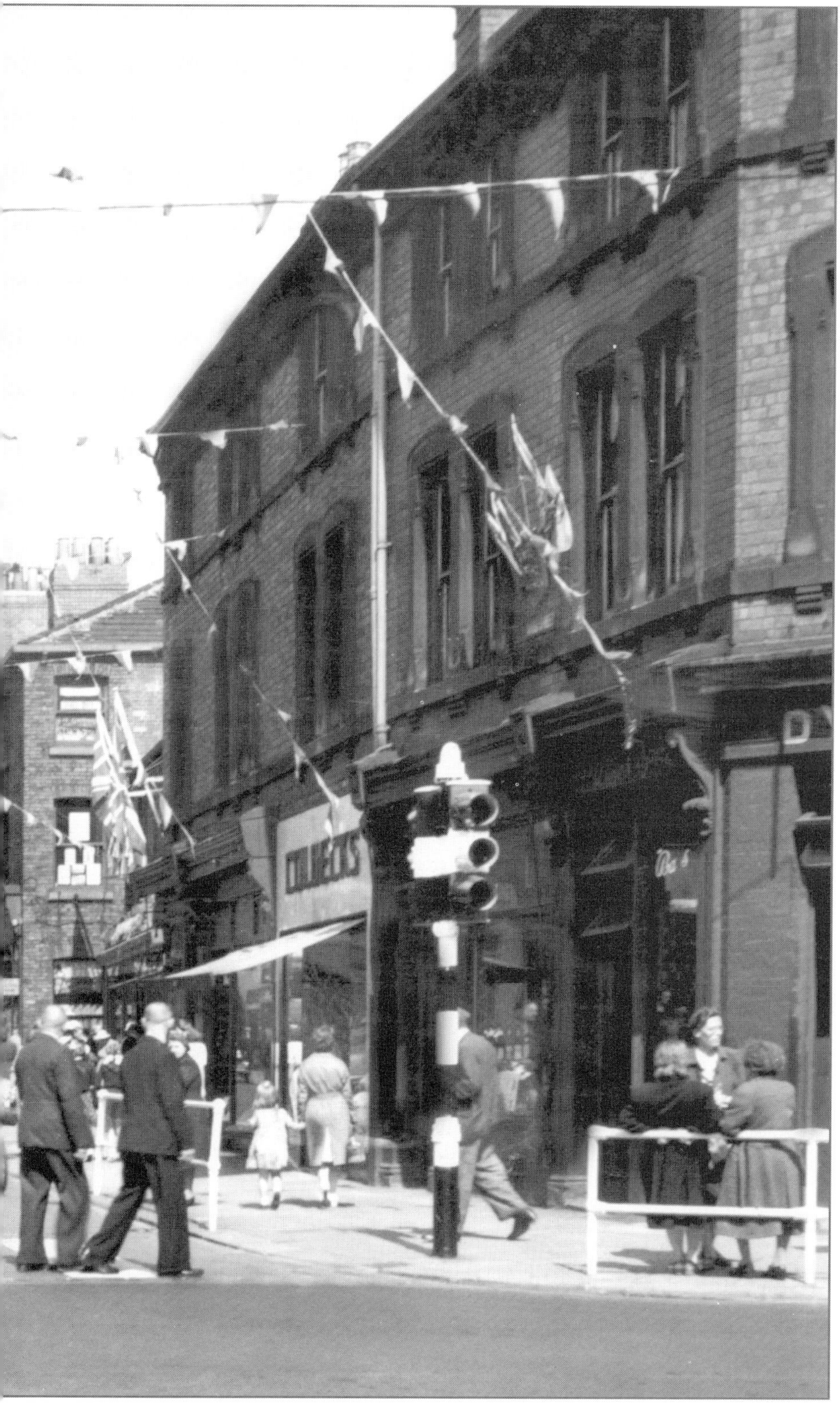

Wakefield
Wood Street c1950
W464005

This is the administrative centre of the city, with the late 19th-century County Hall, the Court House and the Town Hall. The Mechanics' Institute, later a dance hall, is now the charming Wakefield Museum, custodian of the Charles Waterton natural history collection. Also in Wood Street in the 1920s was Hyland's Car and Boat showrooms.

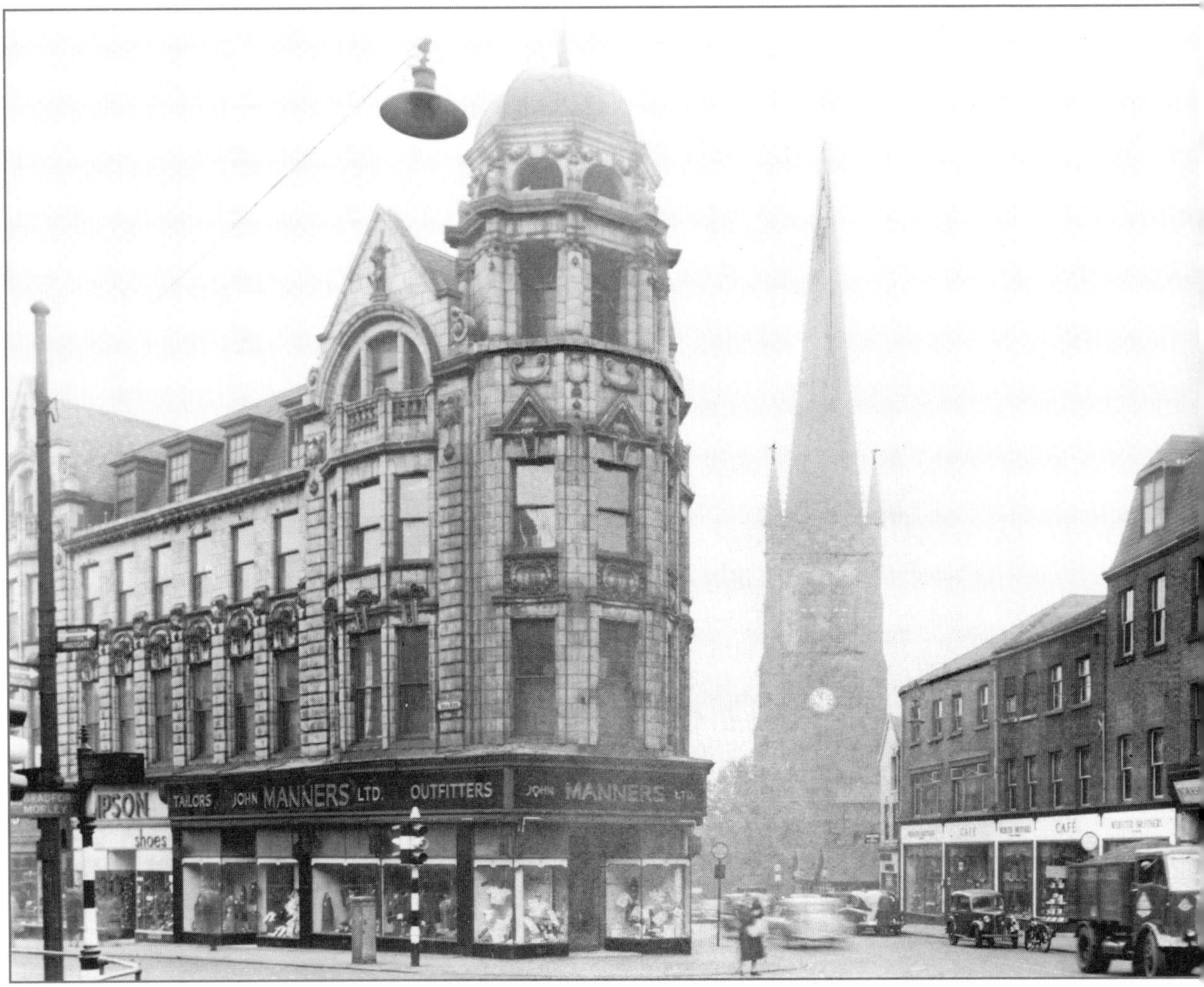

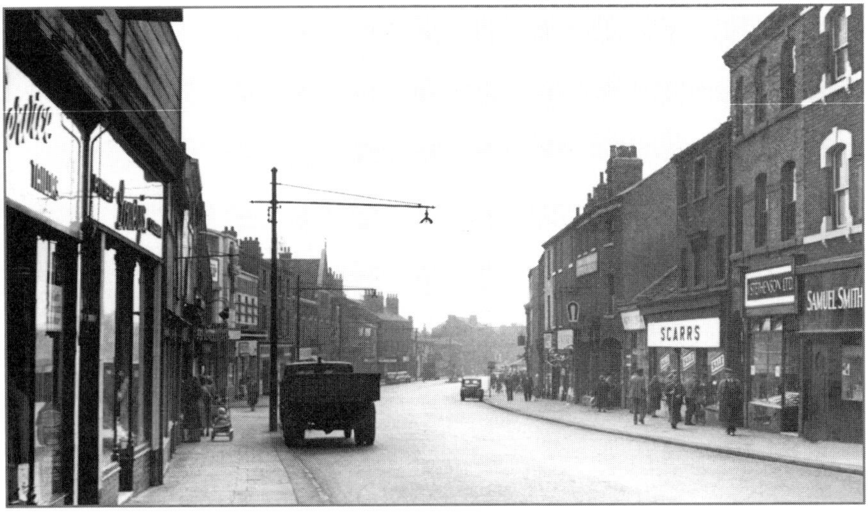

◄ **Wakefield, Kirkgate c1955** W464013
Many of Wakefield's 118 pubs and hotels were along this central road through the city. At the lower end is the Kirkgate railway station, which replaced an earlier station built in 1840. Along the line is the ninety-nine-arch bridge containing 800 million bricks.

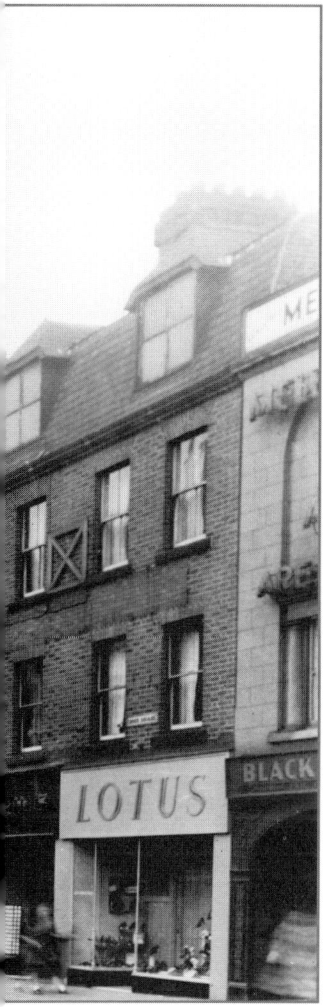

Wakefield Cross Square c1955 W464019

We are looking down Cross Square to the magnificent Cathedral. On the left is the Grand Clothing Hall, a well-loved outfitters, built in 1906. A market cross was here in 1707, but it was demolished 160 years later. Opposite the Cathedral's west door was a jeweller's shop displaying the City Time Ball. The ball slid down a metal rod at exactly 10am and 1pm; it was activated by a direct line from the Greenwich Observatory. Sad to say, it was taken down in 1938 - time never stands still in Wakefield.

Wakefield, The Market Place c1965 W464056

Built in 1963, this modern market replaced a century-old shopping hall. Many German families traded here from the 1880s, including firms such as Haganbach's the bakers and numerous pork butchers like Ziegler's, Oesterlein's and Weegman's.

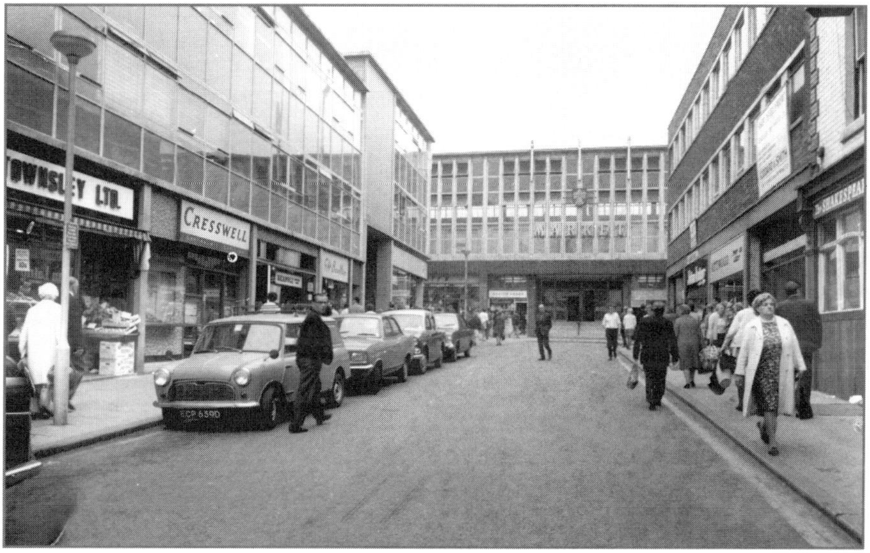

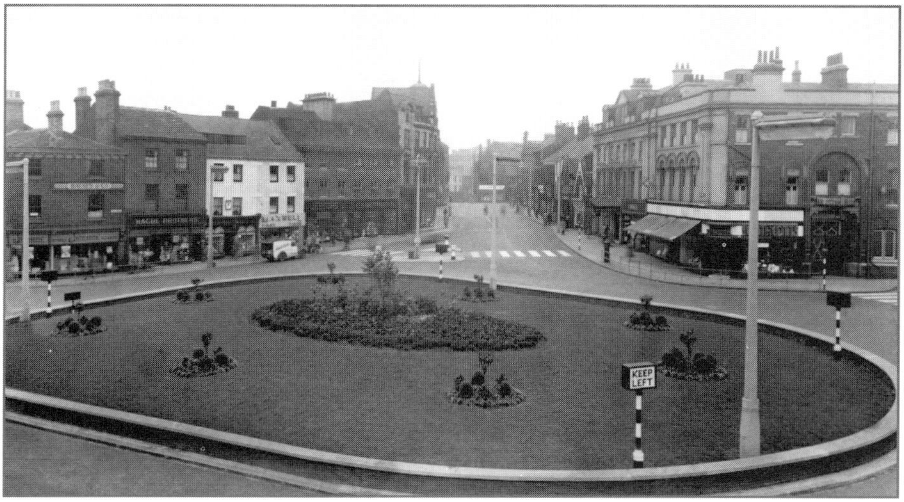

Wakefield, The Bull Ring c1955 W464017

In the first half of the century this roundabout was filled with hansom cabs, and later from 1904 by the rattle of trams. The statue of Queen Victoria had been in the centre and was unveiled in 1905; she was later removed, but she was not amused to be banished and returned to take her rightful place here in 1986.

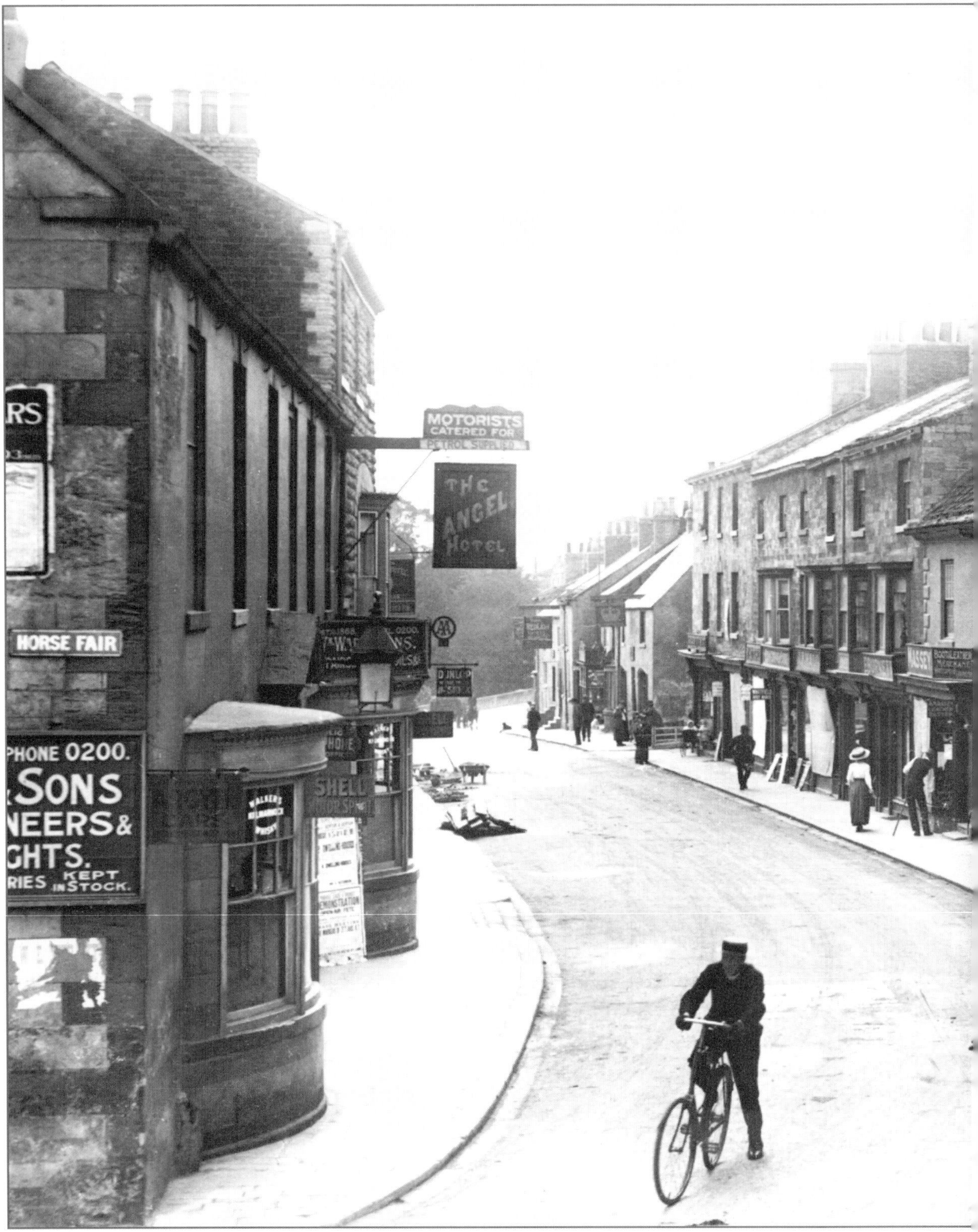
MOTORISTS
CATERED FOR
THE ANGEL HOTEL
HORSE FAIR
PHONE 0200.
SONS
NEERS&
GHTS.
RIES
KEPT IN STOCK.

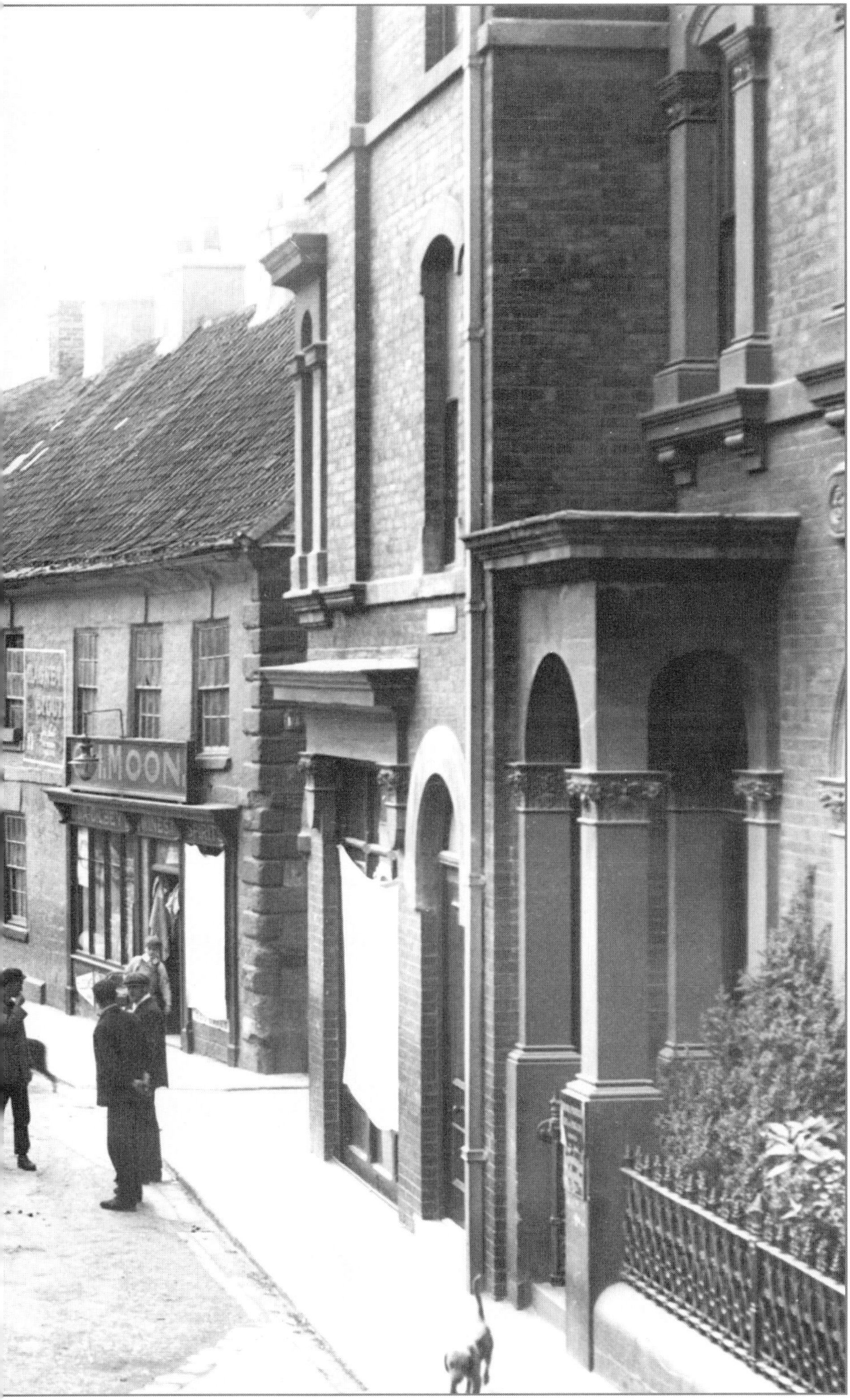

Wetherby, High Street 1909 61730
The Angel Inn on the left has recently been refurbished after many years of closure. Next to Moon's shop is the now-demolished White Hart Inn, formerly the Blue Boar. By 1909 the Cattle Market would have spilled out into the High Street. The Parish Council ingeniously annually auctioned the right to collect the manure. The sign on the left, Horsefair, still leads to the weekly cattle market.

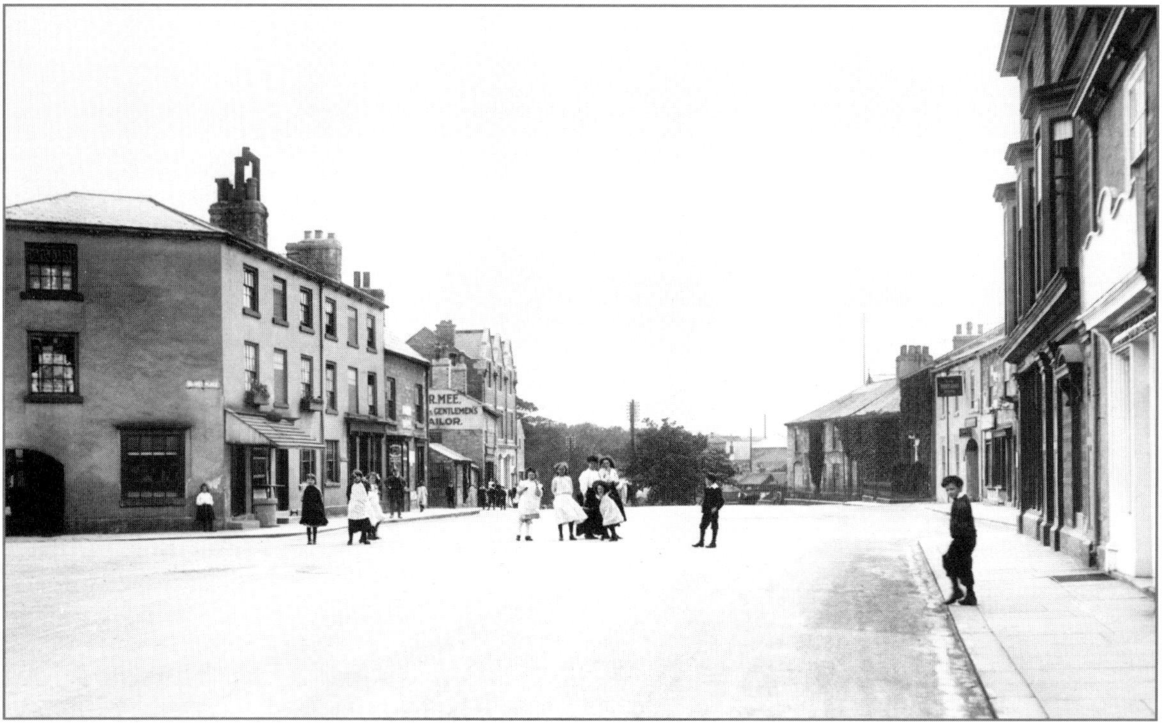

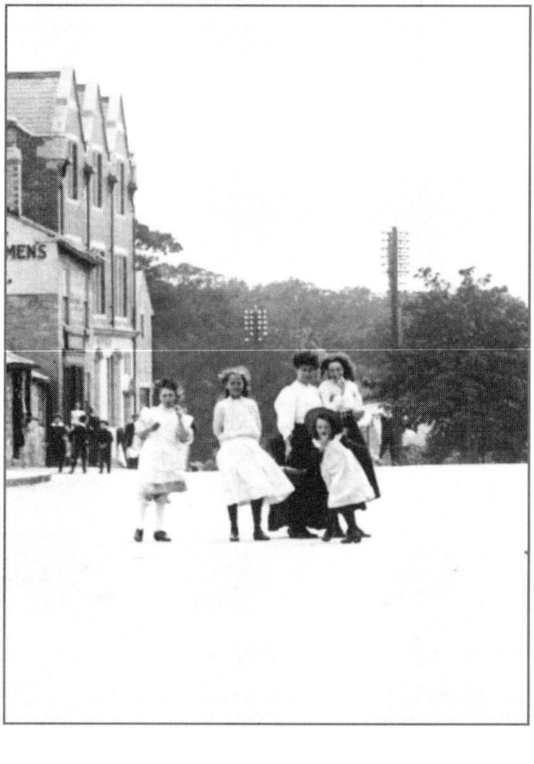

Wetherby
Market Place 1909 61729

This scene is a contrast with the one seven years earlier, when the town packed into the Market Place to commemorate the coronation of Edward VII. The tall telegraph pole in the background now bears the town's Coat of Arms. The building on the left is now a bank, while a few doors down was the old lodging house for down-and-outs. Finally, on the left is the old Post Office.

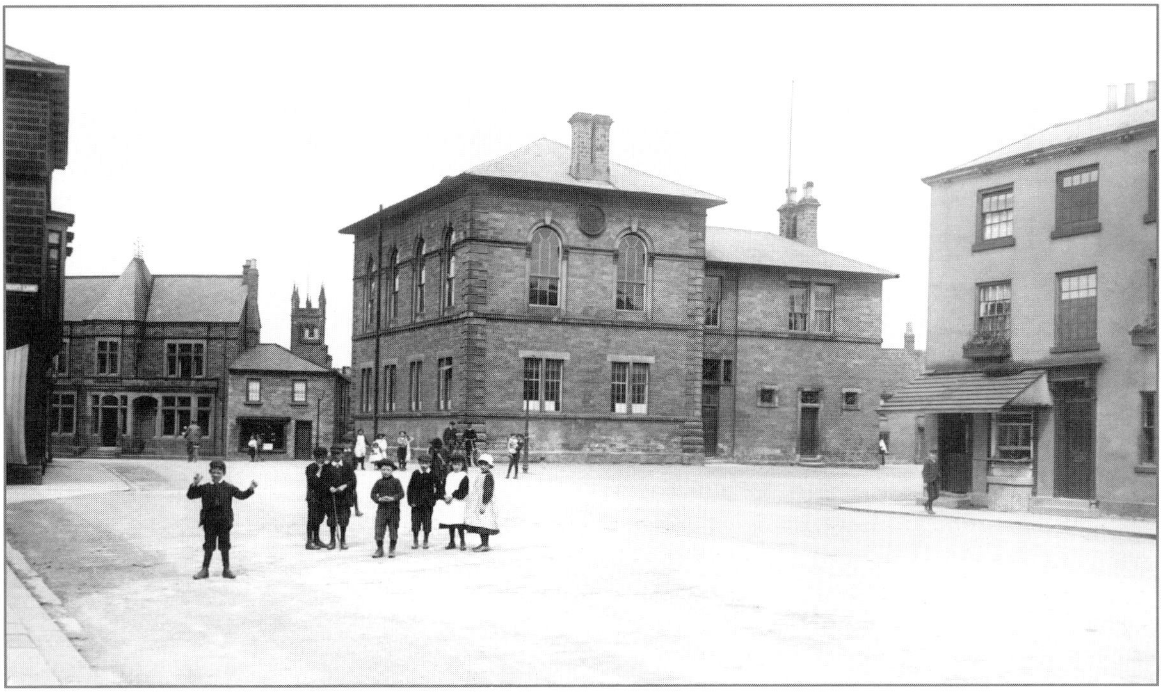

Wetherby
Market Place 1909 61728

The Town Hall was built on the site of the old chapel-of-ease. Its foundation stone was laid on 11th June 1845 and the cost of the building was £1,300. Little here has changed today, except that the Town Hall chimneys have been shortened. In between those on the right-hand side was a bell to summon the Fire Brigade. The magistrates court was held in the Town Hall from its opening in 1845 up to 1982. Prisoners were led to the upper court room through a discreet side door. A day school was held in the lower rooms. The playground was the street, with the girls allowed on the south side, the boys on the north side near the Black Bull. The building just behind the animated young boy was the Conservative Club, built on the site of the Devonshire Arms, named after the Duke who owned the town until the great sale of 1824.

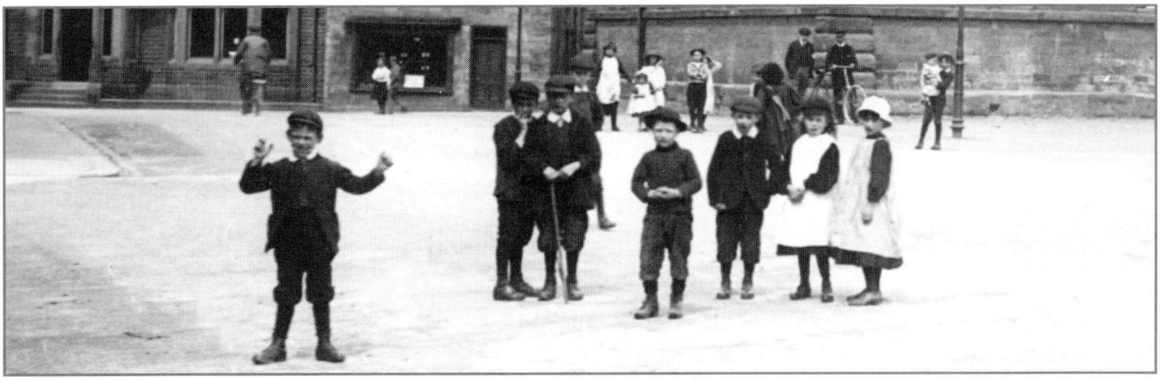

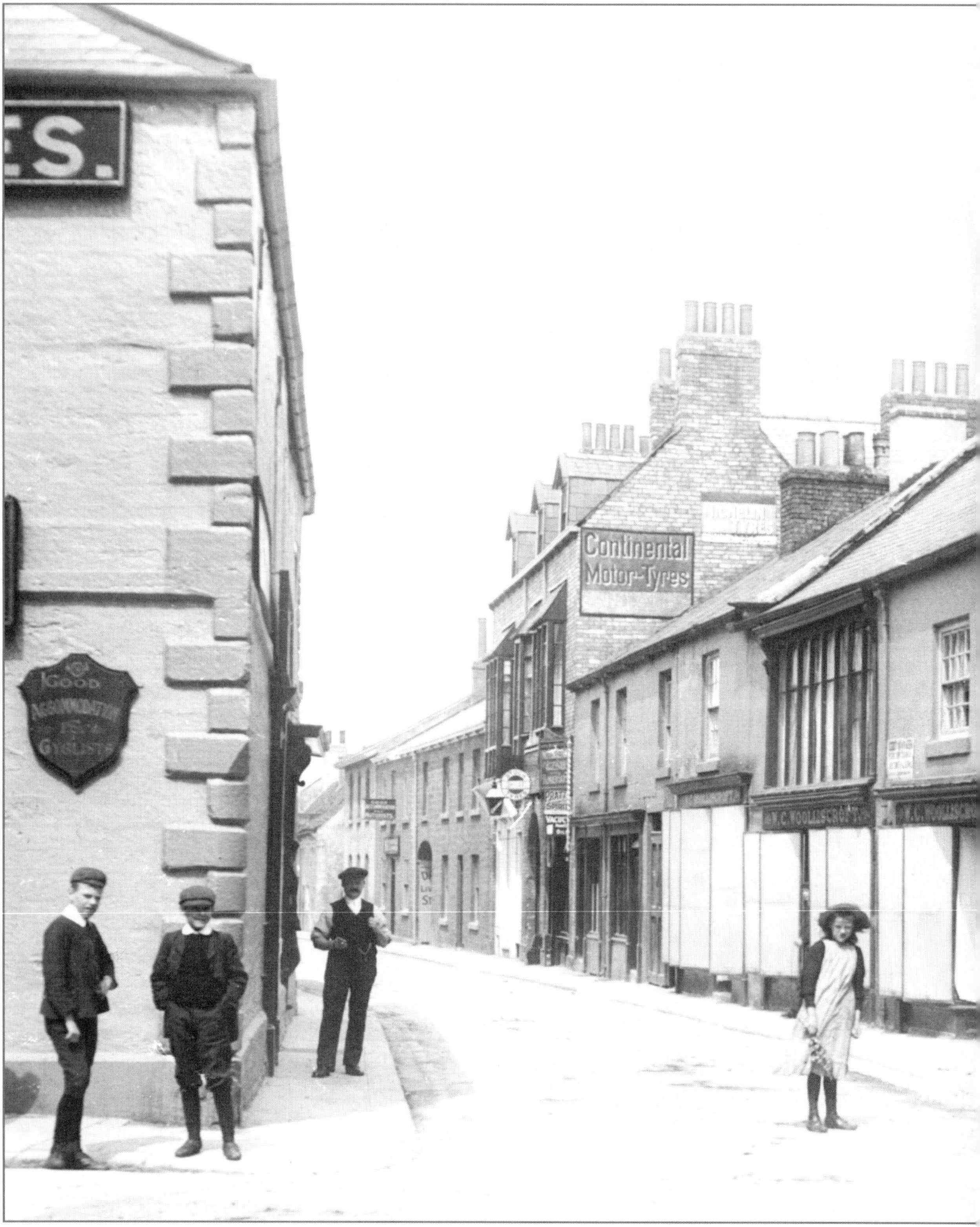
ES.
Continental
Motor-Tyres

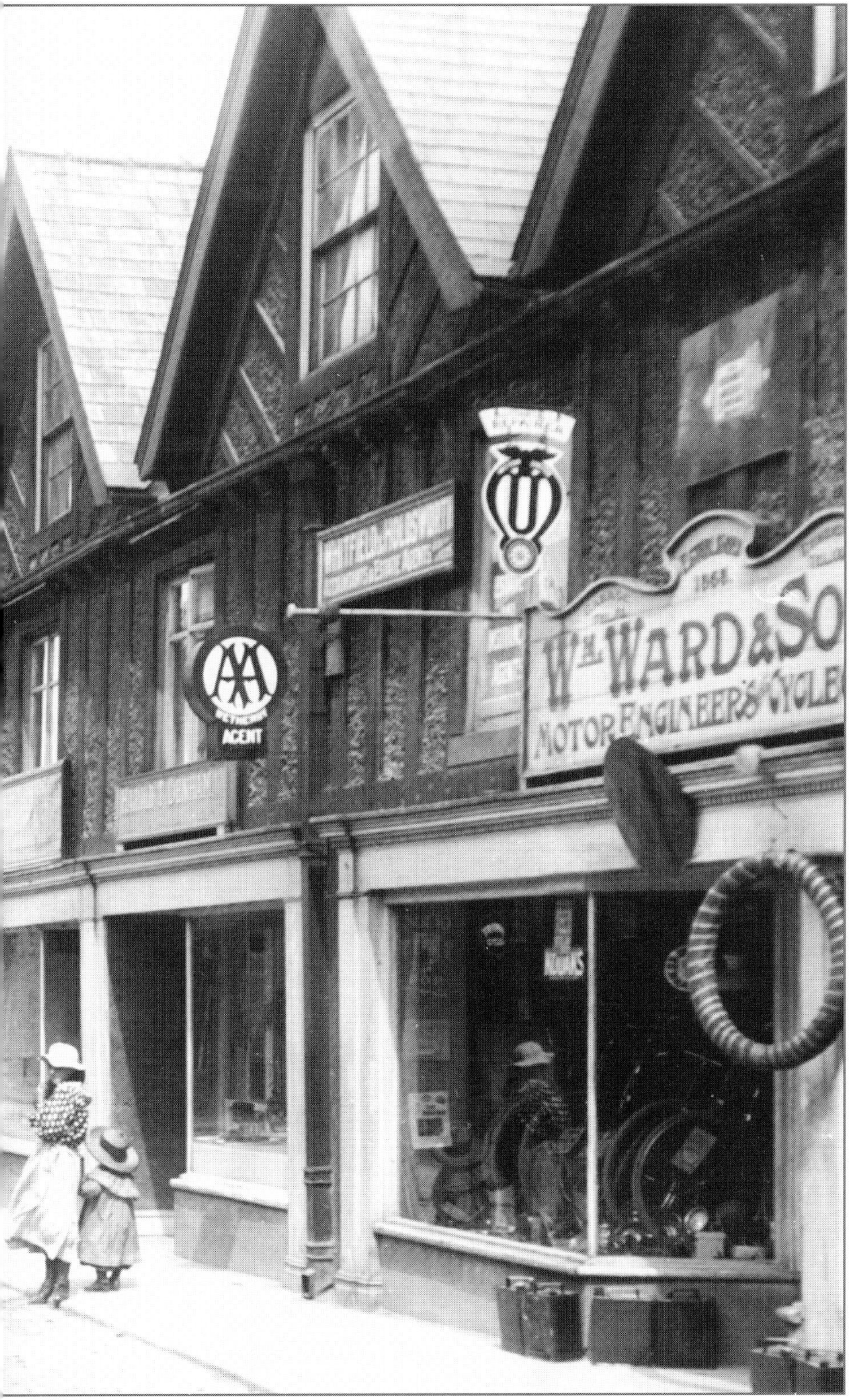

Wetherby, North Street 1909 61731
The complete sign on the left, Tetley's Fine Ales, was fixed to the old Bowling Green Hotel; it marked the narrowest point on the London to Edinburgh Great North Road. The hotel, together with Brigg's shop, was demolished in 1929 for road widening. The Gardens of Rest now occupy the site. Wm. Ward and Sons, established 1868, the first garage in the town, was set up by William for his two sons, Cliff and Philip; William was the landlord of the Angel Inn at the time. From 1924, Cliff Ward ran the North End Garage on York Road, complete with a Shell petrol pump.

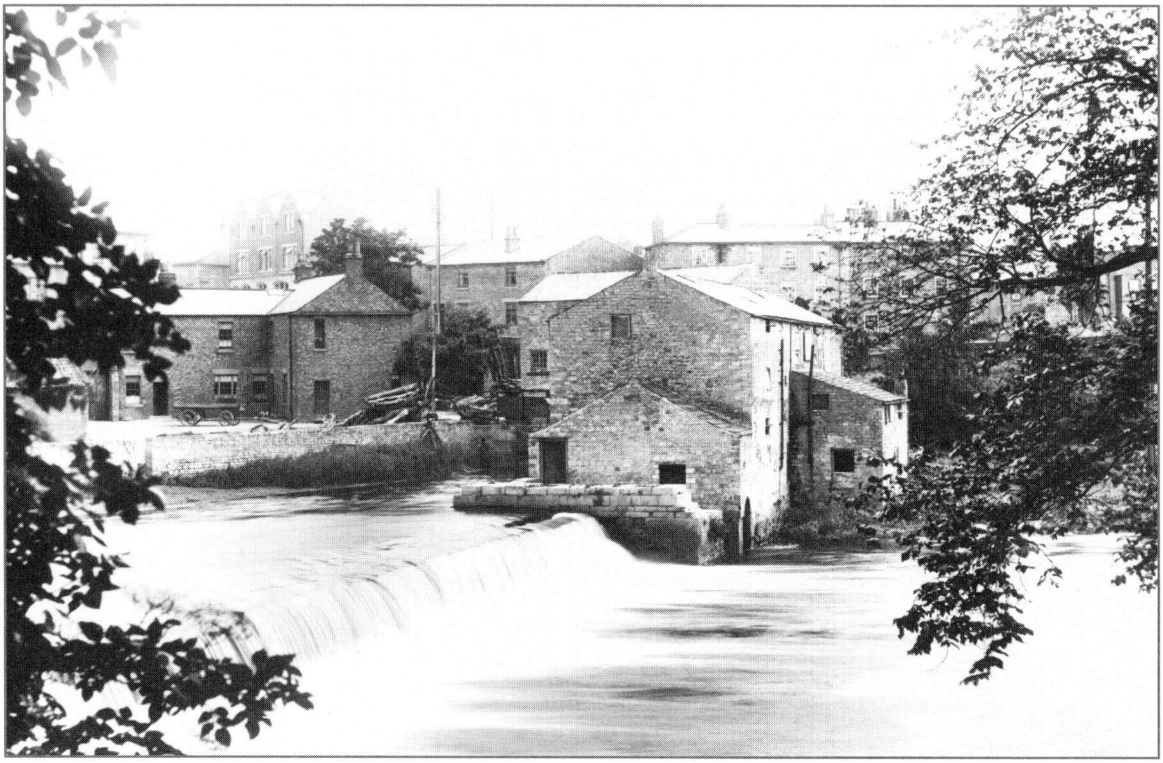

Wetherby
A Weir on the Wharfe 1909 61737

Behind the disused mill was the Wharfedale Brewery, which supplied many of the town's fifteen taverns. The brewery closed during the First World War, and was then used as billets for troops. Its many buildings were gradually taken over by other businesses: during the General Strike of 1926 the wood mill supplied 500 police batons; later it became Oxley's Mineral Water factory, and in 1943 even produced Coca Cola for American troops stationed nearby; during the war German prisoners were quartered here, and another part was let off for dancing, which was popular for many decades. The old brewery chimney smoked for the last time at 3pm on 29th October 1937, and was then taken down brick by brick by two skilled chimney jacks. The archway to the factory bore the cross of the Knights Templar, who obtained the town's market charter in 1240. On the skyline is the newly-opened (1909) Post Office.

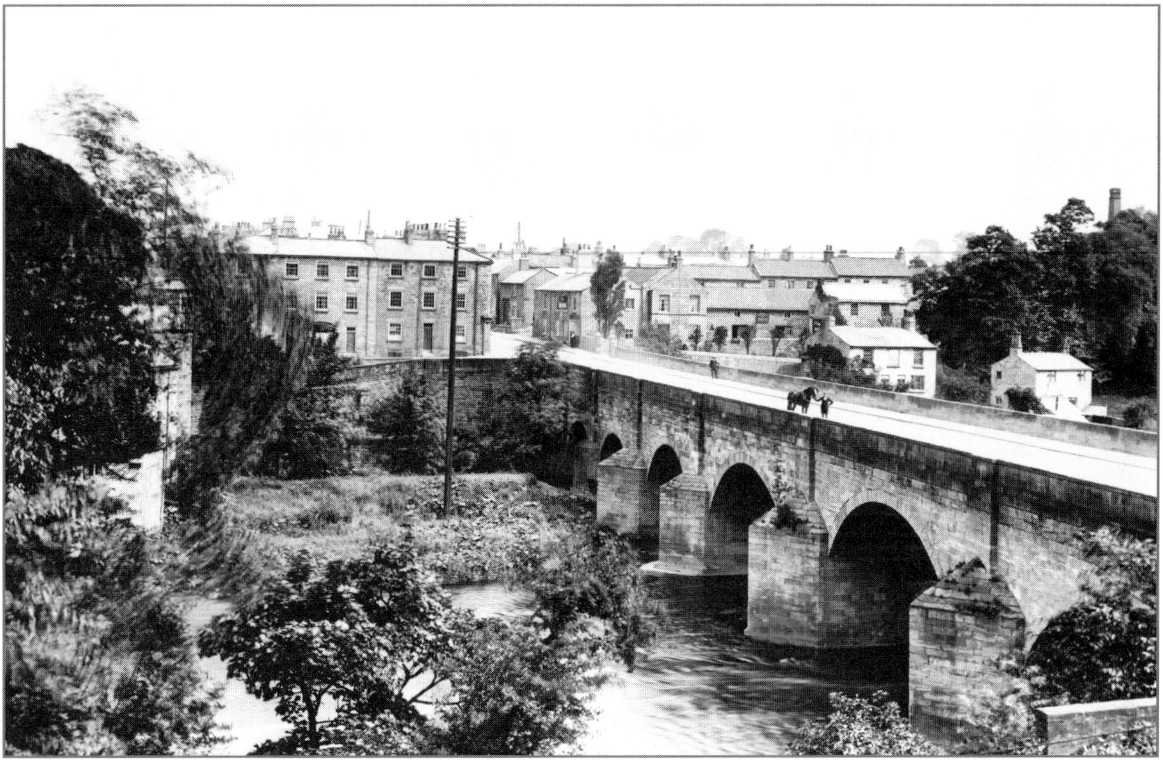

Wetherby
A View from across the Bridge 1909 61726

The first bridge, built in 1235, was eleven feet wide. By 1773 the hump was lowered, and a second widening took place in 1826. All three stages can be seen from underneath the present bridge. Famous travellers over the Wharfe include Mary, Queen of Scots and Oliver Cromwell; the bridge was also used over many years by drovers, who took thousands of cattle south. Up to 1959 the bridge carried all the traffic of the Great North Road; then a new and very welcome by-pass bridge just to the east was opened by Ernest Marples, the Transport Minister. The telegraph pole, seen centre, was erected in the same year as the photograph.

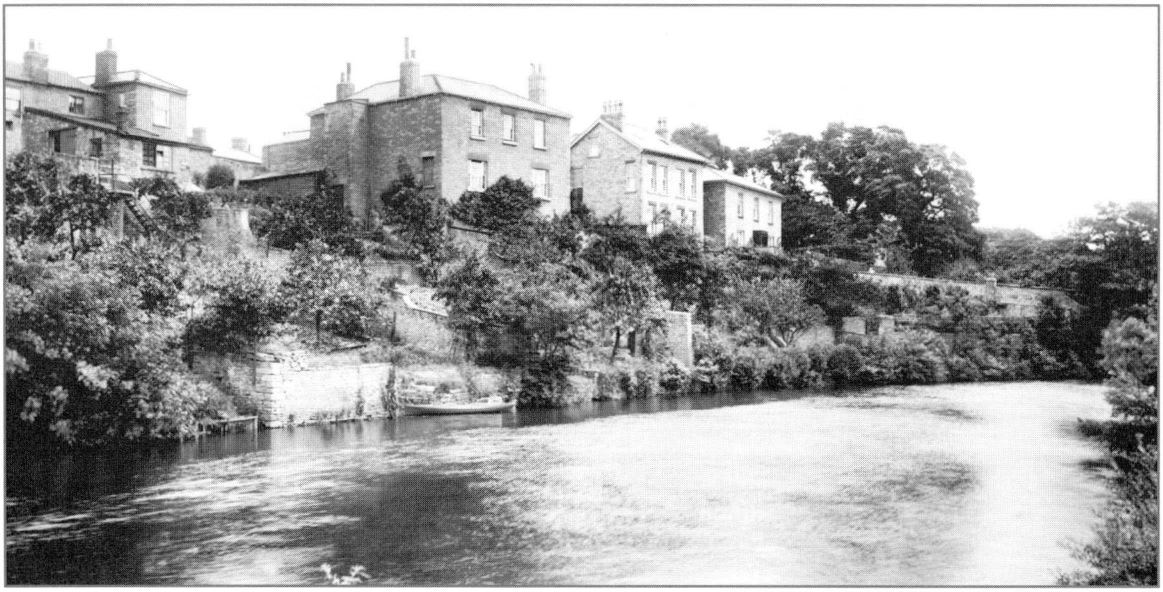

Wetherby, The River Wharfe 1909 61732

In the 1920s, Tom Richmond's West End Boating Stage offered rowing, Canadian-style skiffs and punts. A motor boat plied between here and Collingham Bridge. Behind the houses was Raby Park, an imposing housing development stimulated by the arrival of the railway. The area was named after the Vicar of Wetherby, the Rev William Raby, whose name was also taken by the local cinema which opened in 1915 to entertain the troops. In the 1940s it became the Rodney, and it remains open as the Wetherby Film Theatre.

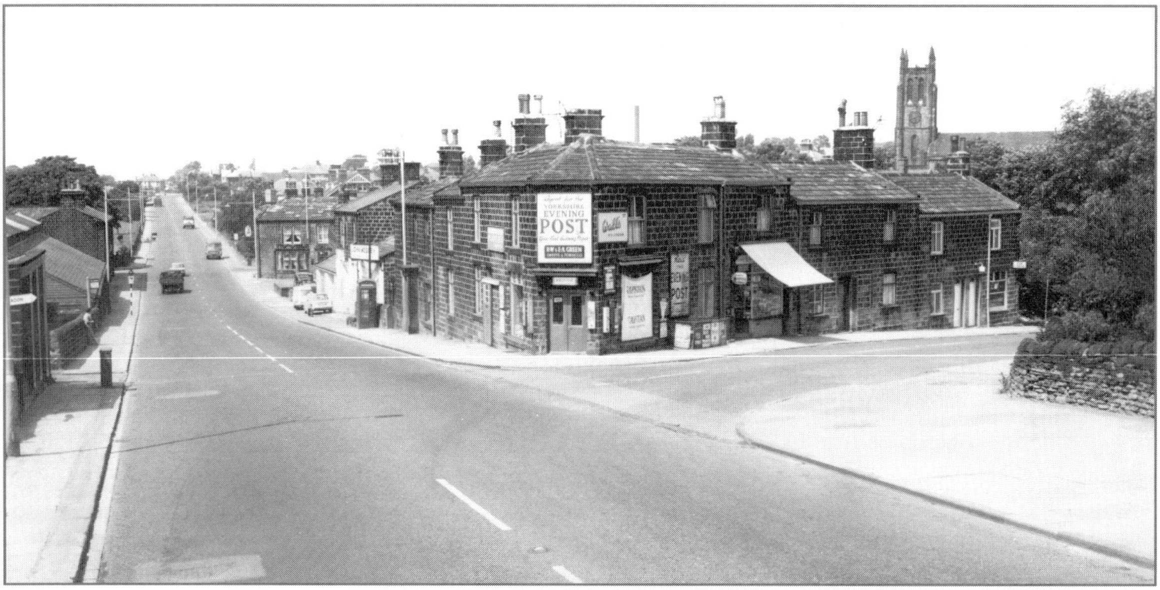

Yeadon, New Road c1960 Y37014

New Road was part of an old turnpike road, where a wagon drawn by five horses was charged 1/6d. In the mid 19th century, there were over twenty-five mills working in the town, but the boom and bust years of trade protection caused much unemployment. This former agricultural village gave way to rows and rows of workers' cottages, many of which remain. Nearby Yeadon Airport began as the Yorkshire Aeroplane Club in 1933, and in the Second World War it was used as a test site for Lancaster bombers. Jet planes arrived in 1984.

Index

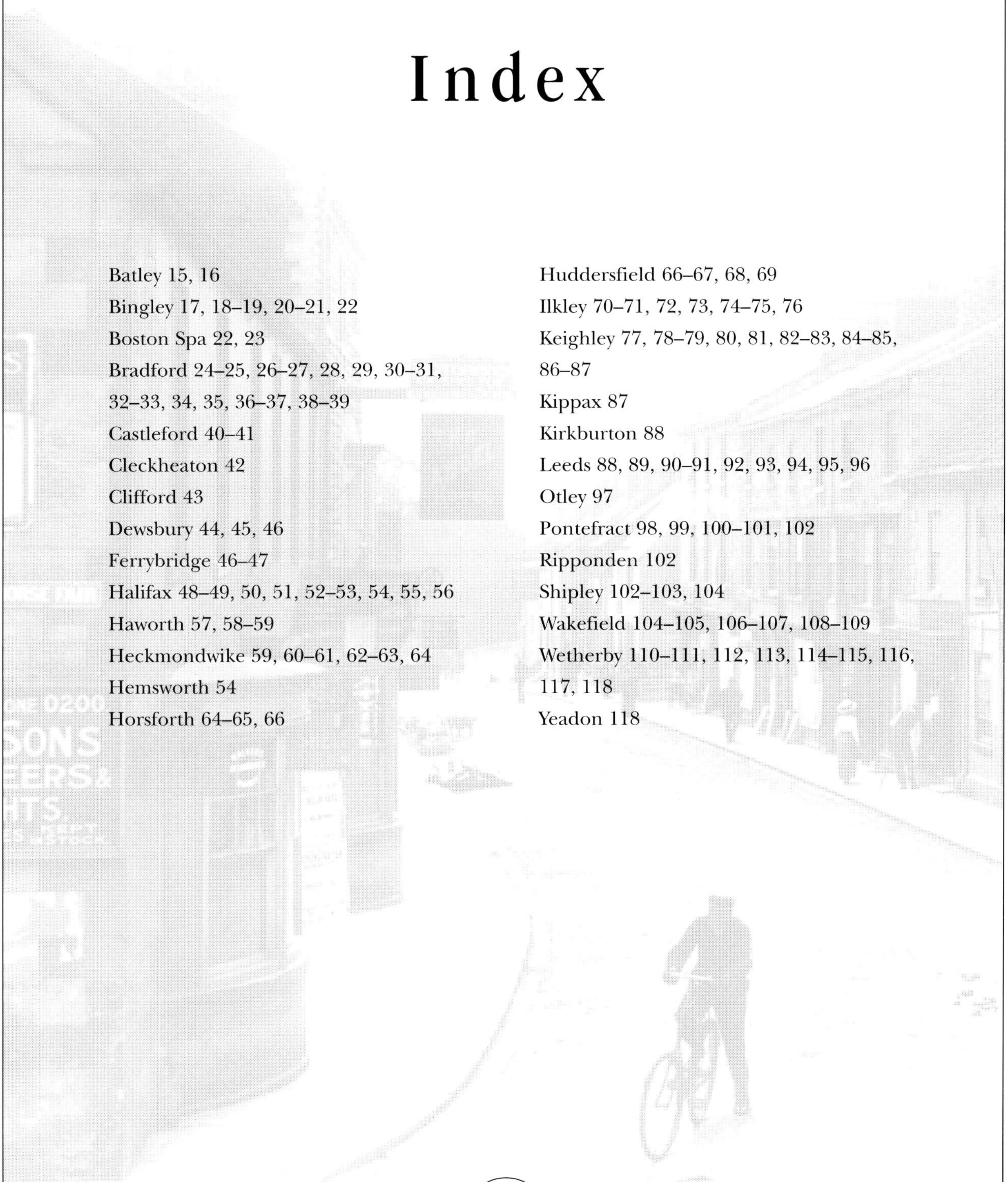

Batley 15, 16
Bingley 17, 18–19, 20–21, 22
Boston Spa 22, 23
Bradford 24–25, 26–27, 28, 29, 30–31, 32–33, 34, 35, 36–37, 38–39
Castleford 40–41
Cleckheaton 42
Clifford 43
Dewsbury 44, 45, 46
Ferrybridge 46–47
Halifax 48–49, 50, 51, 52–53, 54, 55, 56
Haworth 57, 58–59
Heckmondwike 59, 60–61, 62–63, 64
Hemsworth 54
Horsforth 64–65, 66
Huddersfield 66–67, 68, 69
Ilkley 70–71, 72, 73, 74–75, 76
Keighley 77, 78–79, 80, 81, 82–83, 84–85, 86–87
Kippax 87
Kirkburton 88
Leeds 88, 89, 90–91, 92, 93, 94, 95, 96
Otley 97
Pontefract 98, 99, 100–101, 102
Ripponden 102
Shipley 102–103, 104
Wakefield 104–105, 106–107, 108–109
Wetherby 110–111, 112, 113, 114–115, 116, 117, 118
Yeadon 118

Frith Book Co Titles

www.frithbook.co.uk

The Frith Book Company publishes over 100 new titles each year. A selection of those currently available are listed below. For latest catalogue please contact Frith Book Co.

Town Books 96pp, 100 photos. County and Themed Books 128pp, 150 photos (unless specified). All titles hardback laminated case and jacket except those indicated pb (paperback)

Around Bakewell	1-85937-113-2	£12.99
Around Barnstaple	1-85937-084-5	£12.99
Around Bath	1-85937-097-7	£12.99
Berkshire (pb)	1-85937-191-4	£9.99
Around Blackpool	1-85937-049-7	£12.99
Around Bognor Regis	1-85937-055-1	£12.99
Around Bournemouth	1-85937-067-5	£12.99
Brighton (pb)	1-85937-192-2	£8.99
British Life A Century Ago	1-85937-103-5	£17.99
Buckinghamshire (pb)	1-85937-200-7	£9.99
Around Cambridge	1-85937-092-6	£12.99
Cambridgeshire	1-85937-086-1	£14.99
Canals and Waterways	1-85937-129-9	£17.99
Cheshire	1-85937-045-4	£14.99
Around Chester	1-85937-090-x	£12.99
Around Chichester	1-85937-089-6	£12.99
Churches of Berkshire	1-85937-170-1	£17.99
Churches of Dorset	1-85937-172-8	£17.99
Colchester (pb)	1-85937-188-4	£8.99
Cornwall	1-85937-054-3	£14.99
Cumbria	1-85937-101-9	£14.99
Dartmoor	1-85937-145-0	£14.99
Around Derby	1-85937-046-2	£12.99
Derbyshire (pb)	1-85937-196-5	£9.99
Devon	1-85937-052-7	£14.99
Dorset	1-85937-075-6	£14.99
Dorset Coast	1-85937-062-4	£14.99
Down the Severn	1-85937-118-3	£14.99
Down the Thames	1-85937-121-3	£14.99
Around Dublin	1-85937-058-6	£12.99
East Sussex	1-85937-130-2	£14.99
Around Eastbourne	1-85937-061-6	£12.99
Edinburgh (pb)	1-85937-193-0	£8.99
English Castles	1-85937-078-0	£14.99
Essex	1-85937-082-9	£14.99
Around Exeter	1-85937-126-4	£12.99
Exmoor	1-85937-132-9	£14.99
Around Falmouth	1-85937-066-7	£12.99
Around Great Yarmouth	1-85937-085-3	£12.99
Around Guildford	1-85937-117-5	£12.99
Hampshire	1-85937-064-0	£14.99
Around Harrogate	1-85937-112-4	£12.99
Around Horsham	1-85937-127-2	£12.99
Around Ipswich	1-85937-133-7	£12.99
Ireland (pb)	1-85937-181-7	£9.99
Isle of Man	1-85937-065-9	£14.99
Isle of Wight	1-85937-114-0	£14.99
Kent (pb)	1-85937-189-2	£9.99
Around Leicester	1-85937-073-x	£12.99
Leicestershire (pb)	1-85937-185-x	£9.99
Around Lincoln	1-85937-111-6	£12.99
Lincolnshire	1-85937-135-3	£14.99
London (pb)	1-85937-183-3	£9.99
Around Maidstone	1-85937-056-x	£12.99
New Forest	1-85937-128-0	£14.99
Around Newark	1-85937-105-1	£12.99
Around Newquay	1-85937-140-x	£12.99
North Devon Coast	1-85937-146-9	£14.99
Northumberland and Tyne & Wear	1-85937-072-1	£14.99
Norwich (pb)	1-85937-194-9	£8.99
Around Nottingham	1-85937-060-8	£12.99
Nottinghamshire (pb)	1-85937-187-6	£9.99
Around Oxford	1-85937-096-9	£12.99
Oxfordshire	1-85937-076-4	£14.99
Peak District	1-85937-100-0	£14.99
Around Penzance	1-85937-069-1	£12.99
Around Plymouth	1-85937-119-1	£12.99
Around St Ives	1-85937-068-3	£12.99
Around Scarborough	1-85937-104-3	£12.99
Scotland (pb)	1-85937-182-5	£9.99
Scottish Castles	1-85937-077-2	£14.99
Around Sevenoaks and Tonbridge	1-85937-057-8	£12.99
Around Southampton	1-85937-088-8	£12.99
Around Southport	1-85937-106-x	£12.99

Available from your local bookshop or from the publisher

Frith Book Co Titles (continued)

Around Shrewsbury	1-85937-110-8	£12.99
Shropshire	1-85937-083-7	£14.99
South Devon Coast	1-85937-107-8	£14.99
South Devon Living Memories	1-85937-168-x	£14.99
Staffordshire (96pp)	1-85937-047-0	£12.99
Stone Circles & Ancient Monuments	1-85937-143-4	£17.99
Around Stratford upon Avon	1-85937-098-5	£12.99
Sussex (pb)	1-85937-184-1	£9.99
Around Torbay	1-85937-063-2	£12.99
Around Truro	1-85937-147-7	£12.99
Victorian & Edwardian Kent	1-85937-149-3	£14.99
Victorian & Edwardian Yorkshire	1-85937-154-x	£14.99
Warwickshire (pb)	1-85937-203-1	£9.99
Welsh Castles	1-85937-120-5	£14.99
West Midlands	1-85937-109-4	£14.99
West Sussex	1-85937-148-5	£14.99
Wiltshire	1-85937-053-5	£14.99
Around Winchester	1-85937-139-6	£12.99

Frith Book Co titles available Autumn 2000

Croydon Living Memories (pb)	1-85937-162-0	£9.99	Aug
Glasgow (pb)	1-85937-190-6	£9.99	Aug
Hertfordshire (pb)	1-85937-247-3	£9.99	Aug
North London	1-85937-206-6	£14.99	Aug
Victorian & Edwardian Maritime Album	1-85937-144-2	£17.99	Aug
Victorian Seaside	1-85937-159-0	£17.99	Aug
Cornish Coast	1-85937-163-9	£14.99	Sep
County Durham	1-85937-123-x	£14.99	Sep
Dorset Living Memories	1-85937-210-4	£14.99	Sep
Herefordshire	1-85937-174-4	£14.99	Sep
Kent Living Memories	1-85937-125-6	£14.99	Sep
Leeds (pb)	1-85937-202-3	£9.99	Sep
Ludlow (pb)	1-85937-176-0	£9.99	Sep
Norfolk (pb)	1-85937-195-7	£9.99	Sep
Somerset	1-85937-153-1	£14.99	Sep
Tees Valley & Cleveland	1-85937-211-2	£14.99	Sep
Thanet (pb)	1-85937-116-7	£9.99	Sep
Tiverton (pb)	1-85937-178-7	£9.99	Sep
Victorian and Edwardian Sussex	1-85937-157-4	£14.99	Sep
Weymouth (pb)	1-85937-209-0	£9.99	Sep
Worcestershire	1-85937-152-3	£14.99	Sep
Yorkshire Living Memories	1-85937-166-3	£14.99	Sep
British Life A Century Ago (pb)	1-85937-213-9	£9.99	Oct
Camberley (pb)	1-85937-222-8	£9.99	Oct
Cardiff (pb)	1-85937-093-4	£9.99	Oct
Carmarthenshire	1-85937-216-3	£14.99	Oct
Cornwall (pb)	1-85937-229-5	£9.99	Oct
English Country Houses	1-85937-161-2	£17.99	Oct
Humberside	1-85937-215-5	£14.99	Oct
Manchester (pb)	1-85937-198-1	£9.99	Oct
Middlesex	1-85937-158-2	£14.99	Oct
Norfolk Living Memories	1-85937-217-1	£14.99	Oct
Preston (pb)	1-85937-212-0	£9.99	Oct
South Hams	1-85937-220-1	£14.99	Oct
Suffolk	1-85937-221-x	£9.99	Oct
Swansea (pb)	1-85937-167-1	£9.99	Oct
West Yorkshire (pb)	1-85937-201-5	£9.99	Oct

See Frith books on the internet www.frithbook.co.uk

Frith Products & Services

Francis Frith would doubtless be pleased to know that the pioneering publishing venture he started in 1860 still continues today. A hundred and forty years later, The Francis Frith Collection continues in the same innovative tradition and is now one of the foremost publishers of vintage photographs in the world. Some of the current activities include:

Interior Decoration

Today Frith's photographs can be seen framed and as giant wall murals in thousands of pubs, restaurants, hotels, banks, retail stores and other public buildings throughout the country. In every case they enhance the unique local atmosphere of the places they depict and provide reminders of gentler days in an increasingly busy and frenetic world.

Product Promotions

Frith products are used by many major companies to promote the sales of their own products or to reinforce their own history and heritage. Frith promotions have been used by Hovis bread, Courage beers, Scots Porage Oats, Colman's mustard, Cadbury's foods, Mellow Birds coffee, Dunhill pipe tobacco, Guinness, and Bulmer's Cider.

Genealogy and Family History

As the interest in family history and roots grows world-wide, more and more people are turning to Frith's photographs of Great Britain for images of the towns, villages and streets where their ancestors lived; and, of course, photographs of the churches and chapels where their ancestors were christened, married and buried are an essential part of every genealogy tree and family album.

Frith Products

All Frith photographs are available Framed or just as Mounted Prints and Posters (size 23 x 16 inches). These may be ordered from the address below. From time to time other products - Address Books, Calendars, Table Mats, etc - are available.

The Internet

Already twenty thousand Frith photographs can be viewed and purchased on the internet. By the end of the year 2000 some 60,000 Frith photographs will be available on the internet. The number of sites is constantly expanding, each focussing on different products and services from the Collection.
The main Frith sites are listed below.

www.francisfrith.co.uk
www.frithbook.co.uk

See the complete list of Frith Books at:
www.frithbook.co.uk

This web site is regularly updated with the latest list of publications from the Frith Book Company. If you wish to buy books relating to another part of the country that your local bookshop does not stock, you may purchase on-line.

For further information, trade, or author enquiries please contact us at the address below:
The Francis Frith Collection, Frith's Barn, Teffont, Salisbury, Wiltshire, England SP3 5QP.
Tel: +44 (0)1722 716 376 Fax: +44 (0)1722 716 881 Email: uksales@francisfrith.com

See Frith books on the internet www.frithbook.co.uk

To receive your FREE Mounted Print

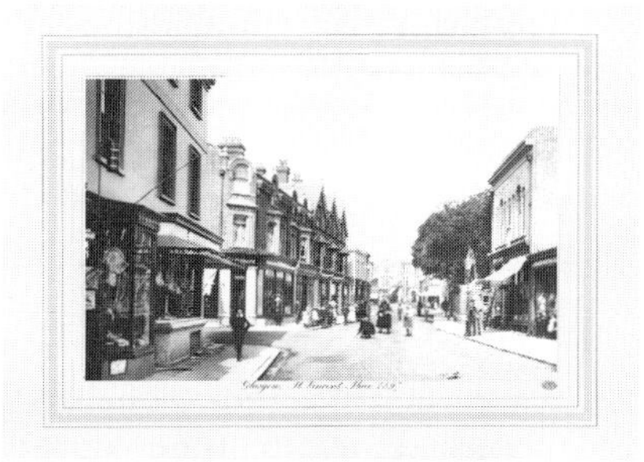

Mounted Print
Overall size 14 x 11 inches

Cut out this Voucher and return it with your remittance for £1.50 to cover postage and handling, to UK addresses. For overseas addresses please include £4.00 post and handling.
Choose any photograph included in this book. Your SEPIA print will be A4 in size, and mounted in a cream mount with burgundy rule lines, overall size 14 x 11 inches.

Order additional Mounted Prints at HALF PRICE (only £7.49 each*)
If there are further pictures you would like to order, possibly as gifts for friends and family, purchase them at half price (no additional postage and handling required).

Have your Mounted Prints framed*
For an additional £14.95 per print you can have your chosen Mounted Print framed in an elegant polished wood and gilt moulding, overall size 16 x 13 inches (no additional postage and handling required).

*** IMPORTANT!**
These special prices are only available if ordered using the original voucher on this page (no copies permitted) and at the same time as your free Mounted Print, for delivery to the same address

Frith Collectors' Guild

From time to time we publish a magazine of news and stories about Frith photographs and further special offers of Frith products. If you would like 12 months FREE membership, please return this form.

Send completed forms to:
The Francis Frith Collection,
Frith's Barn, Teffont, Salisbury,
Wiltshire SP3 5QP

Voucher for FREE and Reduced Price Frith Prints

Picture no.	Page number	Qty	Mounted @ £7.49	Framed + £14.95	Total Cost
		1	**Free of charge***	£	£
			£7.49	£	£
			£7.49	£	£
			£7.49	£	£
			£7.49	£	£
			£7.49	£	£
Please allow 28 days for delivery			*** Post & handling**		**£1.50**
Book Title			**Total Order Cost**		**£**

Please do not photocopy this voucher. Only the original is valid, so please cut it out and return it to us.

I enclose a cheque / postal order for £ ....
made payable to 'The Francis Frith Collection'
OR please debit my Mastercard / Visa / Switch / Amex card
Number ....
Issue No (Switch only) .... Valid from (Amex/Switch) ....
Expires .... Signature ....
Name Mr/Mrs/Ms ....
Address ....
....
....
....
.... Postcode ....
Daytime Tel No ....   Valid to 31/12/02

The Francis Frith Collectors' Guild

Please enrol me as a member for 12 months free of charge.

Name Mr/Mrs/Ms ....
Address ....
....
....
.... Postcode ....